The Bridges of Washington County

Spanning Work and Nature

DAVID P. BRIDGES

*This book is dedicated to my father,
Shelby Powell Bridges, for his years of love and
encouragement along with his devotion to the Bridges'
family story.*

Library of Congress: Control Number: 2002094256
ISBN: 1-932301-12-7

TABLE OF CONTENTS:

INTRODUCTION

The impetus for this book began in 1973 in the basement of my home in Wilmette, Illinois. It was here I became "master of the universe," at least on a HO model train scale. It all began with a standard Christmas gift of a train set which soon expanded into a 25x20 foot layout. Cold Chicago winters were the impetus for making a scenic panorama where the trains ran on time.

My grandfather, Thilo Max Best, often visited on birthdays and holidays. One such time he brought along a vast collection of photographs from the Jacob Best Coal Company of Chicago. The pictures were entrusted to me, and I put them to good use as the inspiration for a Best Coal Company in miniature as part of my train layout. First I did the Mayfair Yard and then the Edgewater Yard. Pa, as I called my grandfather, served as my technical advisor. The layout grew ever more elaborate with the addition of the Appalachian Mountains.

I had a partner in all this, my younger brother Robert. Eventually, we agreed on a leveraged buyout. Some money changed hands, along with a baseball hit by the Cubs' Jose Cardenal. I was now the sole proprietor of a world where coal still ruled as king.

In 1974, we took a family trip to Maryland and visited the Pennsylvania Glass Sand Corporation, once owned by the Bridges' side of the family. The tour of the Corporation fascinated me to the point of collecting samples of raw silica and photographing the yellow thirty-ton trucks used to move rock. I was an eleven-year old with a plan. Back home in Wilmette, I added a silica mining pit to the layout. My ancestral past in rock and coal now showed in HO.

After my grandparents passed, the railroad layout reminded me how their lives had been shaped by hard work and an entrepreneurial spirit. My subsequent education and entry into the Presbyterian Ministry did not lessen this fascination with the Bests and Bridges. In 1997, I began writing two family histories from the time my ancestors arrived in America. It took me five years to write the two books that chronicle their stories.

This account of the Bridges spans the period 1816-1957. If anything, it is a story about the intersection of faith and capitalism; these two undertakings are not always antagonistic. The way in which faith develops character and personal habits outside of church is one of the central themes of this book. Many Americans have created vast fortunes. Far fewer have been devoted to spiritual principles along the way to acquiring their wealth. The Bridges were definitely in the minority.

The narrative begins in 1816, when Robert Ferguson Bridges made his way from Kirkcaldy Scotland to the port of Baltimore. Within a year, Bridges joined a great westward migration that took him to the mountain region of Maryland. In time the Bridges' family became influential in Baltimore, western Maryland and West Virginia. Robert Ferguson's son Robert was the wealthiest individual in western Maryland at the time of his death in 1908. And Bridges' grandson Henry became not only a leading businessman but one of the premier conservationists of the region. Henry's efforts made possible his having a hand in saving the wild turkey from extinction in America. His pioneering conservation of land and game species came at as time when Americans considered wildlife and land as self-replenishing resources. Bridges' efforts on behalf of conservation brought him into contact with four presidents and other notable Americans during a public life that spanned more than half a century.

In 1960 the two families were united through the marriage of my mother, Barbara Ann Best, granddaughter of Jacob Best, (*The Best Coal Company in Chicago, And How It Got That Way.*) and my father, Shelby Powell Bridges, son of Henry P. Bridges. My life has consisted of the Best Bridges imaginable.

ACKNOWLEDGEMENTS

I could not have produced this book over the course of the past five years without the instruction received from The University of Chicago and its Divinity School professors. I would especially like to thank Dr. Martin Marty, Dr. Clark Gilpin and Dr. Catherine Brekus. I am also grateful for the encouragement and advice I received from my good friend, Dr. John Mulder, president of my alma mater, Louisville Presbyterian Theological Seminary.

My family has offered every support and encouragement during this book project. My father, Powell Bridges, has utilized his writing skills as a lawyer to begin editing this manuscript from the day I began writing in January 1997. My Uncle Henry Bridges Jr. has been instrumental in helping me find invaluable primary documents and research materials. My mother, Barbara Best Bridges, listened patiently as the Bridges' story unfolded.

I am indebted to Mr. Richard Gaynor for his excellent computer technology skills. With his computer input and knowledge of writing publishable materials, the project took on its desktop-publishing format. Many Chicagoans also have graciously listened and encouraged the project, including Linda DeLeon at The University Club of Chicago. Linda is a fellow author who listened when I needed to talk and shared her thoughts on the plight of writers. In addition Cindy Wietell at ABS Service did an excellent job typing all the primary research documents needed to complete the project.

In West Virginia, Mrs. Maxine Newbraugh graciously shared the local history collection amassed by her husband Fred. Mrs. Newbraugh's eighty years of wisdom together with her command of stories and facts concerning Berkeley Springs was nothing short of extraordinary. Mr. Toby Tobias, my second cousin, excelled as content editor. His love of genealogical research on the Bridges' family proved to be "just what the doctor ordered" at a crucial point in the project. Mr. Richard Goodell, former CEO of the Better Minerals and Aggregates Company, and Mr. Bill Farell, the Quarry Plant Manager, put me in touch with papers, people and photos I otherwise might have missed. Professor Douglas Bukowski also worked to edit this book and give it that final look and polish. His effort is greatly appreciated. Thanks to all readers of the manuscript who freely gave valuable insight into the writing and re-writing of this book!

CHAPTER 1

ROBERT FERGUSON BRIDGES, 1796-1845 & ROBERT BRIDGES 1830-1908:
From Scotland to Maryland

ROBERT FERGUSON: 1816-1845

In 1650 the first Andrew Bridges of known record was born. Bridges married Agnes Pryde in 1684. The couple were early followers of the Scottish Presbyterian leader John Knox. They would eventually pass their beliefs, heritage and family traditions down to ten generations of faithful Bridges. Andrew's line begot Robert Bridges who married Mary Forgan in 1781. They lived on the 1,600-acre King's Moor Farm in Fife County where they labored as sharecroppers. Bridges later became a skilled mason and stone-cutter. In the year of our Lord 1796, a child by the name of Robert Ferguson Bridges was born to Robert and Mary in Dunino Parish of Fife County, Scotland.

**The Presbyterian Church of St. Andrews, Dunino
Parish, Fife County, Scotland. Though great, the ties
of hearth and church could not keep Robert Ferguson
Bridges from setting off to America in 1816.**

Robert Ferguson was born into a large Presbyterian family, one of nine children, seven of them boys. In 1816, at the age of twenty, he made a difficult decision for a man of such young age and decided to immigrate to America. He no doubt said good-bye to his parents and siblings before traveling to the coastal city of Kircaldy. There Robert had first cousins to give him room and board until his departure for the New World.

While no evidence survives to indicate why young Robert Ferguson left his family and homeland, there is no lack of clues. As a middle child he would not benefit from the Scottish law dictating that only the oldest son could inherit a father's estate. And at the time Scotland was a land where population outstripped opportunity. Robert Ferguson must have seen that better opportunities lay on the other side of the Atlantic. He most likely landed in Baltimore.

Bridges did not need Horace Greeley to know he should head west. Whether by intent or circumstance, his eventual destination was the small town of Hancock Maryland, established by hunters and trappers in 1730. Known as Williams Towne, the settlement was formally laid in 1749. The town name changed to Hancock in honor of Joseph Hancock, a veteran of the Revolutionary War and survivor of Valley Forge. In 1820, Hancock was home to 266 residents, including forty-four slaves and three freedmen.

Robert Ferguson soon found himself courting a sixteen-year-old woman from Reading Pennsylvania. In 1819 Robert married Rebecca Leopold. The couple had eight children: Mary, born in 1819; James, 1822; William, 1824; Katherine, 1828; Robert, 1830; Rebecca, 1832; Helen Mar, 1836; and Sarah Mae, 1838. Bridges had little choice but to work hard and feed his family.

On March 30, 1826, in the Washington County Court of Hagerstown Maryland, Robert Ferguson "declared his intention on oath to become a citizen of the United States, and to renounce and abjure all allegiances and fidelity to any foreign Prince, Potentate, State or Sovereignty whatsoever and particularly to the King of the United Kingdom of Great Britain and Ireland, as required by the law establishing an uniform rule of naturalization, and several additions thereto." Bridges was nearly as interested in real estate as he was citizenship. He had begun buying property in Hancock by 1824 from James Duke, and on March 7, 1829, he bought the old John Donavan public house (built in 1784) on Main Street from "Samuel L. Gregory, Trustee for the estate of John Donovan deceased for $100.00." Robert Ferguson had acquired a substantial home on the eastern end of town with ample living space for a large family. The house also sat directly across the street from that marvel in then-modern transportation, the Chesapeake and Ohio Canal.

Robert Ferguson's home in Hancock Maryland. The demands of an expanding family dictated the purchase of the house in 1829.

The canal, known as the "Ditch," reached Hancock in 1833; by way of contrast, the Baltimore and Ohio Railroad would not reach Hancock until June 1842. The canal made Hancock a center for commerce and transportation. Some people traveled by canal boat, others by stage along the National Pike. Either way, they might stay at establishments like the Barton House, Ferry Inn or Western Hotel. Among the famous travelers passing through Hancock were Andrew Jackson; Davy Crockett; James Polk; Henry Clay; William Henry Harrison; and Zachery Taylor.

On March 27, 1834, Robert Ferguson bought an 81-acre farm from "Jonathon Rowland for $133.32." This allowed him to grow crops that he sold in Hancock. Bridges was an industrious man who, together with Rebecca, sold produce at the weekly market day in town. On July 28, 1840, Bridges bought another half-acre plot in Hancock from "Nathaniel Summers for $130." Robert Ferguson was the proud owner of four parcels of land.

Bridges Presbyterian faith crossed the Atlantic with him. He continued to practice his beliefs in Hancock at a small all-denominational church. It might be said that the faith preceded the immigrant by nearly 175 years. In 1657, Presbyterianism reached the Eastern Shore of Maryland via a poor mechanic. This man, Ninian Beall, "rose at last to be a wealthy planter, a brave soldier, whose services were rewarded by a special grant from the Assembly," wrote J. William McIlvain in 1890. "He was also one of the founders of manufactures in the colony in the shape of flourmills and iron furnaces. And living to a great age (he died in 1717, aged 92), he was well acquainted with the men who formed the first presbytery. He lay claim as the father of Presbyterianism in Maryland, indeed in America." Since the Episcopal Church was already legally established on the Eastern Shore, Presbyterians found the less populated mountainous regions of Maryland more to their liking.

Robert Ferguson Bridges continued the Presbyterian tradition of establishing churches in Maryland. The Session record of the Hancock Presbyterian Church reports:

> *This Church was Organized on the Nineteenth of June AD one thousand eight hundred and forty one by Rev. Jonathan Dickinson and Rev. F. Creigh, a committee of the Presbytery of Carlisle appointed for that purpose. At this time David Neil was chosen and ordained ruling Elder. Since which time the ministry of the Gospel has been maintained agreeably to its original design and form of worship. Has no records of the Church or of the doings of the Session are in existence prior to this date. The members who are mentioned are as follows... Cap. John Johnson, Isabella Johnson, Rebecca W. Lanahan, Sarah B. Presley, Martha Bowles, Mary Fortney, Priscilla M. Ferran, Robert F. Bridges, Rebecca Bridges, Mary F. Brown, David Neil, Ellen Neil, Jane Steele, Robert Bennett, Agnes Bennett, Martha Davison.*

The first Session meeting was held July 28, 1844, moderated by Reverend Terros F. Wilson of Virginia. The congregation must have been meeting in members' homes since there was no church building, a situation which changed in 1848 with the construction of a church building. On August 2, 1845, Bridges was ordained a Ruling Elder. He died eight weeks later.

Probate records show that Bridges owed twelve creditors $189.01, and he had ninety debtors who owed him a sum of $903.63, leaving a net balance of $714.62. His land was passed through his estate to his wife Rebecca. The estate was not finally settled until 1854. During this time an additional thirty indebted Hancock citizens paid the Bridges' estate $471.40. In all debtors paid $1,186.02 to the estate. Bridges' land was valued at $398.32, for a total estate worth $1,584.34.

This total did not leave Robert Ferguson's family with much. Prior to 1845, son Robert felt called to the Presbyterian ministry. But as the only surviving male child, Robert also felt a responsibility for the care of his mother and two sisters. So after his father's death, young Robert helped to work the farm. Robert tilled the soil as best he knew how for the next five years. In 1848, the Presbyterians of Hancock built a new church building in which Robert Ferguson's family worshiped and remembered their father.

Hancock Presbyterian Church, ca. 1870. Robert Bridges was expected to apply the sermons he heard here on Sundays to his business dealings the other six days of the week.

On January 15, 1851, Bridges became a Communicant and formally studied the faith of his Scottish forefathers. On December 9, 1851, Bridges was ordained a Ruling Elder of the Hancock Presbyterian Church. The book of Genesis in the Bible notes, "This is the book of the generations…when Adam had lived 130 years, he became the father of a son in his own likeness, after his image." And so Robert Bridges grew in the image and likeness of his father, Robert Ferguson Bridges. In this way a son kept alive his father's Presbyterian faith.

ROBERT BRIDGES, BUSINESSMAN

In 1850 Robert began a partnership with Charles W. Henderson, originally from Hedgesville, Virginia. The two men opened Bridges & Henderson Merchants and Proprietors General Store on Main Street in Hancock. At twenty, Bridges now had his first business venture. The front of the store was no more than fifty yards from the bustling Chesapeake and Ohio Canal while the back faced the National Pike. It was an ideal business location. Receipts from the store indicate that Bridges and Henderson were selling hardware, home supplies, grains and other food supplies to the people of Hancock and to the canal boat crews and passengers. Goods traveled both directions on the canal.

The stuff of Sunday had a profound effect on the young man. Robert Bridges' character and faith were formed by what he heard preached in Hancock: The Holy Spirit, not the individual virtue of a man molded his morals and ethics. The Holy Spirit restored man to God, and the individual to his neighbor. Bridges was inspired by what he heard preached to live out his religious life by his outward actions towards those around him, including those who came to buy his merchandise at the General Store. Bridges' reputation as a trustworthy merchant spread throughout Hancock. People trusted him as someone informed by his faith and its principles. They were not surprised that the merchant also served as Superintendent of the Sunday School.

ROBERT BRIDGES AND THE QUESTION OF SECESSION

As a well-respected businessman and citizen of Hancock, Robert could not escape the heated debate over slavery. Maryland was a border state where sentiment ran high on both sides of the issue. On November 27, 1860, the people of Hancock called a meeting to gauge public sentiment. Thirty-two years after the fact, J. Thomas Scharf wrote that, "A large meeting of citizens of the Fifth Election District of Washington County, without respect to former party associations, was held at the house of Lloyd H. Barton, for the purpose of taking into consideration the present crisis [not least of which was the election of Abraham Lincoln] in our public affairs, and to appoint ten delegates to represent the district in the State Convention to meet in Baltimore on the 6th of December, 1860." The committee of ten Hancock men included Robert Bridges.

The committee adopted a series of resolutions by unanimous vote. After an expression of regret over the formation of sectional parties and the triumph of Northern sentiment, the group declared:

Resolved, That we believe that under the provisions of our Constitution the legislative and executive departments of our national government possess ample powers to cause the people of the North to do justice to the people of the South in the rendering up of fugi-

tive slaves, and that by a judicious exercise of these powers, and proper appeals to the justice, the sense of right, and the patriotism of the people of the North, all causes of complaint may be easily and speedily removed.

The committee favored upholding the Fugitive Slave Act, which had caused controversy since its passage in 1850. Northerners objected to the right of slave owners to go into free states and take back runaways; Southerners objected to the criticism of what they saw as a right. But the real question for Bridges and all other Americans that November was the future of the Union.

The author John Pendelton Kennedy wrote his novel *Swallow Barn* depicting the state of slavery in Virginia. Kennedy based his characters on people in Morgan County, just across the Potomac River from Hancock. The author treated slavery as morally wrong and emancipation as economic, if not social, ruin. If these were not the fears of Robert Bridges, they were for his friends, customers and fellow worshippers.

Bridges clearly was a man of deep moral and spiritual conviction based on his Presbyterian faith. It is also clear that he stood on the wrong side of the debate. While it does not appear that he ever actually owned any slaves, his selection to the committee of ten strongly suggests he was a Southern sympathizer. Bridges' would have four brothers-in-law who fought for the Confederacy: James Breathed, 1st Virginia Cavalry and 1st Stuart Horse Artillery; John W. Breathed Jr., 35th Virginia Cavalry; and Isaac Breathed, 43rd Virginia Cavalry and Francis who fought at the Battle of Gettysburg.

As a border state Maryland felt the touch of war, and the presence of Union troops in Hancock did not stop at least one memorable visit from General Stonewall Jackson and 8,500 troops on January 4, 1862. During his "Bath Campaign" while commanding a bluff outside of town, Jackson made known his desire for the town's surrender.

Union Brigadier General Frederick West Lander, assisted by Robert Bridges and Charles Henderson, entered into negotiations with a Confederate emissary. When the talks failed, Lander sent back a message: "Colonel Ashby, give my compliments to General Jackson and tell him to bombard and be damned. If he opens his batteries on this town he will injure more of his friends than he will of the enemy, for this is a damned 'Secesh' place anyhow." Jackson did precisely that and after allowing two hours for the citizens to evacuate he defiantly opened up with a cannonade raining shot and shell into Hancock.

A neighbor of Bridges recorded in his diary, "At one o'clock they came cannonading, but we replied, which silenced them before night. About 100 shots were exchanged, one part of a shell hit my house and smokehouse, a ball lodged in the garden in the ground and many other places in town." The Bridges' home was under fire for three hours, with damage to the Presbyterian Church, buildings and trees. This was war, and the people of Hancock were fortunate the engagement resulted in the destruction of property only. Jackson and his Confederates quickly moved on to Romney, Virginia.

FAITH AND FAMILY

But the war did not stop Bridges from getting married. On November 5, 1861, he wed Priscilla Williams Breathed of Breathedsville, Maryland; the wedding took place in Bi-Yuka, the plantation home of Judge John W. Breathed south of Hagerstown at the Episcopal Antietam Parish of St. Mark's, officiated by Reverend J. H. Coith. Robert and Priscilla would have thirteen children, including two who died in infancy. The surviving children were: Ann McGill, born 1863; Robert Willis, 1865; John Breathed, 1866; Helen Mar, 1869; Priscilla, 1871; James Taliaferro, 1872; Addison, 1874; Llewellyn Dupont, 1875; Rebecca, 1876; Henry Percival, 1878; and Wilbur, 1880. They frequently vacationed with their children at the birth place of Priscilla at the Fruit Hill Manor in Berkeley Springs.

Robert Bridges, ca. 1895, with his sons, left to right from bottom: Henry Percival and Wilbur; second row: James Taliaferro, Robert Sr. and John Breathed; third row: Robert, Eugene Addison and Llewllyn. The elder Bridges expected his children to live by the Golden Rule, no matter their profession.

The everyday devotional life of the Bridges began with their children gathered around the breakfast table. It was the practice of the time to reflect on faith and begin each day with memorized Scripture passages. Writing in 1852, C. John Backus declared, "It may be remarked in passing that the genius of Presbyterianism was specially adapted to towns, where people met frequently and discussed the intellectual side of religion. It certainly has always fostered the intellectual in those who professed it." Scripture was central to the Bridges' family, and the family patriarch was expected to take the lead in spiritual matters. According to historian Colleen McDannell:

> *In theory, a father exercised absolute authority over his household that included wife and children as well as servants and apprentices. He was to support his family and rule over them with a firm but just hand. Fathers negotiated for their families in the public world and women and children had few legal rights....As wives submitted to and cherished their husbands, so children were to honor and obey their parents. Bible reading was a serious effort to shape and discipline children so they would be concerned about the state of their souls. It was believed that children were not born innocent and sinless but, as Jonathan Edwards preached, were "young vipers...in a most miserable condition...and they are naturally very senseless and stupid...and need much to awaken them." Children's wills needed to be broken because unless they were obedient to their parents the young would never understand what it meant to be obedient to God or to secular rulers.*

The daily practice of faith was very important to Robert Bridges and his family. As a Presbyterian Elder (since 1851) who lived across the street from Hancock Presbyterian Church, Robert was conspicuous to the people of Hancock for his virtue, or possible lack thereof. Henry Percival spoke often about his father's simple faith in "Father God":

> *My father was a wealthy man. He had, by hard work, accumulated an abundance of money and, by steadfastness of spirit, an abundance of wisdom and love. I think it was this wisdom and love that led him to see that his children were brought up neither spoiled nor ignorant. In his light, the man who had no acquaintance with the world's best-selling book was an ignoramus. I mean, of course, the Bible. The book has figured heavily in our lives....For instance I remember breakfast time in our home. We children, all eleven of us, stood around the table, the food hot on our plates. Father stood at the head of the table, looking at us with a calm face and steady eyes.*

"You may begin, Henry," he'd say softly, nodding at me. And so I would speak up, saying perhaps, "But I say unto you, that whosoever is angry with his brother without a cause shall be in danger of the judgment and whosoever...."(Matthew 5:22) Next, in their turn, my brothers and sisters would recite in high, piping voices. For each morning we had to recite, from memory, a verse from the Bible and it had to be a new verse each breakfast time.

Robert Bridges received his faith from his father Robert Ferguson and passed it to his own sons and daughters. The Presbyterian traditional devotional practices helped children to live and act according to the important Christian principles of faith. The day began and ended with devotion, recalled Henry Bridges:

There were evening services each day, too. When there were no services in church, Bible readings and family prayer took place in the living room. It was a pleasant custom and a profitable one. For one thing, we children had few if any nightmares: such unwanted nocturnal visitations seldom bother the mind, young or old, that has been calmed by the reading of the Holy Scriptures. But make no mistake, my parents' religion had nothing of the impractical or the effete about it. It was a religion to live by and live with. God watches over us all, my mother might have observed. Yes, my father might have added, but He helps those who help themselves.

Robert Bridges sitting in the living room of his home, ca. 1895. The picture is a perfect reflection of the individual, showing success without ostentation.

Bridges' sons were involved in numerous business endeavors in and around Hancock. Robert Willis was both poet and postmaster of Hancock. In 1899 John Breathed and Ernest C. Henderson bought the mercantile interests of their fathers, to bring that business new blood under old names. They operated the store until 1905, when Henderson sold out and the store became Bridges and Breathed. John was also a banker. James Taliaferro had interests in a lumber company, hotel and bridge-building firm; he also tried to mine glass sand in Hancock. Henry and Wilbur were trained as lawyers while Addison was a soldier who fought with Teddy Roosevelt in Cuba. Although Llewellyn Dupont lived and worked in Hancock, the particulars of his work life are unknown. The four girls—Ann, Helen Mar, Priscilla and Rebecca—lived at home until married.

Priscilla Bridges and her four daughters, 1903.

Addison Bridges, "Rough Rider," with Teddy Roosevelt in Cuba. TR's influence on the Bridges' family extended beyond military matters.

The children were raised under the watchful eyes of their parents. The elder Bridges were stern but not unmindful that young people need to enjoy themselves from time to time. So, friends were picked up in horse and buggy for "Tally Ho" parties at the house, and there was the tradition of family picnics not to mention swimming, be it in canal, river or creek. Hunting was another favorite pastime for boys growing up in Hancock. In particular, the Bridges' boys relished snaring rabbits and tracking them after a snowfall.

Bridges family picnic, without a hint of Gilded Age excess.

Oftentimes, deer were seen wandering down the middle of Main Street, only to be scared back up into the mountains that surrounded town. The rolling terrain came right up to Main Street. It was said that, "Horse, cattle, sheep and hogs were driven east along the National Pike and drovers always needed help to get stock through town. Boys would meet them at the covered bridge at the west end of town and drive to the east line of town for a dime or nickel." The Bridges were the most fortunate of Victorian Era children. Town life was never dull for youngsters growing up in a prosperous and caring family. There had once been a war that touched the town and its people as well the Bridges' very house, but it was so long ago as to be the stuff of make-believe.

LAND OWNERSHIP AND CHRISTIAN ETHICS

Bridges eventually became principle owner of 32,000 acres of coal, sand and timberland in West Virginia and Maryland. The holdings were called The West Virginia Coal and Timber Company. During the course of his life, Bridges took part in some 380 land transactions in Maryland alone. Like other Americans during the Gilded Age, Robert treated land, timber and minerals as means to an end rather than resources to be conserved. The economy agreed, to the point that Bridges' land carried an estimated value of nearly $500,000. The following gives a sense of the businessman, the chances he took and the ethics he lived by:

> It was known in Western Maryland that it was not necessary to have any writing in reference to any of Bridges business transactions--that his word was his bond--and after his death Mr. Slaymaker, a member of the lumber firm of Robert Whitmer & Sons of Philadelphia, stated he had told over a hundred persons about a business transaction he had with Mr. Bridges...that Bridges sold them 16,000 acres of spruce and hemlock timber, intending to close the deal in about a year while their company did not have in writing anything to hold him to the sale. He told them he would take $125,000 for the timber. Before the year expired he was offered $300,000 cash for the tract of timber. Mr. Whitmer stated that they certainly did not expect to get the property.

In commerce, the words of a practicing Christian had to be congruent with his deeds. If Bridges had failed to keep his word and instead demanded the additional $175,000 in profits, townspeople would have questioned his character. Bridges knew full well that he would one day stand before God. The question he would have to answer would concern the Golden Rule, not the rule of gold.

According to the Presbyterian theology of the period, land was God-given and created for humanity. People were charged with the responsibility of being good stewards of this resource. If Robert Bridges worked to be a good steward, so did his son Henry. This goal bridged the space between father and son. What changed was the definition of stewardship. Come a new century and people began to see land in a new light.

CHAPTER 2

ROBERT BRIDGES, 1863-1908:
Entrepreneur, Family Man and Community Leader in Western Maryland

THE ROUNDTOP HYDRAULIC CEMENT COMPANY

On May 17, 1785, the Potomac Company was created for the purpose of planning, building, and operating the Chesapeake and Ohio Canal; George Washington acted as its first president until a more important presidency came along. Promoters envisioned the canal as part of a transportation system linking the Mississippi River with Chesapeake Bay. The project was abandoned in 1820, taken up again and completed in 1850 at a cost of over $11,000,000.

In 1837 George Shafer became the first local entrepreneur to process limestone, which he sold under the brand name "Shafer Cement." Shafer found a ready buyer for his product in the C & O Canal Company, which used the material in construction and repair work. Robert Bridges and Charles Henderson bought the Shafer Cement Company in 1863, when it employed as many as 100 men in mining operations. The hydraulic cement works went by the name of The Roundtop Hydraulic Cement Company due to its location on Roundtop Mountain. The business was one of the most important in western Maryland.

The Roundtop Hydraulic Cement Company, ca. 1872. The product kept together the Capitol and Washington Monument. (The Maryland Historical Society, Baltimore, Maryland)

The C & O was not the only customer. In 1850 Philadelphia architect Thomas Ustick Walter won a congressional competition to expand both wings of the Capitol Building. Shafer Hydraulic Cement kept a building, if not a nation, intact. Later, Robert Bridges provided the cement that helped to complete work on the Washington Monument. Other Washington projects using Roundtop Hydraulic Cement included the offices for the Departments of War, State and Navy as well as the Washington Reservoir. Baltimore erected the Gunpower Waterworks, city hall and the gas works with Roundtop. The cement was also used on projects by the Baltimore and Ohio Railroad.

The Chesapeake and Ohio Canal. What looked to be slow-paced travel actually allowed for an extraordinary expansion of the American economy in the first half of the nineteenth century.

Everyday, with the exception of the Sabbath day, Robert Bridges saddled his horse or caught a canal boat to his cement works. It was a beautiful horse ride with the Canal on his right and the Potomac River on his left. For a half mile he traveled by the town, and he then was alone riding peacefully through the undulating mountains of western Maryland. It was a serene commute to work, and Bridges must have enjoyed this time alone to reflect upon all God's blessings and his good life.

The rock from which the cement was made was mined out of Roundtop Mountain above the works. There were five tunnels that stretched hundreds of yards back from the face of the cliff. Two of the tunnels ran through the hill and came out on the other side of the mountain. There was some surface mining on top of the mountain, but most of the limestone was mined underground. The works was, to say the least, dangerous.

Limestone cropped out in several places on the north bank of the Potomac River. The rock was fired at the factory in eight kilns, each twenty-one feet deep and ten feet in diameter at the base. Running night and day, the mill had a capacity to produce 400 barrels of cement every twenty-four hours or 2,200 barrels a week. Each barrel weighed 300 pounds, which may explain why so many of them slipped off a transport cable over the Potomac. Their remains are scattered on the river's bottom.

The mill for grinding the cement was driven by a water wheel, sixteen feet in diameter and sixteen feet in width, with buckets thirteen inches in depth. Water for turning the wheel was supplied by the C & O Canal, which ran by the side of the factory. The grinding was done with four pairs of French burrstones, each one five feet in diameter; the remaining product was then sifted to remove any unwanted rocks. Barrels of Roundtop were shipped east and west via the Baltimore and Ohio Railroad or the C & O Canal. Rail spurs connected the Baltimore and Ohio main tracks to the warehouse on the property across the Potomac. The canal was also utilized to bring in coal for running the steam-powered engines.

Work ground to a stop at the complex every Sabbath. Robert took his Book of Genesis very seriously, "Thus the heavens and the earth were finished, and all the host of them. And on the seventh day God finished his work which he had done, and he rested on the seventh day from all his work which he had done. So God blessed the seventh day and hallowed it, because on it God rested from all his work which he had done in creation." Bridges was a principled man who did not let profit outweigh principle. His wife Priscilla recalled an incident that showed clearly his approach to business, life and God:

> *An ardent Sabbatarian, he kept the Sabbath after the Scots custom of his fathers, and when, in connection with his cement business, he put a boat on the canal to ship his goods to Washington, he gave strict orders that every Saturday night the boat should be tied up till Monday. Once, when he had a contract with the government for a supply of cement, with a forfeit of several thousands of dollars if the cement failed to be on time, his boat was delayed so that Saturday evening found it one day's journey of Washington.*

> *The contractor telegraphed that his supply would be exhausted by Saturday night. The boat captain telegraphed that he could reach Washington by Monday morning by traveling Sunday and Sunday night. Though thousands of dollars would be forfeited by failure to*

be there, Mr. Bridges ordered the boat to be tied up over Sunday, as usual, saying that the question of financial loss was independent of living one's principles. He dismissed the matter from his mind, leaving the result to the Lord. Early Monday morning the contractor wired him that, owing to a strike among his hands, the cement would not be needed: and thus the Lord honored the keeping of His day.

None of this would have struck Roundtop workers as out of the ordinary. Robert Bridges was not only a boss but a fellow worshipper and neighbor. No doubt, when Bridges' wife Priscilla joined the Presbyterian Church in 1867, workers and townspeople rejoiced, and, no doubt, when Bridges' mother Rebecca died in 1878, they mourned too. The birth of Henry Percival that same year, though, was different. Only a parent could truly rejoice.

As a Presbyterian in Victorian America, Robert Bridges could be expected to spread the word of God as he understood it. In 1872 Robert helped establish Berkeley Springs Presbyterian Church, the first such institution in Morgan County. With the application of the Presbyterians living in Berkeley Springs to the Baltimore Presbytery, Robert became a part of a committee to found a church in this town. And, as a church elder, he applied his religious zeal close to home with an intent to bring more into the fold in his region of the country. Presbyterianism grew rapidly in America due to the establishment of new churches like that of the Berkeley Springs Presbyterian Church.

SILICA SAND MINING IN BERKELEY SPRINGS, WEST VIRGINIA

Bridges was always on the alert for his next business opportunity, and he found it in the sand, so to speak. According to the Morgan County Deed Book for May 12, 1868, Bridges was mining on land across from William Crosfield. The town was just six miles from Hancock. Bridges was familiar with the area from 1860, when he helped make possible the construction of a bridge over the Potomac that connected the two communities.

The pure silica sand which Robert and others mined came from the buried pressurized beaches of the continent during the Paleozoic time period. The pressure of the earth over millions of years formed the pure SiO_2 Silica sand. The period in which the sand developed ranged from 600,000,000 and 230,000,000 years ago and was characterized by the development of the first fishes, amphibians, reptiles and land plants. The Appalachian Mountain range, the oldest mountain range in the world, erupted volcanically during this ancient period, and it sporadically pushed these beaches of pure white sand to the surface of the earth. In places along the range the pure silica sand pushed up close enough to the surface where it was economically feasible to mine the sand. One of these locations was in Berkeley Springs. Among the early pioneers of mining this Oriskany Sand in West Virginia was N. Q. Speer. Bridges and Speer were involved in mining from the very beginning of the development of sand mining in Berkeley Springs. In 1748, a young surveyor by the name of George Washington, had overlooked this valuable resource. The prehistoric leftovers made for good sand to use in the Industrial Age.

The Berkeley Glass Sand Works officially opened in 1878 with Bridges as president. The new mill was, for its time, state of the art. Steam moved the giant millstones that crushed the coarse sand into its finished state. The product went to market on a narrow-gauge railroad that serviced the site.

**Sand quarry ironworks shop. The men knew Robert Bridges
as an employer who tried to live by the Golden Rule.**

The combination of steam and iron must have given Bridges an idea. In 1883 a local newspaper announced the incorporation of the Susquehanna and Southern Railway Company at Annapolis. Among the incorporators were Bridges and his longtime associate Charles Henderson, along with other Hancock business leaders. The idea was for a short line to connect with the narrow gauge railroad from the plant. This would give Bridges and Henderson a reliable connection to the main line of the Baltimore & Ohio Railroad.

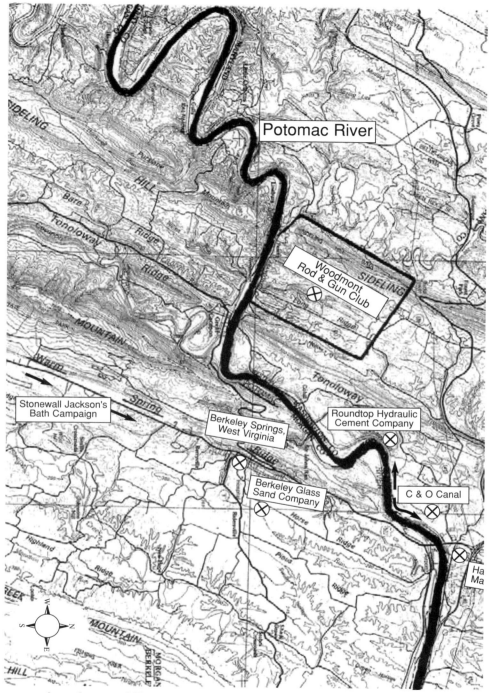

Local map of Hancock and Berkeley Springs. The area was both beautiful and blessed with an abundance of natural resources.

The production of silica was little more pleasant than that of sausage or legislation. After the sand rock was blasted away from the walls of the quarry with black powder, the men went to work with their sledgehammers. The workers, many of them immigrants, then carried smaller rocks to mule-drawn rail carts. The carts moved over another narrow gauge tramway that went from the mines to the crushers at the plant. The millstones did their job, and the product was ready for transport, to glass manufacturers and other customers.

**Early sand miners at Berkeley Glass Sand Company.
The work here was not work for the weak or the
asthmatic. (Fred T. Newbraugh Collection)**

The business flourished under Bridges' leadership. On May 9, 1892, it incorporated under the laws of West Virginia as the Berkeley Glass Sand Company and issued capital stock valued at $50,000. Among the investors were two gentlemen from Pittsburgh. Their presence foreshadowed the development of the largest glass manufacturing company in the United States, The Pittsburgh Plate Glass Corporation. Along with more investors, Bridges looked to secure access to water; the production of his sand depended on water-cleaning the product after crushing. In June 1892, the town trustees of Berkeley Springs granted him riparian rights to Warm Springs Run, a nearby creek running into the Potomac. This control of water gave Bridges a strategic advantage in business because he was located first in line to use the clean water as it then ran by other plants on its way to the Potomac River.

Bridges the businessman did not ignore matters of faith. In October 1893 he authored a report on the state of the Presbyterian Church in Hancock. This narrative illustrates a tender concern for the church together with an understanding of its importance in community life:

In the making of our annual report to Presbytery, we hope we can say that the official fidelity of Minister & Elders (we have no Deacons) has been good. And it is with pleasure we record the fact that the attendance from the services of the sanctuary has been improving & a general interest seems to be manifesting itself. Many portions of our field are already whitening to the hawses. God's Spirit has been poured out & we have cause for devout thanksgiving in the gathering of eight precious souls we hope to welcome others at our next communion.

With one or two exceptions the Christian Department & Growth in grace of church members have been good. Commendable zeal is shown in S.S. work especially in the outlying mission fields. Catechetical & Bible instruction are attended to in S.S. & families. But we fear that family worship is not as generally maintained as it should be. In the congregation the Sabbath is observed but in the Community at large God's day is sadly desecrated. We fear that God's people do not worship Him with their substance as liberally as his word enjoins or his cause demands. It is with sorrow that we have still to report the malevolence of interference and worldly amusements in some parts of our mission field. It hinders our work, but notwithstanding these hindrances the Church has had remarkable success in reaching the destitute in its vicinity- with these kindly greetings which meet us by the wayside we feel called reborn like the Apostle—"thank God and take courage." Robert Bridges, Clerk

The wonder is where Bridges found the energy to devote to both work and worship.

**Certificate from Chicago's 1893 World's Fair for purity of silica.
The award testified to the quality of the product Robert Bridges
sold as it invited competitors to try their hand at mining too.**

Bridges' product made a splash in Chicago during the Columbian Exposition of 1893. This extraordinary event attracted some twenty-one million visitors, many of whom were introduced to Berkeley sand. The Morgan Messenger boasted, "Morgan County is not so bad after all, as can be witnessed by the World's Fair awards for glass sand and limestone … H. H. Hunter [a local resident] was given an award in the World's Fair for glass sand from this place. Good for Berkeley." The sand from rural Morgan County won a blue ribbon for its 99.9 percent purity.

If Robert Bridges had about him the touch of Midas, he also had to deal with those times when a person, inevitably, feels more like Job. That happened to Bridges in September 1897, when the two-story cement mill at

Roundtop burned. This was the first major setback Bridges and his partner Henderson had faced. In addition, a bridge connecting the mill with its cement kilns fell into the C & O Canal. But there was no question that Bridges would rebuild, and quickly. A year later, Bridges settled out of court a suit that charged him with underground trespass—Roundtop allegedly took material that did not belong to it one-hundred feet below the ground. The suit filed for $10,000 alleged some 32,000 barrels of cement rock were removed from the underground mines. It was at times like these that a person drew on his faith to accept the bad along with the good.

Quarry of Berkeley Glass Sand Company. A product mined so primitively had many modern uses.

The Protestant Work Ethic taught industrialists like Bridges to work hard and create wealth. Their success in turn was to be taken as a sign of God's blessing. But this was not enough for Bridges, who struggled to apply the Golden Rule to all aspects of his life, business as well as personal. A Presbyterian writer of the time suggests the dilemma Bridges confronted in trying to do both right and well:

What is a Trust? It is a combination of those engaged in a special kind of business for the purpose of controlling that business....This Trust Company determines how much sugar shall be refined, what shall be the wages of the workmen, and what the price of the refined product will be....Manifestly these Trusts, conducted by prudent, Christian Men, may be a blessing to the land. Why, then, the out-cry against them? Because, in addition to the good purpose already noted, they have all the evils that are incident to monopolies when in the hands of selfish men....As the purpose of the combination is to control the business, it must be so managed, it is often thought, as to crush out all competition. As the Trust is able to create the product somewhat cheaper than an individual firm can do, sugar is undersold by the combination long enough to drive the competitor to bankruptcy, into the Trust, or else out of the business. Is this ac-cording to the Golden Rule? Would Christ do such a thing?

The writer J.A. Quarles asked two other questions that were sure to have made Bridges take pause and think. "But when a Trust uses its power to grind the faces of the poor, it violates the golden rule, and acts contrary to the Spirit of Christ....The Sugar Trust is said to have arbitrarily raised the price of its product this past season some twenty-five per cent, and thus real-ized millions of dollars, most of which came from the hard earned wages of the poor. Is this the Golden Rule? Would Christ have acted thus?"

The question of salvation weighed heavily on the heart of at least one Presbyterian businessman. If there were doubts, Quarles offered comfort by way of a challenge. "The Christian is expected to love his neighbor in the manner and to the extent that Christ has loved him. The Christian law, therefore, not only binds men to the Golden Rule of reciprocity, but, makes Christ's love to us the measure of our duty to others....More than this, we must do for others what we judge Christ would do for them were He in our stead."

Bridges' faith influenced his business practices. Robert would not have been considered a robber baron in the image of Carnegie or Rockefeller. He operated his company not as a trust, but as a locally-run business sensitive to the needs of customers and workers. Every barrel of sand and cement had to pass inspection with the Golden Rule. His pastor, Reverend James S. Webster, a Scotsman would have been available to advise Robert in issues of faith as well as business.

During the last decade of his life, Robert Bridges could better appreciate the travails of Job. In May 1902, Roundtop burned down a second time. Al-though the factory was rebuilt, Bridges' business faced increasing competi-tion from the makers of Portland cement, which was growing increasingly popular for its quick-drying properties. At the same time, Berkeley Glass Sand was facing expanded competition. There were at least eight firms active in the area including Samuel S. Woods' Pennsylvania Glass Sand Co. which had recently bought Hancock White Sand Works in the Warm Springs Valley of Berkeley Springs.

In August 1905 yet another competitor emerged and was chartered as West Virginia and Pennsylvania Glass Sand Company of Baltimore. "The company will operate in the sand district just north of Berkeley Springs, in Morgan County," one of the local papers reported, "and will build several plants for different purposes in connection with their business. The promoters are all residents of Baltimore...." The future of a local business, if not the Golden Rule by which it operated, was in doubt.

In December of this same year a Sand Men's Banquet Supper was held in Berkeley Springs at the grand old Hotel Washington. The twenty gentlemen present represented the companies along the Warm Springs Valley, and Robert attended on behalf of the Berkeley Glass Sand Company. "the repeat was greatly enjoyed and a very pleasant evening spent. The guests were also pleasantly entertained by a male quartette of colored boys at the conclusion of the banquet while they were enjoying their Havana's. The companies in the sand business near here are the Pennsylvania, the Berkeley, the West Virginia and Pennsylvania, the Speer, the National Milling and Mining Company and once being opened by Messrs. Fouse and Bechtel. These works employ quite a number of men and the payroll each month is a big item, adding very materially to the prosperity of Berkeley Springs."

A year later Bridges entered into an agreement with Frank Ehlen of Baltimore to lease the Berkeley Glass Sand Company for ten years, preserving the name of the company so long as he owned it. Bridges basically turned over the operation of the plant at an annual rental rate of 15 cents per ton of sand mined and for a royalty of $2,500 per year. "The party of said Part to pay $10,000 in advance royalties $5,000 at the signing and $5,000 Nov. 2, 1906....Further Ehlen has an option to buy all the property mentions within 3 years for $100,000 to be paid in $30,000.00 payment at signing and each 6 months thereafter until $90,000 is paid and the $10,000 advance to be remaining due....Lessee also agrees to spend $10,000 in improvement on the plant within 1 year after Nov. 20, 1906 --- and $8,000.00 annually on upkeep and improvement." Bridges would collect rent from the two houses on the property and till the fields then used by the company.

At no point did Robert let business get in the way of family. In July 1906 he wrote to Henry, then practicing law in Baltimore. "Hope you may have a happy Christmas Holiday, and many returns. [Continue] Growing in grace, as you advance in Jesus. As you know our Catechism teaches, when justified in God's sight, through Christ, we are then adopted into his family. Then the work of sanctification begins and continues until death. It is a progressive work. Affly, Your Father."

Henry P. Bridges and his two bird dogs in front of First Presbyterian Church, Baltimore, ca. 1906. Life in the city would help Bridges appreciate the countryside.

Henry valued such letters from his father. "In time of sorrow and in time when the world seems cold," he wrote to Robert, "friends seem to be un-true-our parents are dear to us. They are always true--faithful--and I always try to do everything for them and their happiness."

In another letter Robert advised Henry, "I hope this Sabbath you are with us and it maybe a blessing to you spiritually. Life is uncertain, death certain then 'what will it profit a man if he gain the whole world and loose his soul.'" Bridges understood the temptation to sell one's soul for profit in business. But he had stayed faithful, even while becoming the wealthiest man in western Maryland. Henry, a Baltimore lawyer, was now being put to this same test of faith in Baltimore. Would he respond as his father had?

Only four months before his death, Bridges' close friend Andrew Carnegie and fellow Scotsman came to Hancock for the dedication of a new Moellor pipe organ at the Church. The plaque reads,

I Hereby dedicate this organ to the glory of God and the service of man to commemorate the memory of Andrew Carnegie, Philanthropist and friend of this Church, and of Robert Bridges, an Elder of this Church for 57 years, Whose father, Robert Ferguson Bridges, preceding him as an Elder for more than six years, was the first Elder of this Church, together with Robert Wasson, Whose dust sleeps by the doorway....May it ever remind us of those who loved the Lord and walked in service before us.

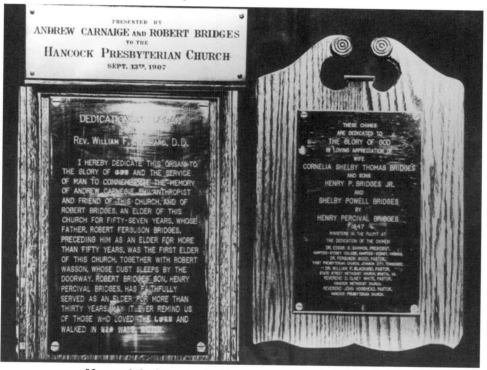

Memorial plagues dedicating organ and chimes for Hancock Presbyterian Church, given by Andrew Carnegie and Robert Bridges. Each industrialist struggled with the challenge of bringing faith to bear on business.

The second-to-last letter Robert sent to Henry is dated December 13, 1907. It reads:

Dear Henry,

You referred to your "loneliness on the Sabbath"--any suggestion I make is prompted by affection and deep interest in your spiritual welfare. Never forget what our heavenly Father has stated in his Word, "What will it prophet a man if he gains the whole world and lose his own soul, or what can a man gain in exchange for his soul?"

You will observe there is no answer in the Bible to this, because nothing can be compared in value to the soul. It plainly teaches you are immortal, will live forever eternally happy or miserable. This is a momentous thought. If you on the Sabbath will go to a Bible class and Church twice where you have such fine preaching (Baltimore City) then in the interval read Mathew Henry's Commentary, you will doubtless realize much comfort. My children are remembered daily at a throne of grace by your Father. Doubtless your Mother doth not forget you in her prayers. Hoping soon to see you, also have your X-mas visit,

Affly, Your Father.

Bridges was in his seventy-seventh year, and he still held fast to his faith convictions. He advised his son, a twenty-nine year old bachelor alone in the busy city of Baltimore, to do the same. Robert's last letter to Henry is dated December 18, 1907. In it Bridges writes of the death of his sister Katherine:

My Dear Son:

It is with a sad heart I notify you of the death of my dear sister. She will be buried Friday at 10 A.M. Either Drew or Eugene will be here. Flora Witherspoon is here, I expected Millard on Thursday. Sammie was going home on Friday, will now remain until Monday the 23rd. It might suit you and Mr. Ingram to make Jim visit about that time--you could attend to your business either Friday P.M. or Saturday. It is a call to all of us be ready, the young may die, the old must. It is a source of great consolation, she felt prepared for the change, therefore we can think of her in company with those who preceded her in that house of eternal happiness. It is my prayer that all as a family may spend an eternity there.

"The old must" die—Bridges no doubt felt the approach of his own death, which he faced with courage and faith. When a man knows of his death, and yet faces it with faith, he is certainly a man to be remembered as an example of faith. Bridges' faith in God led him to believe that all his family would join him in heaven, "that house of eternal happiness."

ROBERT BRIDGES OF HANCOCK

On January 11, 1908, the Hagerstown Morning Herald reported that Robert Bridges had died early Thursday of pneumonia at his home in Hancock.

> *"He will be buried from Hancock Presbyterian Church this afternoon at 2 o'clock....Services will be conducted by Dr. James Webster, of Scotland."*

> *Mr. Bridges enjoyed excellent health until about ten days ago, when a slight attack of grippe developed into pneumonia. In a final effort to save him, a special train left Baltimore over the Western Maryland Railroad, with Dr. Joseph Bloodgood and other specialists aboard, and oxygen was liberally used, but a slight attack of heart failure resulted in death.*

> *Few men in western Maryland were more widely known or respected by a wider circle of people than Robert Bridges. For over half a century he was identified with the commercial development of the western part of the State, and in that time he amassed a fortune estimated at considerably over a million dollars. Many years before West Virginia's great coal and lumber wealth was exploited he foresaw the great possibilities of that region, and at the time of his death owned many thousands of acres of coal land and other vast lumber tracts. Few men ever kept themselves so completely out of the public eye yet at the same time exercised so great an influence over a large part of the State.*

Bridges' obituary offered:

> *When the pulpit was vacant he would assemble the congregation and read to them from some volume of approved sermons, and during the week he would conduct the prayer service, though speaking and praying in public always a severe cross to him. Several years ago, at his own expense he remodeled the little church and bore half the cost of a beautiful organ, (the other half bore by Andrew Carnegie) and in his will he set aside a sufficient sum to pay annually his regular contribution to the pastor's salary.*

The obituary could have added that Presbyterian spirituality and preaching affected Bridges' practice of commerce in Hancock. Faith and commerce intersected in the business place through inspiring Bridges' faithful entrepreneurial endeavors. The church played a central role in the life of

Robert. He lived out his faith convictions in relation to keeping the Sabbath; to the creation and the land; to his employed laborers; to his moral and ethical life; to his Elder responsibilities to the Church and most importantly to his family life. But this is not to say that Bridges was a saint. His support of the Fugitive Slave Act shows him to be an all-too-flawed human, just as Robert Bridges knew he was.

He was a man of substantial wealth in relation to others in the region. His wealth was accumulated through hard work and solid business management. He raised eleven children to adulthood in a faith that demanded practice beyond Sunday at church. The faith of Robert Bridges was passed from his forefathers to his offspring. Bridges remained a citizen of Hancock his whole life, and he served as public school commissioner for many years. He was a good Democrat but an unsuccessful candidate for the state legislature. What did this life amount to? Perhaps it was testament to the old Scottish adage, "Every tub stands on its own bottom and makes its own way in life."

Robert Bridges, humble servant of God, Presbyterian Elder and businessman who believed, "Every tub stands on it own bottom and makes its own way in life."

CHAPTER 3

HENRY P. BRIDGES, 1878-1906: *The Making of a Capitalist*

HENRY P. BRIDGES: A BOY WITH A DREAM

Suddenly the awful weight of that old, twin-hammered, double-barrelled blunderbuss I proudly called "my shotgun" had vanished. The weapon might have been feather-light for all I was aware of it. My whole attention was fixed on the thick patch of laurel just beyond the old rail fence in front of me. I was stiff with tension. I was twelve years old and I had just spotted my first wild turkey. A flock of them were in that laurel. You could hear them scratching around, gobbling to each other. But you could not see them in the thick growth.

There were three of us behind that fence. Three boys, all with shotguns about as large as themselves. We had flushed the turkeys from the buckwheat field behind us. The birds had run into the laurel. "We can hear 'em, but how can we shoot what we can't see?" Ray Faith whispered, with desperation on his young face. "Be quiet!" hissed my other pal, Bob Hughes. I said nothing. As if hypnotized, I stared at the laurel. And then I saw it: an oval, blue head weaving back, and forth, sharp, black eyes peering through the brush, a wild turkey! In an agony of silence, I raised the gun and aimed for the head. I pulled the trigger.

The blast of the gun nearly knocked me flat. The thunderous echo of the shot seemed to reverberate madly with the wild and frantic squawks of the turkeys as they suddenly flew from the laurel every which way. "Come on, come on!" my buddies screamed, now dancing a hysterical jig. Over the fence we scrambled and into the laurel we ran. There was a thrashing sound just ahead. We pushed on in. Then we saw it. I had killed my first wild turkey.

Henry P. Bridges, second youngest son of Robert Bridges, came of age as a hunter a few miles outside of Hancock off Long Hollow Road. The town provided middle-class families an ideal mix of work and nature—the cement mill and mines along with a textiles' factory to go with apple and peach orchards, not to mention the abundant game.

The boy showed an entrepreneurial spirit at an early age. He often heard his father talking about business dealings and he learned early to create wealth by his father's example. He began by raising pigeons. With the revenue from selling pigeons he bought sheep and kept them with local farmers. He sold a portion of the wool to the farmers in return for their boarding his sheep. As he saved, Henry dreamed of ever-more opportunities.

Bridges did not recall where the idea came from to start his own zoo. He just envisioned people coming to see his animals and paying admission for the privilege. He set about building game pens and cages for his newest enterprise. He trapped the local indigenous game of ruffed grouse, rabbits, quail, deer, wild turkeys and bobcats for the zoo. He was comfortable in the wilds of the Maryland mountains and trapped with great skill. His love for the animals increased and he learned to care for wild species of all kinds. Zoo admissions actually grew over time, and this enterprise enabled Henry to learn business practices that became bedrock in his life.

**The "zoo" bear Israel and keepers. Animals
fascinated Henry Bridges from an early age.**

Bridges saved enough money by age fourteen to travel to Canada. His sights were set on the main attraction for his zoo, two bears. After negotiating with the owner, he faced the problem of getting them back to Hancock. The deal was made for $250, and Henry found himself the owner of Nellie and Israel. Provided he could find a proper iron cage to ship them, the railroad arranged for their transport for another $250. Bridges left for home and his bears followed shortly after him. When he arrived home his father said to him, "Henry, you beat any boy I ever saw in my life. I never know what you're going to do next!" The youngster replied, "Why, I'm going to make my way, I'm going to make money."

EDUCATION AND BALTIMORE

At the age of seventeen Bridges received his high school degree in Hancock. He then attended Hampton Sydney College in Virginia. He left after two years without a degree and came to Baltimore. In order to complete his college education, he entered Bryant Stratton Business College for a year. Next, he entered the University of Maryland with the intention of becoming a doctor. But the sight of blood during the operation he attended caused him to pass out cold. So began the pursuit of another career. Henry entered the University of Maryland Law School, where he received his degree in June 1903.

Henry P. Bridges (seated far left) with his classmates from the University of Maryland Medical School, 1900. The occasional skull upset Henry far less than the sight of blood in an operating room.

Henry P. Bridges and friend at University of Maryland Law School, 1902. The law proved a better fit for young Bridges.

Henry spent the first part of his career in Baltimore looking for business. He soon ran through the $250 his father lent him to get started. Fortunately, one of his first clients was the Western Maryland Railroad. He was principally a real estate lawyer and Baltimore was in the midst of a booming housing construction period with forty thousand new homes being built. Though eager for any kind of business, he focused on housing and eventually owned many new homes which he leased. Bridges lived in Baltimore during a time of unprecedented growth. As a real estate lawyer with capital, he would have been poised to take advantage of this boom. But in the same way he was not destined to be a doctor, Bridges would become something other than a real estate mogul. But the time in Baltimore allowed him to meet Addison E. Mullikin, a fraternity brother in Alpha Zeta Chapter, a friend he would hold dear for the rest of his life.

Major industrialist and financiers were all scrambling to take advantage of a robust commercial economy. The founders of The Continental Trust, were the Warfields, Alexander Brown, George Jenkins, and Isidor Raynor, with $2 million capital and $2 million surplus. The Honorable S. Davies Warfield was a friend of the young attorney. Bridges met the Governor of Maryland, Edwin Warfield and his wife through, S. Davies Warfield. Baltimore was a great place for a young attorney to get his start and make life long business contacts by virtue of his law profession. Business was growing in Baltimore City principally because of the Inner Harbor and the trade in coal and other important resources.

GETTING STARTED: WORK AND FAMILY

As much as he enjoyed the outdoors, Henry Bridges also possessed a serious side. It is revealed in this article, *THE TRUTH REVEALED*, which he wrote in 1901. The story concerns a young woman, Julia Abbott, who was sent to prison for a crime she did not commit:

Gradually the shadows of night passed away and the faint red tint in the eastern sky foretold the approach of the day. A few minutes later and the sun arose majestically over the distant peaks and with his glowing beams chased away the few lingering shadows and kissed the morning dews from the grass and flowers.

Higher and higher rose the sun and more beautiful became the day, until at length one little ray of sunlight crept in through the window of cell No. 13, of Rockville prison and kissed the face of a fair young girl lying there on a cot. What effect that little sunbeam had on that girl's life no one can tell, yet it aroused her from her slumber and awakened her to the realization of the fact that she must content herself for ten long years with only such freedom as penitentiary life affords.

But why should one so fair be so imprisoned? The story is a simple one and shows plainly the fallibility of man in executing justice. It seems but a few years since the local papers of Rockville had announced the birth of a girl baby in the family of Judge Abbott. Her advent on that beautiful May morning brought such joy into that home as only parents can realize. As the rosebud under the nourishing and protecting care of nature gradually unfolds and develops into a perfect and beautiful white rose, the pride of roses, so this little bud of humanity, under the tender and loving care of her parents gradually developed into a full blown flower of womanhood a pride not only to her parents but to the people of the town in general. She was a woman of beautiful and symmetrical form, fair skinned, deep blue eyes and hair of a golden hue. Her future was most promising, the young people admired her and the old people caressed her; and happiness seemed to be in store for her forever, but alas, as life's pathway is not always strewn with flowers, so dark clouds were gathering in this girl's life.

Much to the astonishment of her friends she was charged with the murder of Mrs. Johnston. The law claims she must be considered innocent until proven guilty, thanks to the Code of Justice for even this charitable expression toward this beautiful young woman. It was whispered that she might be the first in her state to pay the extreme penalty of the law, and die the sad and ignominious death of a murderess upon the scaffold.

She was brought into the court room and tried before a jury and while she claimed to be innocent, still all the evidence seemed against her. When the trial ended, the court room was crowded and many anxiously waited for the verdict. When her jury filed in one by one, a hush went over the crowd, and all breathlessly awaited the announcement of the verdict. Amidst the stolid quiet and solemnity of the room the foreman arose, and in a deep voice said, 'guilty in the second degree.' The grief of the heart-broken parents and the sobbing of the convicted girl touched the heart of the old Judge, and he arose and with tears in his eyes and in a low and trembling voice said, "It is a sad task for me, but I am obliged to sentence this girl to ten years in the penitentiary." Cold chills seemed to creep over the crowd and as the girl was led out all heads were bowed in sorrow and tears.

Seven years of the ten had passed since she was sentenced but on account of good behavior she had been pardoned before the expiration of her term. As she rode along toward her home, one thing came into her mind, that troubled her, and that was how could she meet her lover, who for many years had given her advice, and in whose mind she held first place both before and after alleged guilt? True, his love for her had apparently not grown less, for while she was in prison, he had written her several letters and sent her flowers. She knew she was innocent and often hoped that something would happen that would wipe out this stain and leave her free to meet her lover and the public as a pure innocent girl as she was. Often while in prison she felt that surely some day the truth would be made know and that this cloud which hung over her would be removed, yet she dared not even let her mind dwell on it as it seemed improbable.

As she was sleeping on her cot at home and dreaming, she seemed to see an officer approach, and as he came nearer she recognized him as the one who had taken her to the prison seven years before, the officer spoke, and as she heard his words she awoke with a shudder, and found that her dream was true for there stood the officer clad in blue with his big brass buttons shining like gems. Her face began to whiten with fear, and the officer said in a gentle tone, "Be *not frightened, my girl. Come with me right away, there is a man in cell No. 14 who is dying and wants to see you right away, lose no time, for he wants to tell you something which he says will clear you from the stain that hangs over your life."*

She with the officer hastened to the prison, and was met at the gate by the warden, who urged them to hasten as the man was nearly gone. A reporter joined them at the gate, and the three hastened to the cell. There on a couch lay a man, rolling and tossing in the greatest agony. Julie knelt at his bedside and as he rolled back his dark eyes and looked into her face he recognized her, and in tones of deepest distress cried out, "Forgive me for what I have done for I have blighted one of the purest lives, and I could not go without telling you that it was I who murdered Mrs. Johnston, and my dying wish is that my confession may be made known all over the country and that you may be restored to your social position from which my cowardice and wickedness has dragged you." Then he expired, and with tears in her eyes she kissed his death-like forehead and stole out of the cell.

Her burden had been removed and what a change it made in her life, her very countenance seemed to change and she seemed another girl. The next day the papers were filled with long articles explaining how she had innocently suffered disgrace for another and had come back ....as she had left them....

Although a sportsman by nature, Henry approached life with a strong sense of fair play. He was moved by the plight of someone who had been punished wrongfully. He understood conservation from the same perspective: Neither the land nor its creatures should be made to suffer for no good reason.

Henry P. Bridges in his law office, 1906.

Henry's literary venture may also be explained as an influence of his older brother Robert Willis Bridges, a writer and poet. Help came from other quarters as well. Twelve years Henry's senior, his brother John Breathed was also a noted financier in Hancock with interest in the Hancock Bank. Brother Taliaferro had interests in the Wabash Railroad and the lumber industry. Whenever possible, John gave his lawyer brother business to transact for him. Other siblings helped in this way, too.

Less than three months before Henry's graduation from law school, Chicago meatpacker Gustavus F. Swift. Bridges clipped this article from the Chicago Tribune on Swift's life philosophy:

> *Don't drink.*
>
> *No man, however rich, has enough money to waste in putting on style.*
>
> *The richer a man gets the more careful he should be to keep his head level. The man that doesn't know his business from the top clean down to the bottom isn't any kind of a businessman.*
>
> *Business, religion and pleasure of the right kind should be the only things in life for any man.*
>
> *A big head and a big bank account were never found together to the credit of anyone, and never will be.*
>
> *No young man is rich enough to smoke 25 cent cigars.*

Every time a man loses his temper, he loses his head, and when he loses his head he loses several chances.

Next to knowing his business, it's a mighty good thing to know as much about your neighbors as possible, especially if he's in the same line.

The best a man ever did shouldn't be his standard for the rest of his life.

The successful men of today worked mighty hard for what they have got, the men of tomorrow will have to work harder to get it away.

You can never make a big success working for anybody else.

These maxims were universal for such Victorian business titans as Rockefeller, Carnegie, Morgan, Swift and his fellow packers. Each observation struck Henry as important. He had a bit of the baron in him too, although his father taught him it was a sin to rob.

Henry was a winsome and attractive young man. He had a bounce in his step and a sparkle in his eyes that women had a hard time ignoring. He was an optimist and a person of faith. His looks and his nature made him a popular date for the young ladies of Baltimore. He kept a log in his diary of the women he dated:

Girls met 1901 - 02 - 03 – 04

Miss Helen Wheeler nice looking, sweet manners. Met her at Hancock, MD, Aug. 1898. Baltimore girl Miss Amie Hart met four years ago became good friends, good Christian girl, right large, nice looking. Baltimore girl Misses Levening on Oak Street two very sweet girls, one my friend Patterson had case with, good looking, sweet manners Baltimore girls.

... Miss Namie and Mary Sullivan, 1728 N. Calvert Street became very good friends. Very charming girls. Balto girls Miss Rosalie Conor, 214 E. Biddle Street one of the best friend I had in the city. Very good looking girl, dark hair and large eyes. Splendid character. Balto girl Miss Hulda Bennett, 1200 N. Calvert Street very pretty and handsome, impressed me as a big flirt.

... Miss Reynolds, N. Charles Street, met two years ago, Balto girl Miss Ethel Panter, N. Calvert, great society girl afterwards became engaged to [Confederate] General [John B.] Hood's son.

Bridges fell in love with none of the above. Instead, he gave his heart to Ella Vaughan Patterson. After asking Ella to marry him, Henry heard from her mother. Mrs. Patterson informed him, "My daughter will need a chauffeur, a person to clean house, a home in the country and a home in the city, fine clothing and jewelry, and the best there is to offer a woman of the times." For all intents and purposes, Mrs. Patterson ended the courtship with this comment. In his diary entry for January 2, 1904, Henry sadly wrote this poem, *A Lover's Soliloquy*:

> *Who am I that I dare to aspire, To woo you and wed you, my heart's desire!*
>
> *To dare to pay court to one in your station, When you are desired by the wealthiest man of the nation.*
>
> *Of the aristocracy of gold -- for money is king. Personal merit counts nothing - the dollar's the thing.*
>
> *Then go to the bride you've purchased with gold. And do not tell me her caresses are cold.*
>
> *You can buy her jewels and dresses - models of art; You've bought her body - you can't buy her heart.*
>
> *Then take your bargain -- I have the best, I have the heart - you can have the rest.*
>
> *When your wife is sad - Oh I do not complain; And the tears on her pillow - ask her not to explain.*
>
> *But think of the other - you ruined his life, And blighted his future - he loved your wife.*
>
> *Did she love him? Tis sad but true, With her heart and soul, she but tolerates you.*
>
> *She warned you she'd never be true; You forced her to marry - that bargain you'll me.*
>
> *Her life in mine was blended - our hearts were as one, And they died together when the ceremony was done.*
>
> *Then a toast to your bride in her setting of gold, May our love for each other never grow cold.*
>
> *Sometimes, only work can mend a broken heart.*

BRIDGES AS ATTORNEY AND MAN OF FAITH

In 1904, Bridges served as the attorney for, Isaac Swain, an African American who sued the New England Mutual Company over a policy. Henry's choice of client was more than a little noteworthy. While Baltimore looked to be a modern city with its impressive sanitation and public transportation systems, it still clung to some old and bad habits, particularly in the matter of race relations. When Bridges won the case for his client, news of the decision found its way onto the pages of the Baltimore Sun. If the paper was surprised, it obviously did not know the makeup of the lawyer in question,

> *JURY AWARDS NEGRO $600- Isaac O. Swain Gets Verdict Against Insurance Company Isaac O. Swain, colored, obtained a verdict for $600.95 in the Superior Court yesterday against the New England Mutual Insurance Company of Massachusetts in his suit to recover an additional life insurance premium, alleged to have been paid by him because of false and fraudulent representations of an agent of the company. The verdict was for the full amount claimed, with interest. The declaration described Swain as "an ignorant and inexperienced farmer residing in Allegheny County, Maryland." The testimony showed that on August 2, 1897, Swain insured his life in the defendant company for $10,000 giving his note for $420 for the premium. Subsequently, in the same month, an additional premium of $429 was collected from him.*

> *The case was tried by Henry P. Bridges, E. R. Dickerson and W. Burns Trundle for the plaintiff and Edward Duffy for the defendant.*

To Henry, Isaac Swain may have been another Julia Abbott, someone wronged and in need of help. A good deal of Henry's compassion was the product of a simple and yet deep Presbyterian faith. While living in Baltimore, the young man cut many sermons out of the Monday morning Sun; the paper printed the sermons from selected area churches. Henry's diary is filled with these clippings. Of particular interest are those from James Cardinal Gibbons, Catholic prelate of Baltimore. Given the level of friction that then existed between these faiths, Henry showed that he could move beyond yet another of the prejudices of the day.

Gibbons was one of the great figures in American Catholicism. According to historian Sherry Olson,

> *Born in Ireland, James Gibbons is more often remembered for his concern for the new immigrant nationalities. In 1880 he had created*

an Italian parish, St. Leo's. He was building a larger church for the Bohemian parish of St. Wenceslas. He dedicated three new Polish churches in East Baltimore: Sacred Heart, St. Stanislas Kostka, and Holy Rosary. But it was the German experience in Baltimore that stamped his views of American society. As he watched the rapid expansion of ...St. Michael's, St. Alphonsus, St. James and Holy Cross, he saw their German parish schools become Americanized. Both his social concern and his intense patriotism were part of the loyalty and development of East and South Baltimore.

Here is an undated sermon Henry pasted into his diary. The subject matter suggests a religious side to the budding sportsman and lawyer:

APPEALS TO THE LAITY- Cardinal Cites Example of The Primitive Christians.

ASKS PROFESSION OF FAITH-Citizens of the Republic of the Church, He Says, Is the Most Glorious of Titles.

Gave Rational Idea of God

The Christian religion gave the pagan world a rational idea of God. It proclaimed a God essentially one, existing from eternity to eternity. It proclaimed a God who created all things by His power, who governs all things by His wisdom, and whose superintending Providence watches over the affairs of nations as well as of men, without whom not even a bird can fall to the ground. It spoke of a God infinitely just, infinitely merciful, infinitely holy, and infinitely wise. This idea of a Supreme Being so consonant to our intellectual conceptions was in striking contrast with the low, debasing and sensual notions which the pagan world ascribed to its divinities....

The Christian religion gave not only light to man's intellect, but also peace to his heart. It brought him that peace of God which surpasseth all understanding, and which springs from the conscious possession of the truth. It communicated to him a triple peace. It taught him how to have peace with God by the observance of His commands; peace with his neighbor by fulfilling the law of justice and charity, and peace with himself by keeping his passions subject to reason, and reason guided by the light of faith....

Christianity Universal

The religion of Christ, on the contrary, was cosmopolitan, worldwide, universal, restricted by no state lines or national boundaries.

Christ came as the world's Physician. He alone could feel the pulse of humanity and prescribe to each man the remedies to assuage his fever and restore him to spiritual vigor. It was the first and only religion that proclaimed the fatherhood of God and brotherhood of Christ....But when you came into our midst, knowledge of the fact was brought home to us that this court had for its chief one who from long experience and long study recognized that law is a science; one who had acquired knowledge from the sources of the law; who recognized, in the language of Lord Coke, that "ratio est anima legis," and again in the language of Coke, "One in the sunshine must descend deep in the well of learning to view the bright stars of knowledge overhead; one who had for his object the ascertainment of truth, and who brought to the attainment of that object more than usual ability, with no horror for work; one in whose hands the sword of justice became a staff upon which the innocent, and those in whom the right was, might lean for support and feel its safety."

Bridges collected sermons reflecting his personal beliefs. Here is another of the cardinal's:

FAITH ALONE SATISFIES: So Declares Cardinal Gibbons, In All Saints' Day Sermon.

Let us take up one by one the various sources of human enjoyment. Can earthly goods adequately satisfy the cravings of the human heart and fill up the measure of its desires? Experience proves the contrary....My brethren, it is only an unclouded faith and the eternal life to come that can give man an adequate sense of his dignity and more responsibility. It is this belief alone that satisfies the loftiest aspirations of the human soul and that gratifies the legitimate cravings of the heart.

While it may not show on the surface, Henry was a believer in turmoil, a college-educated man in the Age of Darwin and a man who struggled with his faith in the light of modernity. A sermon such as "Faith Alone Satisfies" could only bring peace to a troubled soul. In a way, so did a humorous postcard Henry kept. It shows a scene where evolution has run riot and apes dress as humans. If evolution brought out the fundamentalist in Henry, he was not alone. Democratic presidential candidate William Jennings Bryan, who for decades symbolized the aspirations of millions of Americans, felt the same.

Darwin's critics strike back with sharp-edged humor.

Bridges attended church in Baltimore at First Presbyterian Church. A diary reads, "The Rev. Dr. Donald Guthrie, pastor of the First Presbyterian Church, Madison Street and Park Avenue, preached the baccalaureate sermon to the graduating class of the John Hopkins University yesterday morning....The church was crowded to the doors, and the service was very impressive." Dr. Guthrie's simplistic understanding of faith no doubt reflected Henry's, and his address was certainly directed at the Modernist Movement's theory of evolution.

SERMON TO HOPKINS MEN-Dr. Guthrie Urges Simple Faith to Spiritual Kings.

ONLY WAY TO GET KNOWLEDGE- With Jesus as the Sure Foundation Men Will Attain A Calm Against Intellectual Storms,

His text was: And there was a great calm. (St. Mark, iv., 39). The storm upon the Gallilean sea was graphically described and Dr. Guthrie used it as a simile to represent the intellectual storms that confront the thinking young men of the present time, especially in the realm of religion. He admitted that utter lack of demonstrated proof in religious questions but pointed out the virtue and necessity of simple faith as the only way to gain knowledge of spiritual things. "Men today don't deny," he said, "they merely question.... It is only as our minds, hearts and wills recognize and bow in authority to the religious sovereignty of Jesus, become voluntarily obedient to His word, as were the winds and waves, that the higher storms subside and there is a great calm. The storm of intellectual uncertainty in regard to religion is a vast present day storm raging in many quarters and involving us all more or less. Men are today prepared to deny very little, but they question everything. Religious knowledge is contrasted with knowledge in the sphere of the natural sciences and seems to lack in truth is demonstrable and provable. Religious truth seems undemonstrable and unprovable."

Bridges' faith was undoubtedly a cornerstone in his life. He responded to the Modernist Movement with a simplicity of faith that shows in this poem he wrote about Jesus:

Jesus, Thy boundless love to me. No thought can reach, no tongue declare; Oh, knit my thankful heart to thee, And reign without a rival there Shine wholly. Shine alone, I am Be thou alone my constant flame.

Oh, grant that nothing in my soul May dwell, but thy pure love alone. Oh may thy love passes me whole My joy, my treasure and my crown. Strange flames far from my heart remove My every act, word thought be love.

Oh love how cheering is thy ray. All pain before thy pressure flies. Care anguish sorrow melt away. Where're thy healing beams arise. Oh Jesus nothing may I see, Nothing desire I seek but thee.

Still let thy love point out my way, What wondrous things thy love hath brought. Still lead me, lest I go astray Direct my word, inspire my thought. And if I fall soon, may I hear Thy voices and know that love is near.

In suffering, be thy love my peace In weakness, be thy love my power. And when the storms of life shall cease Jesus in the dark, final hour of death, be thou my guide and friend. That I may love thee without end.

Success only furthered Henry's resolve to lead a moral life. His diary contains this sermon preached at "At Christ English Lutheran Church, by Rev. Dr. L. M. Zimmerman...from Psalm viii, 4: 'What is Man?'"

Only the Pharisee thinks himself an angel. But there are those who are not true types of manhood. The real man is lost in some, and the beast above itself. The man who loses self-respect, who allows his body to rule him instead of "keeping it in subjection," who suffers bad habits to control him, and who with an evil eye and heart revels in the sensual and devilish, such men need making over, for they are not as God made them. Man, true man, is able to keep away from evil, to resist temptation and to rise above debased conditions. Of course, if man plays with the fire he must naturally expect to be burned, and if he walks with the wicked, if he stands with them, if he sits with them as his fond associates, he will most likely soon be one with them. God, however, has given man will power to rise above environments. Man is not the size of his father's pocketbook or home, but is able to start at the bottom round of the ladder and climb up to a respectable height in honor and success. A good man will find his level...serving and worshipping God with all the heart, soul, mind, and body and love his neighbor as himself. Show thyself a man, therefore, that you may not only be loved of God, but that all who know you may love you for your very works' sake. Make the world better because you live in it. Pay your price at whatever cost; be honest, just, true, pure, good.

The Bridges' family did not lack for writers. Along with Robert Willis, there was Henry's first cousin, Robert Bridges, an editor for Scribner's in New York City. This Bridges reviewed the work of Ernest Hemingway, S. Scott Fitzgerald and James Joyce, and he was principally responsible for bringing Theodore Roosevelt to Scribner's. This was no mean feat considering that Robert roomed with Woodrow Wilson at Princeton and the two remained close friends. So, writing was in the family genes, though Henry may have seen it as more of a God-given gift, Henry wrote this poem:

1st -Far Away: what does it mean?

A change of heart with a change of place when footsteps pass from scene to scene. Fades soul from soul with face from face. Are hearts the slaves or lords of space.

2nd -Far Away: what does it mean?

Does distance sever there from here. Can leagues of land part hearts. I mean they cannot: for the trickling tear says 'Far Away means Far Away Near.'

3rd-Far Away: the mournful miles.

Are but the mystery of space that blends our sighs but parts our smiles: For love will find a meeting place when face is farthest off from face.

4th-Far Away: we meet in dreams.

As round the atlas of the night. Far parted stars send down their gleams so meet in one embrace of light and make the how of darkness might.

5th-Far Away: we meet in tears.

That tell the path of weary feet and all the good-byes of the years. But make the wanderer's welcome sweet. The rains of parted clouds thus meet.

6th-Far Away: we meet in prayer.

You know the temple and the shrine before it bows the brow of care, upon it tapers dimly shine: Tis mercy's home, and yours and mine.

7th-Far Away: it falls between.

What is today and what has been, but ah: what is meets what is not in every hour and every spot where lips breathe on I have forgot.

8th-Far Away: I sing its song but while the music moves long from out each word an echo clear falls trembling on my spirits ear. Far Away means Far more near.

In November 1904, Henry pasted the following notice of his brother James Taliaferros's wedding in his diary. It is testament both to family affection and a hope that he too would one day wed:

BRIDGES – HENDERSON-Maryland Couple Married at Berkeley Springs, W. VA.

Hancock, MD, November 26 - Miss Sarah Henderson, daughter of Judge James B. Henderson, of the Third judicial circuit of Maryland, whose home is in Montgomery County, and J. Taliaferro Bridges of Hancock, were married at 3:30 o'clock this afternoon in the Presbyterian manse at Berkeley Springs, West Virginia. Mr. and Mrs. Bridges will reside at Hancock. Mr. Bridges is a son of Robert Bridges, one of the wealthiest residents of Hancock. He is the senior member of the firm of J. Taliaferro Bridges & Co., lumber dealers and contractors, and a brother of Harry P. Bridges, of Baltimore, and Wilbur Bridges, of Hagerstown, both young lawyers. Bridges older brother Taliaferro married into the Henderson family and it is interesting to note that Robert Bridges was a partner with Charles Henderson beginning in 1850. The Bridges and the Hendersons

were good friends and worked together to create fortunes in western
Maryland.

Young Bridges must have wondered why love took so long to find him in
Baltimore. He dated many of the prominent women of Baltimore without
success. He may have been too demanding, as this diary entry implies,

> *Don't Marry this Girl:*
>
> *Who is a flirt.*
>
> *Who can not control her temper.*
>
> *Who is deceitful and is not true to her friends.*
>
> *Who fuses, fumes, and fidgets about everything.*
>
> *Whose highest aspiration has never soared above self.*
>
> *Whose chief interests in life are dress and amusements.*
>
> *Who can not bear to hear anyone but herself praised or admired.*
>
> *Who thinks more of making a fine appearance than a fine character. ...*
>
> *Who appropriates the best of everything for herself and is thoughtless of others.*
>
> *Who attracts attention in public places by 'loud' dress, and loud talk and laughter.*
>
> *If she expects everybody else in the home to contribute to her pleasure, instead of trying to make them happy....*
>
> *Who does not think it worth while to read for self-improvement, or current information, but spends her time reading trashy novels....*
>
> *Who is so tyrannical that the whole household has to be governed by her whims as to where to go, when to go, or what guests to entertain: who sulks about the house and is disagreeable when she can not have her own way; who upsets any plans or arrangements others make, if they do not suit her fancy, and who flies into a rage if opposed or crossed.*

By 1904 Henry was a twenty-six year old bachelor living a good life in
Baltimore. He was wining and dinning the prominent people of Baltimore
and yet felt lonely. He clipped this article on what constitutes happiness,
which he could have answered in one word, Love,

No matter how successful the enterprises a man may achieve in money getting, the possession of riches only tends to depress him if his home is void of a congenial companion. Without her tender administration he sees the loss he has sustained in his headlong push for the filthy lucre, and would give all he now possesses for one tender look or one endearing word from the lips of a wife, whom he might cherish in his old age....He admits now at the pinnacle of fame, that love, not pride and riches is the true happiness of life.... Marion Crawford says, "There is no true criticism of man's happiness but his own belief in it." Again it has been said, "The grand essentials to happiness in this life are something to do, something to love and something to hope for...." On the top rung of the ladder of fame it is supposed to have an abiding place, but men have climbed the dizzy height and found it bare indeed....Contentment is the chief concomitant of perfect happiness and the simple joys of life its surest generator. Ask the great man his happiest day. If he is honest, he will tell you when life held fewer responsibilities and broader measure of affection: when 'the music of the laughing lips, the luster of the eye made his simple abode elysian.'

In January 1904, a conflagration destroyed 60-square acres of the central Baltimore, dating to colonial times; over 1,500 buildings were lost to the flames. As the city rebuilt, Henry relocated his law offices to the prestigious Calvert Building. It was a step up, though one Bridges tried to make light of. He proposed the following rules of conduct for his new digs:

1.Upon entering, leave the door open.

2.Those having no business, will remain as long as possible, take a chair, and lean against the wall, it may prevent its falling.

3.You are expected to smoke, especially during office hours, tobacco will be supplied.

4.Spit on the floor, and put your cigar in the inkstand. Spittoons are only for ornament.

5.When we are busy, talk loud or whistle, if this has not the desired effect, sing.

6.Put your feet upon the desk or lean against it, it may assist those writing.

7.Idlers will call early and often, or excuse themselves.

The fire or his (lack of a) love life may have given Henry cause to stop and take stock of his life. In any case, he left Baltimore sometime after the fire to try his hand at silver prospecting. He and a friend spent a year in Cuba looking for silver in the mountains. There was just one problem: Henry got so seasick he demanded the captain stop the boat until he could recover. Bridges never again set out across a large body of water for fear of sea sickness.

Henry P. Bridges postcard from Cuba. After Baltimore burned, Henry prospected.

Shortly after Bridges returned from Cuba in late 1905, tragedy struck the family. The Hancock Star reported:

"On November 1905 - JOHN W. BREATHED BRIDGES -Passes Away After an Illness of Short Duration PRESIDENT OF HAN-COCK BANK- Recognized as One of the Best Business Men in western Maryland. This Community Suffers an Irreparable Loss in His Death. Funeral, Friday...."

Scarcely had the clouds of sorrow disappeared from our midst until a deep gloom was again cast over this community by the heavy hand of death, when John W. Breathed Bridges was summoned to his eternal home on Wednesday morning after an illness of only ten days' duration, from typhoid-pneumonia, aged 39 years. While many had learned of his illness, very few knew that his condition had reached such a serious and critical stage and that it would terminate so suddenly and sadly was a thought foreign to all, and when the fact, that his life had passed out at seven o'clock, was heralded through the streets, the heads of young and old, who stood in awe, were bowed with grief. Spending almost his entire lifetime in the mercantile establishment of Bridges & Henderson, which has been in existence for over fifty years, the greater portion of which time his father was the senior member of that firm, he became closely identified with the former's business affairs, through which position he formed an acquaintance that reached far beyond the boundaries of this State, and one which few men enjoy.

For eighteen years Mr. Bridges was secretary and treasurer of the Round Top Hydraulic Cement Company. Several years ago he and Mr. Ernest C. Henderson purchased from their fathers the Bridges & Henderson store, and conducted the business under the old name until last January, at which time Mr. Bridges purchased his partner's interests becoming sole proprietor....Mr. Breathed Bridges, as he was more familiarly known by that name, was a man whose word was as good as his bond. His life, although comparatively brief, molded character for others and during his time spent here the most valuable asset he gathered to himself was the respect and esteem of the people who knew him best. There is none to say that he was not upright and honest in all his dealings, a sound Christian gentleman....In the case of Mr. Bridges his friends and the public may well take pleasure in the thought that his was a life well spent and that he died as he had lived, a Christian. - The Funeral for Mr. Bridges. - The banks and stores of Hancock were closed during the funeral as a token of respect of our departed townsman.

Although devastated by the loss of his older brother, Henry returned to Baltimore after the funeral and continued his law practice. Through a combination of hard work and charm, he made the right contacts and expanded his client base. Even his love of hunting came in handy. When he gave a "game dinner" in 1906 at his residence, The Shirley, the event did not lack for well-laced guests.

Bridges character was a mixed bag of high minded thought and competitive business genius. During his early years growing up in Hancock, he learned from selling pigeons and selling the wool from his sheep. He was no bodies fool and could verbally back his adversary into a corner before they knew what had happened. He used his wit and verbal skills to create contacts and win friends in high places. He was a self made man who created opportunity through his own brilliance and charm. He was not willing to work for anyone but himself and his personality bred success. When one entered a room where Bridges stood one could feel his presence. People were attracted to his radiant glow. He believed in himself and this belief radiated from his countenance. His talent both as a litigator and corporate lawyer brought him no lack of business. In addition, he developed an interest in business start-ups.

Bridges was inspired to become a great business leader and he was always aware of what the alternative was--poverty. This clipping in his diary on the dangers of a regular salary reveals a deeply felt sense of independence:

A FIXED SALARY BREEDS EXTRAVAGANCE, This is to be a disagreeable editorial, intended to make the young and old man working for a salary THINK SERIOUSLY about himself. If you talk to a man who has $15 a week salary, he will say to you, "I can just manage to live on it-fairly well-BUT I CAN'T SAVE A CENT. I see no hope ahead for the future." The man with a salary of $100 a week will say, in exactly the same tones, "I can just manage to live on it, and keep my family half decently. BUT I CAN'T SAVE A CENT. I don't know what would become of my children of anything should happen to me." And it is always the same story, no matter what the salary or the wages-the full amount is always spent. It is difficult to make ends meet, and there is nothing left over to show for long years of work....Let us consider, therefore, why it is that the salaried man, with a steady, regular income is nearly always the man who has nothing saved up against a rainy day....But not one salaried man in a thousand realizes that as he draws his weekly salary, he is selling HIMSELF, his youth, his strength and his future prospects ON THE INSTALLMENT PLAN.

This article he saved suggests Henry's understanding of poverty,

Facing the Wrong Way is Fatal

*Poverty itself is not so bad as the poverty thought. It is the con-
viction that we are poor and must remain so that is fatal....As long
as you radiate doubt and discouragement, you will be a failure. If
you want to get away from poverty, you must keep your mind in a
productive, creative condition. In order to do this you must think
confident, cheerful, creative thoughts. the model must precede the
statue. You must see a new world before you can live in it. You must
have faith in yourself. The miracles of civilization have been per-
formed by men and women who believed in themselves. "What the
superior man seeks is in himself: what the small man seeks is in
others." That man has failed who has not been able to keep a good
opinion of himself.*

A drive to succeed and fear of failure, a need to be humble, a love of
nature—Henry Bridges' diary gave ample evidence of the man.

THE WOODMONT ROD & GUN CLUB OF HANCOCK

While living in Baltimore, Henry P. Bridges became involved with the
Woodmont Rod and Gun Club of Washington, DC. The club was located
outside his hometown of Hancock Maryland. Decades later, Henry recalled
the club's genesis as a "combination of people and places far too improbable for the taste of a fiction writer." One of those people was Robert Lee
Hill, a member of the Virginia aristocracy. The sixteen-year old Hill had no
interest in the Blue and the Gray. Rather than choose sides and fight, he left
home to wander the mountains of western Maryland. Hill eventually found
refuge at Sidling Hill Mountain on the Woodmont Estate. Here he built a
rustic log cabin. He lived off the land, hunted game, and fished the bountiful
Potomac River. This was how he put food on the table for himself and his
new bride.

By 1870 Hill had ventured back to civilization and that year traveled to
Washington, D.C. He happened to be riding a streetcar with Rear Admiral
Robley Dunglison Evans, known for his Union naval heroics in the Civil
War. Evans went on to a brilliant naval career. In 1891, he outmaneuvered
superior Chilean forces with use of a single U.S. gunboat in the harbor of
Valparaiso. During the Spanish-American War he commanded the battle-
ship Iowa, and he later served as commander of the U.S. Asiatic Fleet. But
on this providential day, Evans the man of action happened to sit next to Hill
the peaceful mountain man.

Founder Rear Admiral Robley Dunglison Evans. "Fighting Bob" won his reputation at the expense of Confederates, South Americans and Spaniards. He also hunted game in the countryside around the nation's Capitol.

Hill and Evans struck up a conversation about a mutual interest, hunting. Hill invited Evans to come and hunt at Sidling Hill Mountain. After a successful hunt Evans brought the game back to Washington to share with high-ranking in the military and government. The outing led Evans to convince his friends that they should form a club at Woodmont. Initially the new members used an old ramshackle log cabin as their clubhouse located over looking the Potomac River. By 1882 the Woodmont tradition was such that the *Washington Evening Star* reported, "The Woodmont Rod and Gun club celebrated the opening of the bass season on the 8th....That the members and their guests had a grand time, caught bass, sang songs, ate a big dinner, and made themselves unanimously merry, is a foregone conclusion." The membership was limited to fifty individuals holding capital stock valued at $12,500. Each share cost $250. In addition, there was an initiation fee of $500.

The Star also noted, "The club was organized in Washington two years ago, the prime mover being Mr. A. H. Evans, of Washington, president, who is a hale and hearty old gentleman, an enthusiastic sportsman and a prince of entertainment." According to Bridges, the club was first called the Woodmont Rod and Gun Club of Washington, D.C. In 1880 the club authorized its officers to purchase what the paper called, "a large old estate situated in Washington County, Maryland, bearing the appropriate title of 'Woodmont'....The original purchase consisted of 2,023 acres, but this amount has since been considerably increased by later purchases in order to extend the hunting privileges as well as to properly protect game." The group officially incorporated as the Woodmont Rod Gun Club on March 21, 1882. The seal of the club consisted of a stag's head and two fish, with the motto, "Protect and Enjoy."

The first ramshackle Woodmont clubhouse.
With fame came better accommodations.

Bridges identified the first clubhouse as a ramshackle, 140-year old log house set far away from the Potomac in the preserve. In 1882 *American Angler* reported a "new clubhouse was erected just 200 yards from the river." In 1883 *The Evening Star* described the living accommodations of the club as "consisting of a large new fine clubhouse, situated on a high bluff overlooking the river and beautiful range of country beyond, which cost, with its substantial fittings, about $6,000. The building contains a fine club room, a large dinning hall, a magazine room, store room, linen room, servant's room, and ten large fine chambers, all comfortably furnished."

Second Woodmont Clubhouse.

Industrialization, urbanization along with a sense of too many people and life lived too fast were beginning to take an emotional toll on the newly emerging middle class of late 19th and early 20th century America. Many men in particular yearned for more natural surroundings and at the very least some kind of symbolic return to what they saw as a better, pre-industrial society. For those lucky enough to join, there was Woodmont. In 1882 *The Evening Star* described the Woodmont experience, "In short, the year round, by land and water, there is good sport to be had, the pure, sweet air comes to the lungs with the odor of pine and the fragrance of flowers, the distant droning of the dam, the cry of the whippoorwill, the drumming of pheasants, the hooting of owls are among the voices of the night, and here, if anywhere, one is sure of rest and recreation."

Lock #55 of The Chesapeake and Ohio Canal below Woodmont clubhouse. As the canal grew obsolete, club members were tempted to idealize it as part of a simpler time.

Woodmont was part of a wilderness craze that attracted self-made men who often bought large tracts of land for their private hunting and fishing parties. Between 1880 and 1900 numerous hunting and fishing clubs were established in the United States. In comparison to similar clubs, Woodmont was in a class by itself with an elaborate clubhouse and elite membership. The Western Maryland Railroad ran trains from Washington to Cumberland Maryland. The tracks paralleled the Chesapeake and Ohio Canal below the Woodmont clubhouse. With a stop just a few hundred yards from the clubhouse, members felt privileged indeed. They could arrive from Washington via express rail by 10:15 AM., hunt and fish all day, and depart on a 6 PM. train in time to attend a ball or party in Washington that evening.

In 1883 *The Evening Star* described the membership, "To most of the gentlemen comprised in this list the people of Washington need no introduction: but for the benefit of strangers it may be said that it includes prominent private citizens, members of both houses of Congress and distinguished officers in the military and naval services of the country….Among its guests, or guests of individual members last summer, were many persons distinguished in all walks of life, including the President of the United States [Chester A. Arthur]." The first presidential visitor was James Garfield in 1881. Benjamin Harrison first made the trip from the White House ten years later. Robley Evans brought Grover Cleveland along to fish a favorite spot on the Potomac three miles upriver from the clubhouse.

But the privileged status of members and guests did not exempt them from some stringent club rules. The publication *Shooting and Fishing* reported in June 1891 that, "The rules of the club have some admirable features regarding the killing of game and catching of fish, and all fish and game killed are entered on the club books. One article provides that any member who infringes on the game or fish laws of the State or county shall be expelled." Conservation appears to have been a concern of Woodmont almost from the beginning.

In an April 1882 story *The Evening Star* noted, "The rare sport which black bass affords has been but recently developed, and even now fly-fishing is almost unknown." *The Angler's Association* of Washington was the only organization of its time that exclusively fished the Potomac River. Bridges recalled that the early years of Woodmont revolved around fishing the Potomac. In fact, the popularity of Woodmont may have been due in part to black bass fishing at Dam No. 6 (of the Chesapeake and Ohio Canal) in the Potomac, below the clubhouse. "The locality affords opportunities for both deep or still water and rapid water fishing," said the Evening Star. "Below the high dam the river runs for several miles over a rocky bed, thus furnishing a long stretch of tumbling cascades, circling eddies, and quiet pools, ever greatly affected by game fish of all varieties, and always so tempting to the angler's eye."

Woodmont fishing party on the Potomac River
Dam No. 6 below Woodmont. A dam meant for 1800s'
commerce would lend itself to sport in the 1900s.

The club experimented with adding other game fish to the native black bass. The Potomac was stocked with salmon, brook and California trout. Still, bass predominated. During the summer of 1882, club members caught some 1,296 bass, weighing 956 pounds or nearly half a ton in all. *The Evening Star* reported that, "Senator Wade Hampton of South Carolina, is an ardent disciple of Walton and cast a fly equal to any other man in the South." When he ventured onto the Potomac with flies instead of live bait, a guide who rowed his boat bet him fifty dollars he could not bring in twelve bass with flies. A few hours later the Senator brought in his twelve bass, and the guide was made to believe in a Southern fly fisherman on the Potomac River.

Henry records in *The Woodmont Story,* "fire struck in 1903. It leveled the clubhouse to the ground. And it also very nearly destroyed the Woodmont organization, for with their clubhouse destroyed the members were faced with the necessity of building a new one, and this necessity gave birth to a controversy that proved exceptionally bitter." The members were so divided into opposing factions as to what the new clubhouse should look like that they decided to sell Woodmont and dissolve the organization which had held the Club together for thirty-three years.

Henry was never enamored with the great stone and steel buildings of Baltimore, and he professed a desire to return home to Hancock. In 1897 he began raising wild turkeys on fifty acres of a farm he owned near Hancock. While practicing law in Baltimore, he employed a manager to care for the flock. When he heard that the lushly forested acres of Woodmont were for sale, he quickly alerted some of his close friends of the impending doom of the club. A lumber company had put in a bid for the land. With the help of such friends as Eugene DuPont, Jerry Wheelright, Bartlett Johnson, Thomas Clayborn and Nelson Perin, Henry gathered sufficient resources to outbid the lumber company in 1906. The Woodmont Club was then reorganized by Bridges in 1908. Perin was elected president of the club, with Henry as secretary-treasurer. The first task for the new members was to build a clubhouse. They located it directly on the burned foundation of the old clubhouse. Bridges supervised construction.

As the facility took shape, Henry began to dream, "I wanted the Woodmont Rod and Gun Club to be the best of its kind – a true sportsman's paradise. But I wanted more than that. I wanted a place where men might work to resuscitate dying species of wildlife, a place where men might observe and study the needs of the forest, the stream, and the animals and fish that live in them. I saw Woodmont as a kind of jewel with many facets – an excellent place to hunt and fish, a place to raise wildlife for the forests of the nation." Bridges went on to raise wild turkeys by the tens of thousands. He and Woodmont can take credit for having a hand in repopulating the wild turkey in North America.

The Woodmont Rod and Gun Club is the result of the wilderness craze, a love for fishing and hunting, coupled with the Modernist cultural movement of the 1880s. It is a sacred place where self-made men come to re-create their souls by pitting their natural instincts to hunt and fish against nature. The fresh mountain air revived innate instincts that dwell deep within every man. These instincts have been masked in many men by the forces of industrialization and urbanization. Woodmont remained a great outlet for the expression of the innate human instinct to hunt and fish. As a remnant of antiquity and a unique refuge Woodmont would become an important part of the American outdoor adventure. "And it all began when a shy mountaineer sat down beside an action-loving Admiral in a crowed, noisy streetcar in Washington, DC."

Henry P. Bridges, Eugene DuPont and others hunting at Woodmont. No matter their status, club members and their guests were expected to follow the rules.

CHAPTER 4

BALANCING SILICA MINES WITH THE WOODMONT ROD & GUN CLUB, 1907-1930: *Work and Conservation*

CONSERVATION

In the spring of 1874, *Field & Stream* ran a story on the travails of hunting wild turkeys. The account suggests the reasons behind Ben Franklin's choice of a national bird:

But the wild turkey is a beautiful bird, as different from the domestic turkey as the game cock and the Shanghai. He is no relation whatever to the barnyard turkey-the domestic turkey being descended from the turkey of Mexico, which is an inferior breed. It requires more patience and skill to be a successful turkey hunter than any wild fowl or beast I know of, and I pride myself on my skill in this particular line.

Having studied their habits for years, I have learned to imitate every note of the hen, but would give the best horse in my stable for an instrument that could exactly imitate the gobble and strut of the cock. Whenever I hear of an old gobbler, known to be particularly wild, I invariably go for him, and once spent a whole month after an old gobbler. The first morning I took a young friend with me, who was a novice at the business. Getting as near as possible without being seen, we concealed ourselves, and began imitating the yelp of the hen promised. I gave my friend the shot. Soon we saw the patriarch of the forest approaching us; but my friend got nervous, and began to shake with the "buck-ague." The turkey was nearly in gunshot when he became frightened at the shaking of my friend, and left for tall timber.

Next morning I tried him alone, and nearly succeeded in getting him within gunshot, when bang went a gun, off went my hat, and rattle went buckshot all around me. I arose and confronted a mean-looking, coperas-breeched cuss, who had crawled up behind me, and seeing the top of my head, had fired at me for a turkey. To say that I was mad would in no way express feelings – I like to have swore. After I had exhausted my vocabulary of invective, the fellow looked up demurely, and says, "Mister, was that you that went cluck, cluck, just like turkey?"

The next morning I tried again, and every morning for a week; but the cunning bird knew every call I could make, and he became so distrustful he would not even go to a hen. I had hunted him so close he had lost all confidence in turkeykind. He would not gobble until the sun was up, and never until he had left his roost. And probably when I heard him a second time he would be a quarter of a mile off, in some other direction. I flanked him, and headed him off a number of times. I had let a number of young gobblers pass unnoticed, sometimes killing one after I had given up the old cock for the day, rather than return home empty-handed. There always was some "contretemps" that prevented me from my killing the old gobbler.

Once I had, by making a wide circuit, got ahead of him, and saw him coming strutting across a piece of burnt woods directly towards me, when a countryman passed nearby with an ox team, cracking his whip, "Gee, woo, Dobbin, get up here; goin' to town this morning, bully boys?" I almost wished he had been going to the ---. Another time, after crawling for nearly half a mile on my knees, I found myself directly in his walk, and there he comes. My heart bounds with delight – he is within thirty yards of me – my gun is at my shoulder – my eye glances along the barrel – when whir-r, z-i-r-r, a sound that ever appalls the stoutest heart – the rattlesnake rattled almost under me.

The most skillful athlete never left more day light between himself and terra firma on an extemporaneously improvised leap, than your Christian friend did on that occasion. I never looked to see what my gobbler thought of my leap, or which way he went. I shot that snake and cut off his rattle, which counted seventeen buttons, and then eagerly turned myself loose on the home stretch; but I couldn't get my hair down smooth, or rid of the cold perspiration for several hours. In fact, it makes the cold chills creep over me yet when I think how narrowly I escaped being bitten by so venomous a reptile.

The next morning I was out again, and heard my old gobbler fly down from his roost. So, instead of attempting to call him with the hen note, I slapped my old felt hat on the ground several times, and imitated two gobblers fighting. He could not stand this, and supposing it to be a free fight, he came charging up within twenty yards of me, and stopped behind a large oak. I waited, almost without breathing, for what seemed an incredible length of time, for him to step out from behind the tree. I almost had a "buck ague," but my spirits sank below zero when I heard him gobble a quarter of a mile behind me.

How had he escaped? I arose and examined the spot where I had last seen him, and the mystery was revealed. There was a gully some three feet deep leading from the tree, and passing within less than twenty feet of where I had been sitting, and, becoming suspicious, he had quietly stepped down into the gully and walked out by me.....Day after day I hunted that gobbler, but he always outgeneraled me, until the season passed away, and I retired, fully determined to spend next Spring after him, and never give him up until his long black beard shall hang among the trophies of my shooting box.

**One of two rare Audubon prints from Woodmont Rod &
Gun Club. The subject should come as no surprise.**

There was something about this animal that intrigued hunters. Long before the Pilgrims, Native American Indian hunted the wild turkey with a bow and arrow or sarbacane reeds through which they blew poisonous darts. The populations were plentiful, and Indians only killed what they needed to survive. But an increase in population and advances in weaponry devastated the turkey population. By the end of the 19th century, conservationist estimated that there were less than 30,000 of the birds where there had once been millions roaming the woods of North America.

An 1875 article in *Field and Stream* highlights one of the problems, not just for turkey but various game animals--bounties were being paid for the slaughter of indigenous game species. Holmes & Sears was a firm offering hides, furs, game and poultry specialty items. *Field & Stream* reported, "Prairie chickens were in some demand by shippers, but they refused to pay above $2.75 although in some cases $2.85 was obtainable, when wrapped and put in shipping order. Quail were salable at $1.75 @ $1.85 per doz. Venison, good supply. Other descriptions met with a light local demand and

sold at about former quotations. Partridges wanted; Wild Turkey nominal."
Here is a price list for game,

Ruffed Grouse (Northern)	$2.75	@	$2.85 per doz.
Ruffed Grouse (Kan. Or Mo.)	$2.75	@	$2.85 per doz.
Pinnated Grouse	$3.00	@	$2.85 per doz.
Partridge	$3.00	@	$2.85 per doz.
Quail (Northern)	$1.75	@	$1.85 per doz.
Quail (Kan. or Mo.)	$1.75	@	$1.85 per doz.
Wild Turkeys (full feathered)	$0.11	@	$0.13 per lb.
Ducks (Canvas Back)	$4.50	@	$5.00 per doz.
Ducks (Mallard)	$2.75	@	$3.00 per doz
Ducks (Red Head)	$2.50	@	$3.00 per doz
Ducks (Small)	$1.50	@	$3.00 per doz
Jack Snipe	$1.25	@	$3.00 per doz
Marbled Hudsonian Godwit Snipe	$2.50	@	$3.00 per doz
Golden Wing Plover.	$0.75c	@	$1.00 per doz
Pigeons (Flight)	$1.00	@	$1.25 per doz
Pigeons (Dressed)	$1.25	@	$1.50 per doz
Rabbits	$1.50	@	
Venison (carcass)	$0.05	@	$0.06 per lb.
Venison (saddles)	$0.11	@	$0.12 per lb.
Antelope (saddles)	$0.12	@	$0.13 per lb.
Black Bear (whole)	$0.15	@	$0.18 per lb.
Elk (hams)	$0.05	@	$0.06 per lb.
Buffalo (hams)	$0.05	@	$0.06 per lb.
Speckled Trout	$0.30c	@	

The market--or commercial--hunter in America did not call individual turkeys to kill. Instead he created systems of mass destruction to maximize his day's work. This deadly hunting method is credited for the wild turkey's near extinction. The market hunter would build a blind and dig a shallow trench to fill with feed once he located a flock. The turkeys would return to the bait and feed daily, unaware the hunter had set a trap for them. The trench was in line with the blind, where the hunter sat undetected. This setup allowed the hunter to fire a single shot the length of the trench at precisely the right moment, when the flock was feeding. This method of market hunting was so successful the hunter would need help carrying the large number of birds back to camp.

If anything, the situation was even worse for the American Bison and the Passenger Pigeon. It was not until the early 1870s that a conservation movement began, to be led by such luminaries as John Muir, Aldo Leopold and Theodore Roosevelt. Henry Bridges joined their ranks with his takeover of the Woodmont Rod & Gun Club in 1906. Bridges would emerge as a pioneer in local and national conservation circles. It is worth remembering that in turn-of-the-century North America there was nothing as basic as a hunting season for game.

Bridges' approach to conservation and wildlife husbandry set a precedent for the state of Maryland. Never before had any one man worked to propagate wild turkey, deer, fish and other indigenous species in a specific region of the country. The intent was both to hunt the species and return wild game to a healthy, sustainable level. Bridges raised game at Woodmont while simultaneously shipping animals across the United States. Henry understood the importance of reintroducing game into the wild to repopulate respective species.

THE CONSERVATION MOVEMENT IN MARYLAND

Maryland was one of the first states to enlist in the conservation movement. Dr. Paul Knight, an instructor of entomology at the University of Maryland, had a great deal to say about conservation. "To most of us conservation means the preservation of wildlife for hunters, fishers, and trappers. We should think of it in broader terms than this. The conservation of natural resources includes many other things, and we who are interested in game preservation and rehabilitation should also be interested in forest depletion, stream pollution, pest damage, and the depredations of tourists and sightseers."

Dr. Knight believed that early American settlers better understood the harsh conflict with nature and the struggles it presented, including the struggle for life itself. Settlers depended on nature in ways modern society had forgotten. Knight feared that with this change "we have lost contact with a very essential part of our everyday life." In addition, Knight warned that this altered relationship between society and nature would lead to the "ravaging of our streams, woodlands, and fields by pleasure-seeking metro-politans." Without conservation, civilization itself would one day become impossible.

Knight went on to say:

> *The rapidity of the destruction of wildlife by hunters and fishers has led to the formation of many state and Federal game laws, in-cidentally, to the expenditure of immense sums of money on their enforcement. Here in a few cases action has been too late. We of today are paying for the wanton destruction of the past generation. Several species have been wiped from the face of the earth, and they occur now only in museums. Others have had their ranks thinned till their numbers may not be strong enough to be able to perpetu-ate their species. Marylanders are only too well acquainted with the oyster situation, and the diamondback terrapin.*

According to Knight, industrialization had upset the balance of nature between animal and plant life, where no one species increased beyond a reasonable population. Knight thought the "situation as it exists today is an aesthetic disgrace and a crime upon our most priceless gift. What is the solution? The most reasonable answer is public education. From our earliest hours we are in a constant contact with nature. We are a small part of the life of the globe, and not the lord and master of it. If we are brought into an un-derstanding with nature we will be more respectful of it, and will preserve it for the generations to come."

Another Marylander who sounded the alarm was Mr. E. Lee LeCompte, State Game Warden of Maryland and close friend of Henry Bridges. In his "History of Conservation of the Natural Resources of Maryland" LeCompte noted his state's proud heritage in conservation for over one-hundred years. He taught that conservation of natural resources in Maryland dated to 1890, when eight of the twenty-three counties supported initiatives in the General Assembly protecting game birds and animals. In subsequent sessions leg-islation was passed to cover all upland game birds and establish a uniform bag limit. In 1896 the governor was empowered to appoint a state game warden who in turn named game deputies throughout the state.

In 1916 the legislature created the Conservationist Commission of Mary-land, whereby the governor appointed a "commission consisting of three members for a term of four years, whose terms became effective June 1st,

1916, the duties of said commissioners being to take over all departments pertaining to the natural resources of this State....which were authorized to protect our seafood, fish, and game....I [LeCompte] received the honor of being appointed state game warden under the new commission." The game warden was the sole salaried game warden in Maryland until legislation in 1918 created a State Hunters License System, requiring all persons who hunted on property other than that of which they were owners or tenants, to purchase a hunting license. This allowed for salaried district deputy game wardens, whose number reached 24 by 1924.

LeCompte described the establishment of the first game farm in Maryland:

> *In 1919 the department purchased 290 acres of land located at Gwynnbrook, Baltimore County, known as the Dolfield Estate and established thereon a State Game Farm where we have been propagating Chinese and Mongolian pheasants and liberating same in the covers of this state, trying to establish this specie of game bird in addition to our native game. We have been very successful in raising this specie of bird and this past season have distributed 5,356 in several counties of this state. We have also purchased each season, when same was available, bob-white partridge or quail from Mexico and planted them in our covers and we believe they have increased our supply of this specie of game bird.*

LeCompte went on to say, "Leaving the big game out of the question as being of only passing interest to Maryland, there being little big game outside of our three western counties, our small game is constantly preyed upon by its enemies, who know no closed season nor the moral necessity of conserving our natural resources. Foxes, hawks, stray cats and dogs, snakes, and other natural enemies prey upon our game birds, song birds and rabbits throughout the year." Not only did the game species have to defend themselves against natural predators but undisciplined shooters who killed everything they saw. LeCompte offered a provocative solution—limits that would leave enough game to restock the districts for another season.

LeCompte wanted to attack the lack of uniformity in Maryland's game laws and the lack of money to enforce state laws. He believed the first problem could be solved by getting counties together to coordinate the opening and closing of hunting seasons. The solution to the second problem was:

> *The most successful way yet devised is the system of licensing every hunter, charging him one dollar for the privilege, the revenue*

*derived there from being used for game and fish protection. This
has many attractive features and is in force in thirty-four States in
this country and in practically all the provinces of Canada. First, it
puts the cost of maintaining the game and fish upon the persons who
derive the benefit. Very few sportsmen object to paying $1 per an-
num when they know it is going to be used for the protection of game
which will result in direct benefit to them.*

LeCompte was convinced, "The game of Maryland is a valuable state
product and it is most important that we look at the situation seriously and
accomplish many needed improvements before it is too late. Our game birds
are not only the means of giving the residents of the state recreation, but
they are valuable to the farmers on account of the great number of noxious
weed seeds and insects which they destroy."

Both Dr. Knight and Mr. LeCompte could count on the support of one
man in particular, Heary Bridges.

WOODMONT ROD & GUN CLUB AND ITS ARCHITECT

Henry Bridges oversaw the construction of a new clubhouse. This white
clapboard building was ideally situated in the preserve of Woodmont, with
easy access to hunting and fishing. The new facility was complete with large
brick and stone fireplaces, a clubroom and expansive front porch with a
magnificent view of the Potomac River below the C& O Canal.

The men of prominence at the turn of the century valued the club and
many of the aristocratic caste in society were members of fine clubs, "the
club has become, in the course of this century, one of the most important
agencies for assimilating men of talent and their families into an upper-class
way of life and social organization. On a visit to this country before the First
World War, Max Weber observed of our American establishment that "affiliation with a distinguished club was essential above all else. He who did
not succeed in joining was no gentleman. ..." It was, then, one's club and
educational affiliations, rather than family position and accomplishment
alone, which placed one in a secure establishment position in the corporate
and urban world which America had become by the end of the nineteenth
century."

Third Woodmont Clubhouse. This one was a charm.

One of the first men of prominence that Bridges invited to the Club was President Theodore Roosevelt. Bridges wrote Theodore Roosevelt and on August 23, 1907, received this letter from Oyster Bay, New York:

My dear Mr. Bridges:

That is a most attractive invitation of yours. I have not shot quail or anything of the kind for too many years to make it worth my while to try now, but I should greatly love a hunt for deer and turkeys. I fear, however, that it is a simple impossibility. Would you let me write you again in the <u>very</u> improbable event of my finding toward the end of October that I can change my mind?

With many thanks and regard, believe me,

Theodore Roosevelt

The president soon sent Henry a second letter:

THE WHITE HOUSE
Oyster Bay N.Y.
September 4, 1907

My dear Mr. Bridges:

Mea Culpa! I have sinned the sin of vacillation. Down at the bottom of my heart I knew perfectly well I ought not to leave the smallest loophole open in connection with the acceptance of your invitation; but it was so very attractive that I could not bear to make the refusal as definite as I should have done. But thinking it over I am perfectly sure that I shall not be able to leave Washington after I once get back from my Mississippi River trip; so, my dear Mr. Bridges, you must count me out for this season.

With heartiest thanks, believe me,
Sincerely yours,
Theodore Roosevelt

Bridges was determined, as befitting his Scots Presbyterian character, to engage the President. One can image him refusing to take No for an answer from the President of the United States. Consequently, Henry sent some game from the Woodmont preserve directly to the White House for the President's table. Roosevelt responded to this kind gesture with the following letter:

THE WHITE HOUSE
November 27, 1907

My dear Mr. Bridges:

Many thanks for those wild turkeys. How I wish I could have been with you! I would have been amply contended if I had gotten one of the five turkeys that I see hanging up in the photos, and if you had gotten the remaining four and the coon and all the rabbits and birds.

With hearty thanks, believe me,
Sincerely yours,
Theodore Roosevelt

Photo sent along with game from Woodmont to the White House. Henry Bridges was not easily dissuaded.

Had he visited, Roosevelt would have seen that the essence of Woodmont was its front porch. The front porch of the preceding clubhouse had four

U.S. Presidents and many other notables grace its presence over the years. The present clubhouse has a rustic wooden porch that extends the length of the building and the porch overlooks the Potomac River, just 200 yards distant, into West Virginia. The view of the Blue Ridge Mountains is spectacular and sure to impress even the veteran traveler. There is a V-shaped cut where the Potomac divides West Virginia from Maryland.

The Appalachian Mountains that surround Woodmont have an alluring bluish hue, especially visible at dusk. This hue can envelop valleys and mountaintops as much as any fog. So it seems when the rolling treetops turn into a fantasy borne by the cool night air.

The front porch with guests (from left) Mrs. Edwin Warfield, wife of the Maryland governor, and Mrs. Calvin Hendricks, 1908.

Long after the departure of Native Americans from the region, the names they gave to the mountains and terrain live on. Clear Springs, Indian Springs and Falling Waters are reminders to the present users to treat the land as good stewards would.

The mountains are forested with poplar, maple, oak and other leaf-bearing trees. The tall pines are home to the American Palliated Woodpecker, the American Wild Turkey and many other indigenous species. The fall season is spectacular as lush green foliage turns amber, gold, orange and brilliant reds. The lands of Woodmont are a worthy subject for any artist's canvas. The sounds heard from the front porch are equally impressive. They comprise a natural orchestra of crickets, cicadas, birds and more. This musical arrangement begins with no introduction, no fanfare, no applause and no maestro to lead.

The sunsets from the front porch of Woodmont are not to be missed. The bright blue sky and the lily white clouds buffer up against the undulating mountaintops in the distance. When the sun moves behind Sidling Hill Mountain to the west, a great array of spectacular light filters along the horizon. From the front porch day then settles into night. The sound of the hoot owl and morning dove all enrich the senses. This is some of what would have been lost had a lumber company placed the winning bid on the preserve.

There have long been two industrial-age intruders at Woodmont. The tracks of the B & O Railroad and the Western Maryland Railroad parallel the Potomac. But the sounds of a steam engine and, for that matter, a diesel do not offend so much when filtered by tree and mountain. The second in-terloper, the C & O Canal, was always far quieter. The passengers of canal boats pulled by horse and mule spent seven days traversing the 180 miles from Washington to Cumberland. It was a relaxing way to travel and the passersby waved to the Woodmont guests on the front porch.

On the morning of May 7, 1909, club president Nelson Perin and sec-retary Henry Bridges welcomed guests at the Western Maryland Railroad stop below the clubhouse for the grand opening of the newly re-organized club. The railroad stop made it easy for Baltimoreans and Washingtonians to make the trip to Woodmont without much hassle.

Woodmont swimmers survey a stop of the Western Maryland Railroad. Regardless the desires of members, not all signs of modern life could be kept away.

This clipping from Henry's diary describes the event:

A big dinner celebrated the opening of the celebrated resort. Drs. Cullen, Bloodgood and Mayor Mahool had the first swim of the season in the Potomac. The water was as cold as ice but they all came ashore declaring it was fine. Our old friend Robert Hill, who was guide to Presidents Cleveland, Arthur and other distinguished men, attended the dinner and was happily greeted by those at the festal board. Mr. Hill's personal recollections of the sporting proclivities of Grover Cleveland are quite interesting and entertaining.

**First Presbyterian Church of Baltimore
and Pastor, Dr. Donald Guthrie.**

Bridges lived in a room at the Shirley Hotel while he practiced law in Baltimore. The Shirley stood directly across the street from the First Presbyterian Church. Henry attended services there. A church that began in 1763 in a log cabin had since moved into a magnificent building with spires 275 feet tall. Whether hunting, residing or worshipping, Henry sought out beauty.

When possible, Henry sought to mix work with pleasure in a Woodmont sort of way. "Mr. Henry P. Bridges will give a luncheon tomorrow at the Baltimore Country Club and afterwards will start in a touring car for Hancock, MD where he will entertain a party at the Woodmont Club for the weekend." So reported the Baltimore Sun of a certain ambitious lawyer. The following story provides some more details of the event.

Baltimoreans Have Thrilling Experience in the Mountains, J. D. Riley Has Narrow Escape, Wagner Is A Fine Tennis Player, But A Rabbit Will Testify That He Is A Bad Pistol Shot.

Browned by the sun, but delighted with their trip, profuse in their praises of the beauty of the Blue Ridge scenery, and more profuse in their praise of the hospitality of their host, Henry P. Bridges, members of the Woodmont Rod and Gun Club returned yesterday morning in their private car from a visit to their preserves. The program as given in THE SUN of Saturday was carried out to the letter. The fishing was not as good as the party had expected. On Saturday, a heavy wind was blowing along the Potomac and the water was muddy. But with this handicap the party caught 10 good big bass. The honors for high catch went to John Riley, Gresham Poe and Frank B. Stayman.

The article reported that the sojourners were happy to get back to civilization due to the travel on the rough mountain roads:

While driving down the mountainside, John D. Riley was thrown from his wagon into a raging mountain stream, but fortunately Aeronaut Robinson was at hand to win a hero medal by rescuing the unfortunate Riley.

Another accident, which came very near ending fatally for a couple of the members of the party, occurred on the drive to Berkeley Springs. The harness on one of the teams broke and Arthur Seldman and Bernard Fenwick were thrown from the wagon, but were saved from being precipitated down the mountainside by their companions, James Whedby and Mose Coyne.

The article went on to note that the party had a pleasant Sunday in the preserve while seeing pheasant, rabbit and wild turkey. In Berkeley Springs Cy Montgomery, Loring Cover and Alec Groome gave an exhibition of fancy diving and long-distance swimming. Basil Wagner entertained the crowd with fancy revolver shooting. While shooting he spied a rabbit intensely interested in the sport. Wagner "turned on the inoffensive animal and fired three shots at him, when the rabbit, disgusted at the poor marksmanship, walked and turned away unharmed."

Before leaving Woodmont, Bonsal Brooks, on behalf of the party, presented Bridges with a handsome diamond pin as a token of the members' appreciation of Henry's hospitality and untiring efforts for the amusement of his friends. Wagner, Brooks and Bridges did not return with the rest of the party, but stopped at Hancock, where they played in the singles and doubles of the tournament of the Hancock Tennis Club. The Sun could have added that being a good friend did not hurt a lawyer's business.

Bridges enjoyed sharing the mountain refuge with guests from Baltimore and Washington. He was particularly keen on having state and national conservation people share Woodmont with him. The following article, "*Wild Turkeys - - Hunting We Go!*," was written by E. Lee LeCompte, Maryland State Game Warden. In it he describes a hunt at Woodmont:

> *Early in November, that well-known sportsman, Henry P. Bridges, secretary of the Woodmont Rod and Gun Club, Hancock, Maryland, extended a very pressing invitation to Mr. Talbott Denmead, U. S. Game Conservation Officer and me to pay him a visit at the Woodmont Rod and Gun Club for a wild turkey hunt. We accepted the invitation with alacrity.*

> *"Lanky" Den and I left Baltimore on November 18, motoring up through the beautiful autumnal countryside of Howard, Frederick and Washington counties, and arrived at the Clubhouse, located near Pearre Station, on the Western Maryland Railroad, at 5:30 P.M. We received a royal welcome. During the evening eighteen members and guests arrived, and the hunting yarns that were spun around the table that evening would make Meshack Browning, who had a bit of a reputation in the '50's as a big game hunter in the western Maryland hills, drop his head in shame. Everyone was happy, and you could not expect them to be otherwise, with the expectation of a great turkey hunt the following morning.*

Guide William Elkins, Eugene DuPont and Henry Bridges (on horseback).

Monday morning, November 19, dawned fine and somewhat warm. When Denmead and I had feasted to our heart's content on a wonderful breakfast, we were invited to get into a double spring covered wagon, longitudinal seats, to ride to the wild turkey country on Sidling Hill Mountain. "Lanky" Den informed our host that he preferred to walk, as he had been quail hunting for the past week and his muscles were absolutely keyed up to the situation. We insisted that he ride, however, the distance being three miles to where we were dropped at a crossroad in company with Shorty Booth, a guide, and we started on our hunt for this great game bird.

We tramped for about an hour through uplands covered in places by grapevines and running briars to such an extent as to be almost impassable (great turkey country) but we did not locate a bird. After a time, we heard the familiar call from our host Bridges to come to the wagon, where we found he had two small Scotch terriers, which he claimed to be turkey dogs. They wore collars with rings in them, coupled together with a short strap, one dog being much larger than the other. These pups (which reminded me of Mutt and Jeff) followed closely at the heels of their master. Bridges informed us that when released the older pup would hunt turkey by trailing the scent and flushing same.

On the first put down, no results were obtained. Bridges was in the lead and Denmead and I followed. Going down a steep incline on one of the mountain roads, Mr. Bridges' hand suddenly went up as a signal to stop. He had seen turkeys across the road around a bend in the hollow. Now, creeping cautiously along (the rainfall of the previous night assisting materially in muffling our footfalls) to a bend in the road. I saw a turkey feeding under the oaks. Bridges nudged me and said, "Shoot that one." Seeing only one bird, I could not shoot any other. With my sixteen-gauge fox gun I drove for the head, and that turkey spun around and around. It took a second barrel to lay him low.

Henry P. Bridges with Woodmont turkey, 1908.

"Lanky" in the meantime had fired at another turkey, hitting him heavy, but failing to stop him. This bird came running toward me (which was the first time I had seen it, having supposed there was only one) and Denmead's second barrel brought it to the ground dead. Shorty Booth, who was in the rear, came running down the hill and retrieved our birds, which were killed probably forty yards away. Upon examination, we found the tom which I had killed was a tremendous bird. An argument arose immediately between Bridges and Denmead as to the probable weight of the bird, Bridges claiming 20 pounds and Denmead protesting, and offering to bet $25.00 that it would weigh only 15 pounds. Not being far from the camp, which is located three miles from the Clubhouse, we went by and hung our turkeys on a rail placed there for the purpose.

As "Lanky" had informed our host early in the morning that he was in walking condition, we started out again, and Bridges, who is an experienced mountain climber, took us to the top of Sidling Hill, in and out of ravines that were stiff for even a dog to crawl through. How he did walk us, and "Lanky" who had dressed in clothing suitable for the coldest winter morning (the thermometer on that date was hovering around 70 degrees) warmed up. After an hour of hill climbing, he began to shed clothes, until finally he was down to shirtsleeves.

At that point of my story we were introduced to turkey dog work. The dogs were released and the older of the two broke away at a rapid pace. He returned in a short time, having failed to scent turkey. I noted that the dogs were thoroughly broken to the whistle, and whenever Bridges, who is an expert in calling this great American game bird, used the turkey call, the dogs came running to his feet. We again hunted hard, but in vain. Returning to the dinner camp, which is located in the beautiful Sidling Hill Mountain, a feast was prepared by the guides (Millard F. Bishop, Chief of Police of the gun club, acting as chief cook), and, believe me, it was some meal: country ham (smoked with hickory wood), potatoes, fried apples, beans, bread, butter, and coffee, and the most delicious apple butter I ever ate. We ate heartily, as can be imagined.

After lunch, again starting out, I noted "Lanky" crawled into the wagon, the same as the rest of us. Bridges' hour and a half of mountain climbing seemed to have taken some of the pep out of him. At 1:30, while waiting near one of the game fields for our wagon, which we abandoned, a terrific storm arose. From the point where we were standing, we could look over into the valleys of West Virginia and see the storm approaching at a rapid pace. How it did rain and blow! It was over in a short time, however, and by that time the wagon arrived, it had almost ceased. Just about that time we spied in the distance two turkeys feeding. Den and I crept cautiously along the woods road and without much difficulty succeeded in killing the pair. The club does not permit the killing of more than two birds on one trip, and indeed we had no desire to kill more. Therefore, having secured our bag limit, we winded our way homeward. Arriving at the Clubhouse, we found some of the members and guests had returned ahead of us with their bag limits. When the birds were brought in from the wagon quite an argument arose as to the weight of the big gobbler I had killed. Placed on the scales it weighed 22½ pounds, and was said to be the largest wild turkey killed in that section for some years.

We spent the evening with our host and left early on the morning of the 20th, motoring back to Baltimore after a very pleasant and successful hunt for this greatest of American game birds.

Woodmont was an huntsman's paradise, thanks to Henry Bridges. The preserve was majestic, rugged and comfortable all wrapped into one experience. Few places in the country equaled Woodmont for hunting. Every need was catered to at Woodmont, from the fine cuisine, to the warm bed, to the fellowship shared around the two fireplaces. After dinner, talk might turn from the day's hunt to politics, society, conservation or business. While everyone may have been having too good a time to notice, Woodmont thrived because of the business talents of one of its members.

CREATING WEALTH BY DEVELOPING A CORPORATION

By 1908 Bridges was ready to expand his interests in business and industry. He had made many friends in Baltimore while practicing law. The death of his father that year was difficult for the young man. In the elder Bridges' *Last Will and Testament*, he carefully lined out the method of dividing his large estate:

Article #6. All the property in Washington County appraised and sold to any of my children.

Article #7. All indebtedness owed me by my children is not forgiven to be collected and put in the Trust.

Article #8. All the rest and residue to be held in Trust and sold at the best time within twenty years.

Henry's brothers Taliferro and Wilbur were named executors and trustees for their father's estate, of which the lease for the mining rights of The Berkeley Glass Sand Company was a part. Henry and his friend Nelson Perin soon acquired the lease rights to the company. Bridges now put his efforts into continuing his father's efforts in silica sand mining. The success of Berkeley Glass Sand also allowed Henry to continue vital financial support to Woodmont.

Bridges had the mining rights and Perin had access to needed capital for operating Berkeley Glass Sand. *The Hancock News* reported of the events of 1909, "We hear from Baltimore that some important sand developments and reorganizations may shortly be announced here. Baltimore capitalists are figuring on the purchase of the Berkeley plant owned by heirs of the late Robert Bridges, of Hancock and on a reorganization of the West Virginia and Pennsylvania sand plants."

Mining was an inherently dangerous business. Fires, accidents and explosions were a constant threat to the men employed. *The Washington Post* reported on this incident from April 1910. Even a non-fatal accident was frightening. "Boyd Casset met with a serious accident Wednesday at the Berkeley Springs Sand plant. He was one of the truck drivers. At a certain point of approach to the mill, the horse is unhitched from the truck and the latter goes onto the tipple of its own momentum. The truck he was driving was going at a greater speed than usual, and he missed getting the horse loose in time and was caught, the truck passing over one of his feet mashing it severely. The horse was dragged over the tipple and was also injured."

The tipple was the apparatus used for emptying the trucks or mine cars when they came off the mountain full of silica sand. Horses pulled the trucks along a narrow gauge track to the tipple location in front of the plant. Each truck was unhitched from the horse, and the tipple literally tipped it over emptying the sand rock onto a beltway that carried the material to the primary crusher within the plant itself. Casset apparently was unable to unhitch the horse in time for the truckload of sand to pass under weight of its own gravity on the way to the tipple.

Later that month, *The Post* reported on another narrow escape, this one near the Berkeley quarry. Mrs. E.W. Ziler was visiting her father, Mr. Michael Pentoney, when it might have seemed like all hell had broken loose. The company used black powder to blast huge holes in the sand rock and also to collapse layers of the mountainside. On this particular day the blast went off and showered boulders of sand rock onto the public road. The shower of rock proved quite a shock both to Mrs. Ziler and others. "W. Crosfield's team, we understand, driven by G. P. Phillips, (who) was also on the road, and the driver fortunately stopped the team or he, too, may have been injured. More care should be exercised by those having these blasts in charge or else have a watchman employed to notify the traveling public."

By July 1910, Bridges and Perin were still working to settle the many difficult land transactions related to the Berkeley Glass Sand Company and Robert Bridges' estate. On July 13, 1910, the relevant pieces of property were conveyed to Berkeley Glass Sand. It must have been a difficult transfer of wealth, for Robert Bridges at one time owned 32,000 acres of land in

Morgan County and many southern counties of West Virginia. Bridges also bought from his father's estate the West Virginia Coal and Timber Company with a number of other investors. It was mostly coal land in a number of southern West Virginia counties.

A miner at the Berkeley Works. The young visitors do not appeared to be dressed for work.

The rights to the lands that contained the pure silica sand were important for Bridges and Perin, along with the riparian, or water, rights. On November 29, 1910, a conference was held in the office of attorney A.C. McIntire to consider the most feasible plan of securing water for the sand mills of the Warm Springs Valley. Present at the conference were T. F. Sorague, R. C. Ringold, H. P. Bridges, F. R. Reed, W.D. Stephenson, Wm. Noel, F. C. Lasman, E. F. Millard, each representing their individual sand company in the valley. Everyone in the room realized that there could be no finished product without water to wash the sand clean.

The Warm Springs Run was a small tributary that ran through the town of Berkeley Springs. It then flowed by each of the small plants on its way to the Potomac River. The Berkeley Glass Sand Company was the first company the stream passed; it was then harnessed by each of the other companies via holding ponds. Berkeley Glass Sand used water during the day and shut down mining and washing operations at night. The other companies then used the clean water at night to fill their cleaning ponds and have a supply ready for work the next day. The conference considered the idea of a pipeline from the town of Berkeley Springs. A participant recorded that "the matter of construction of a pipeline or raceway to carry water to the sand plants of Millard, Speers, Pittsburgh, West Virginia and Pennsylvania Works…that the pipeline and right of ways as far as Millards be shared jointly by all the works…and each across his property.…It appears that the lie was to start at the north line of Bridges and Perin." This issue of water would grow even more critical when Berkeley Glass Sand began to run mills twenty-four hours a day.

Across the Potomac J.T. Bridges was working to build a sand operation similar to his brother's. The operation began with $25,000 capital and J.T. Bridges as president. The Hancock Building Sand Company reported a great new ledge of pure white sand struck above the town on High German Mountain located on the Bridges farm. On March 31, 1911, *The Hagerstown Mail* reported that, "There is enough glass sand there to run for ages. A sample of it was pronounced by an analytical chemist to be over 99 percent pure and the sand lies only a foot below the surface. It will be pumped to the cars by a hydraulic pump and not handled at all except by shoving the nozzle of the in draft right into the deposit." The sand was initially washed from the mine.

Later the sand was washed through the pipeline that passed by a Methodist parsonage directly into train cars. "The pipeline, 1,610 feet long, is now building. It is composed of 5-inch iron pipes on poles 70 feet high. By means of water the sand will be washed down the big sand mill into bins, each with a capacity of 200 tons and from the bins loaded into cars. The sand is of extra fine quality, containing 99 3/4 percent silica." J. T. Bridges engineered this pipe system that traveled from the mountain across the town and directly to the Western Maryland Railroad. However, this operation had numerous flaws and did not prevail.

There were now eight mills operating on hills surrounding Hancock and Berkeley Springs. Few people knew of the value of the sand deposits. C.W. Henderson, Robert Bridges' business partner, owned the majority of the land on which the sand deposits were located. A Mr. Kessler first came along and took options on the lands owned by Henderson. He then went to Pittsburgh and made a deal with the Pittsburgh Plate Glass Company. Both Kessler and Henderson received substantial royalties from Pittsburgh Plate Glass. The company also found another deposit in the same hill. Royalties were as high as $40,000 a year.

The Berkeley Glass Sand Company was incorporated in September 1911 with a capital of $200,000. Henry P. Bridges was president and Nelson Perin secretary-treasurer. *The Hancock News* noted:

> *[the] present output of sand, which is 120 tons a day, will be increased to 320 tons by the erection of another mill having a capacity of 200 tons, at a cost of $30,000. The increased business of the company necessitated the construction of a new mill. The company owns a mountain of sand with a tunnel 300 feet deep. The sand is used exclusively in the manufacture of plate glass and is sold principally in Pittsburgh and Baltimore. The corporation will also conduct business in all states, District of Columbia and foreign countries.*

Bridges and his mining partners at Berkeley Glass Sand quarry in 1911. There were profits to be made in such rubble.

The newly incorporated company had difficulties from the start with labor unrest one of the first problems Bridges and Perin faced at the plant. One summer's morning in 1911, workers became disgruntled at the action of the owners of the works, in reducing the force from eight to six men to a truck; men with picks and shovels in the quarry loaded the trucks. The men decided that they would strike and collected their pay. Then they "proceeded to Hancock to get a supply of 'canal water' which was entirely too freely imbibed and on their return to Berkeley resulted in about six to eight rough and tumble fights several black eyes, sore noses, and hard feelings, but no arrests." Since these were considered boom times, the men found themselves able to make as much as $1.75 a day.

Disaster struck a year later when the old mill of the Berkeley Glass Sand was destroyed. A fire started from an overheated chimney connected with the large dryer. In less than an hour the mill was reduced to a mass of embers. The old mill was a landmark in Berkeley Springs as one of the first facilities erected. For the past fifteen years it had been turning out high-grade silica sand. Luckily, the company's new mill had just started operating. It had a daily capacity of over 200 tons and a storage capacity of forty carloads of dry sand.

**Berkeley Glass Sand Company and construction
of the new storage hopper, ca. 1912.**

But more than equipment was destroyed in the mining business. On December 11, 1913, one of the Hungarian-immigrant workmen at the Pennsylvania Glass Sand Corporation mine north of town fell from the mountainside into the mine and to his death. He had been assisting other workmen in loosening stones near the mouth of the mine when he lost his footing and fell. The man was married, with a wife living in the old country. *The Morgan Messenger* also reported another accident, "Mr. Marvin Everett while working in one of the sand mines on Tuesday was struck on both legs by a stone that rolled from the side of the mine, skinning and bruising him seriously."

Henry continued to live in Baltimore. He often traveled to Berkeley Springs to check on his company interests. He frequently visited his mother, who continued to live in the Bridges' home on Main Street in Hancock. Henry's older sisters also lived in the area, and they entertained lavishly as this excerpt from Priscilla Breathed Bridges' diary shows:

*A barge party on a recent evening by Misses Helen and Lilla
Bridges was an event of much pleasure. The party started late in
the afternoon for Dam No. 6, ten miles above Hancock on a large
flat boat that was gorgeously decorated and most comfortably fitted*

out. A framework was erected on the boat around the top of which was entwined bunting of orange and black, the colors of Maryland. A beautiful harmony was blended by the decorations of golden rod and sunflowers placed on the pillars supporting the framework. Japanese lanterns were hung under the graceful folds and the effect was very pretty. The party arrived at the Dam after twilight and supped under the softening light from Japanese lanterns. The Dam was viewed under the beams of a moon holding sway in a cloudless sky. Streaks as of dawn were observed in the east as the barge glided up to Wason Street pier and the company sang softly, "Home Again."

Henry attended the barge event with his mother along with his sisters Helen, Lilla and Reba and brothers Taliaferro and Wilbur.

Canal barge below Woodmont at Dam #6 in 1912. The canal was already a transportation anachronism.

While in town he also attended to friends fishing the Potomac at Woodmont. A newspaper story reported:

Henry P. Bridges, of this city, secretary of the Woodmont Rod and Gun Club, will give a large weekend house party at the Woodmont Club and game preserve, which is noted for its beautiful scenery. John D. Riley, who is an expert fisherman, has already engaged Hooper Coyne to help him land a five-pound bass that William Elkins, the guide, wired Riley was staying around Grover Cleveland's Rock. This is the rock Cleveland fished from when he was entertained by the Club a few years ago. [In 1894, Cleveland caught 25 bass from "Cleveland Rock," west of Cox Island in the Potomac.]

Henry, obviously understood the need to balance work with play, for himself and others. His first cousin Robert Bridges also attended family social events and loved to fish the Potomac at Woodmont. In 1914, this Bridges was named editor-in-chief of Charles P. Scribner's Sons a New York-based literary magazine and publisher of world renown. Bridges' fishing talent may also have applied to work. That would explain his ability to catch Theodore Roosevelt as an author for Scribner's.

Robert Bridges of Charles P. Scribner's & Sons at Woodmont. This college dorm mate and friend of Woodrow Wilson managed to work closely with Wilson's political adversary, Teddy Roosevelt.

Bridges spent a great deal of his weekend time at Woodmont as his interest in conservation and the outdoors grew. In April 1916, *The Hancock News* reported that, "Our friend Henry P. Bridges is likely to be appointed on the Maryland Conservation Board by the Governor at a salary of $3,000 per year....Mr. Bridges being a game expert and a lawyer would make an ideal member for the Board and we certainly hope he is appointed." Bridges' friendships with Maryland Governor Edwin Warfield and Game Warden Lee LeCompte contributed more than a little to his success as a conservationist.

His efforts were beginning to make a difference in the wild game populations. Henry raised wild turkeys by the thousands and shipped the birds all over the country. Maryland State Forester John Mash wrote:

There are many successes of the last ninety-odd years, but the two with the biggest are the deer and wild turkey. There are several factors for the return of these two valuable species, as well as, several others that were gone a hundred years ago. Among them was the appointment of E. Lee LeCompte as State Game Warden in 1916, the Mertens Green Ridge Orchard Company bankruptcy in 1917, (orchard owners killed deer because they ate the apples) and the Woodmont Rod and Gun Club.

Bridges pioneering conservation programs at Woodmont had important ramifications nationwide. On April 3, 1916, the Woodmont Club became an Associate Member of *The American Game Protective and Propagation Association*; the association was organized to protect wild game species in the United States. This was all part of a web of conservation Henry spun over the years.

Bridges lived at the Woodmont Clubhouse while he stayed in western Maryland. He had an office in a small white clapboard house where he conducted business for Berkeley Glass Sand. The plant was within walking distance.

**Berkeley Glass Sand Company office
where Bridges ran the operation.**

In March 1917, Bridges signed an agreement to pay Nelson Perin an annual salary of $3,000 plus 10 percent of the company's net income. Berkeley Glass Sand was prospering. The next capital improvement was the construction of three tramways and tipples over the Hancock Grade. This project enabled the company to move the silica sand from the west side of the Grade to the crushers on the east side of the road. The Honorable County Court of Morgan County West Virginia was petitioned on the 17th day of

May 1917, "the Berkeley Glass Sand Company, a corporation, by its Attorney J. Hammond Siler [native of Berkeley Springs and Corporate Council to Berkeley Glass, Western Maryland R.R. and Potomac Light and Power], and asked that a franchise be granted the Berkeley Glass Sand Company, a corporation, for a term of fifty years, to build, operate and maintain an overhead trestle tramway or crossing over and across the County road." The request was granted.

Labor continued to be a major concern for Henry. On October 25, 1917, Berkeley Glass Sand together with the West Virginia and Pittsburgh Sand Company announced a wage increase of 25 cents a day, with an annual 10 percent bonus for full-time workers. Men earned as much as $4.50 a day, a figure which made them the best paid laborers in the county.

By December 1919, Bridges and Perin were interested in operating their mills twenty-four hours a day, which required a steady supply of the water from the Warm Springs Run. Company attorney John T. Siler spelled out the firm's views to another lawyer:

The Berkeley Glass Sand Company is the pioneer company in this town or vicinity and is also the company owning and operating the sand works nearest the Springs just north of the town; and for this reason gets the water fresh from Warm Spring Run stream before it has been used by any other sand company – all the other sand mines and mills being located below the Bridges works.

Up to the present time the Berkeley Glass Sand Company had been using the water from this stream all day long: first taking it from the stream in a clear condition and after washing its sand returning the water in a muddy condition to the stream. As soon as the Berkeley Glass Sand Company would stop work in the evening the other mills (five or six in number) below on the same stream would begin drawing the water from the stream into ponds arranged for that purpose and this process would continue during the night while the water was clear until the ponds were filled, and then the inlet to the ponds would be closed so as to prevent the muddy water from the Berkeley Glass Sand Company coming into the ponds the next day.

This arrangement has been in use a long time, but now a new condition is about to arise, namely, the Berkeley Glass Sand Company is arranging to increase the capacity of its mills so that it will need all the water all the time for washing its sand so that the water as returned to the stream will always be muddy, and the present arrangement for the distribution of water will thereby be disturbed.

I have understood that there was some paper once given Mr. Robert Bridges, the former owner of the sand works, by which he acquired certain rights to lay a pipe in the bed of the stream to convey water from the Springs through the property of the several owners to this mill, but as yet I have not been able to find any record of this paper. If I find such record or the original paper, I will advise you promptly of what it contains.

Berkeley Glass Sand Company was in a position to monopolize the area sand industry on account of its primary access to clean water. On January 2, 1920, Henry advised his attorney to handle riparian rights in this way:

Dear Mr. Siler:

Your one letter received while at Woodmont and your second letter received on my return to the office. My father had J. T. Bridges to start out and see the lot owners to get a right of way to put a pipeline to the Spring at the Grove. I think J. T. Bridges did secure some of the right of way but there is nothing on record or any agreement that I know of. After my father started the matter, he consulted some lawyer in Martinsburg, W. VA and he advised him to not put a pipeline and connect at the Spring, telling him that if he did so that it would open up a question in Berkeley, where he would start lawsuits by the property owners and by the others who used the water from the Spring.

He also stated it would even open up a question that the State could charge a rent for the use of the water taken from the Spring. He advised that my father had the right to use the water at his mill site and that any manufacturing plant or land owners above his mill site could give him no trouble about the water, therefore my father always stated when he owned the property that he thought a wise thing to do was to let the water question alone and not do anything that would cause any contention by the people in Berkeley.

He also advised us if anything should happen to him, not to try to put a pipeline to the Spring or open up questions about the water, therefore I think it would be a mistake for our Company to try to put a pipeline to the Spring and Mr. Perin spoke to me about it four or five years ago and I told him then that we would only be looking for trouble if we did so and that I was strongly opposed to it and that my father was a very wise man and we better let the water question alone and use the water in front of our property and not try to go to the Spring to take the water.

You know as well as I do, in Berkeley, there are some people that would only want the opportunity to give us trouble in reference to this water, therefore I think it will be a big mistake to advise our Company to put this pipeline to the Spring. We have not had any trouble up to the present date in getting all the water we want at our mills, and the water system that Mr. Perin has already installed is a splendid one. The only trouble, as I understand, is that the canning factory in the summer throws in their tomato skins in the water and dirties the same. We can certainly stop that.

You know as soon as we pipe the water from the Spring and divert the same into our pond, that the mills below are going to make a big howl as knowing the law in Maryland which I suppose is the same in West Virginia, we would not have any right to divert all the water from this stream or change the course of the stream or using all of the water that goes down, to go to our pond. I think you will be of the same opinion as to this matter, but if you want to find anything out about the right of way Tol can tell you because he was the one that started it for my father.

Yours truly, Henry P. Bridges

A day later, consulting lawyer Horrest Brown told Siler, "The general trend of authority seems to be that where there are several riparian owners on a stream using the water for mining or power purposes, that each of them may make reasonable use of it for such purposes having regard to the capacity and limitations of the stream and this right of a reasonable use applies both as to the flow of the water and the purity of the water." Although Brown's view seemed to support the competition, the other sand manufacturers were realizing that Berkeley Glass Sand was a power to reckon with.

THE WILD TURKEY CALL, HENRY P. BRIDGES, INVENTOR

Hunting a wild turkey is no easy task. The hunter must scout for the bird as it roosts in tall pines the night before the hunt. The bird roosts off the ground for protection from predators. The hunter then works to position himself before dawn in the vicinity of the roosted bird. The birds "gobble" before flying to the ground in the spring of the year to mate with hens. The call helps them locate any hens receptive to mating.

The hen plays a key role in this process as she yelps and clucks to the gobbler so he can locate her in the woods. Turkeys have eyesight ten times sharper than humans do and hearing twenty times better. The male cautiously approaches the hen wary of predators and other boss gobblers that may be on the prowl. Gobblers are territorial and aggressively defend their breeding territory.

The hunter who takes to the woods after a turkey must play the trickster, with mouth calls, box calls, slate calls, crow calls and gobbler noisemakers to fool the gobbler. The hunter also is fully camouflaged from head to toe. The camouflage details determine the success of a hunt. The bird is extremely cautious and can spot or hear a fake with an uncanny instinctual ability, as Henry Bridges noted:

> *"'Turc! Turc!' calls the wild turkey, scratching for feed deep in a stand of towering oaks. But let so much as a single leaf rustle unduly and the bird is off, either running with the speed of a race horse, or rising into the air on broad wings to fly for half a mile or so to safety. There is nothing keener on the face of the earth than the wild turkey's sense of sight and hearing – the two prime facts a turkey hunter must keep in mind."*

The slightest glimmer of reflection, false movement or wrong cadence of calls can frighten a wise old boss gobbler so that the hunt is over for the day. The successful hunter uses Bridges' diaphragm mouth call and can spend from one to three hours calling. When the turkey is within shotgun range of twenty to forty yards, the mouth call enables the hunter to hold his gun and focus on the all important head-shot. Bridges wrote:

> *Now, a wild turkey is, I believe, one of the smartest creatures on two feet. It is just not an ordinary hunter who can bag him. Your turkey hunter is usually a special breed of hunter. He is a man of infinite patience, much woodmanship and a good shot. Only the man who knows his business stands any chance at all of returning from*

a turkey-hunting trip with a bird. In fact, even the expert hunter is frequently given the run-around by the sagacious bird, a bird that does not hesitate to express its contempt for the dumb, deaf and half-blind creatures that hunt for it.

Calling wild turkey dates back thousands of years to Native Americans. They used hollow turkey wing bones to call the bird within killing distance. The Indians were equally skilled, one writer has noted, as "experts at killing with sarbacane, a hollow cane through which they blew a small dart."

The history of the modern-day turkey call is credited to M. Samuel McCain. Prior to the everyday use of rubber, McCain used animal parts to patent his turkey call, the "Whistle and Bird-Call," patented February 5, 1867. But the call was difficult to master. McCain's patent document put it somewhat more delicately, "[With] a little practice... the power of the instrument is only limited by the perfectness of the ear or taste for music of the performer, and his perseverance."

The wild turkey is one of the most vocal of birds. It relies strongly on its voice and has evolved the anatomical features that make vocalizations possible. Turkey calls have to reproduce these vocalizations perfectly to draw a response from a wary bird. The first commercial box call, known as the Gibson turkey call, was patented in 1897 and made by Gibson and Boddie of Dardanelle, Arkansas. Dwain bland writes, "These boxes enjoyed great popularity and were used by hunters across the South and in what was then Indian Territory, present day Oklahoma."

According to Lovett Williams, the turkey call industry has grown today to include calls in five different categories:

"1) breath-operated by suction; 2) breath-operated rubber mouth diaphragm; 3) breath-operated tube with a rubber membrane; 4) wooden sounding boxes operated by friction of a scrapper, and; 5) slate or other rough surface scraped with a hand-held peg. There are also calls of hard plastic and rubber that gobble like a wild bird when shaken and many automatic pushbutton friction calls."

Bridges would further the development of the call and apply for a patent on March 20, 1920. This call, the diaphragm mouth call, has become essential for hunting turkey in the wild. The call was no more than a piece of latex rubber stretched across a metal horseshoe-curved mouth piece. It was a derivative of an old-time hunters' call that used a simple green reed leaf to call turkey. A patent was granted February 1, 1921:

UNITED STATES PATENT OFFICE
HENRY P. BRIDGES, OF BALTIMORE, MARYLAND
SOUND-PRODUCING DEVICE
1,367,176Specification of Letters PatentPatented Feb.1, 1921.
Application filed March 20, 1920.Serial No. 367,484

To all whom it may concern:

Be it known that I, Henry P. Bridges, a citizen of the United States of America, residing at Baltimore, State of Maryland, have invented certain new and useful Improvements in Sound-Producing Devices....My invention relates to sound producing devices, and is particularly adapted to devices to be used in imitating the sounds made by birds and other game...to imitate the call of a wild turkey.

Bridges' patent of turkey mouth call.

Advertisements selling the call ran as early as December 1920 in *Forest & Stream* and also ran in the December 1923 issue of *Field & Stream*. The cost of the device was first listed at $2 before coming down to $1 in 1923. Another call, the work of Jim Radcliff of Mobile Alabama, did not appear for sale until 1926 or 1927. Henry's call was the first modern-day mouth call in the United States.

There were two unique styles of hunting wild turkey at Woodmont. Bridges wrote that the best ways were "by scattering a flock and then calling them up again, or by staging a turkey drive, much as a deer drive is staged." The Woodmont style of naturally hunting and calling the wild turkey also relied on the turkey dog. Bridges' turkey dog was named Billy, and he had a series of turkey dogs that he hunted with over the years, all named Billy. Bridges reported that, "To scatter a flock of wild turkeys, the hunter needs a specially trained dog. The dog is turned loose in turkey country; it hunts out a flock of turkeys, charges them and barks as the flock scatters. The hunter then creeps up to the point where the dog is barking and then both dog and hunter begin to wait in silence for about an hour. They must remain in perfect silence and they must be out of sight, behind a tree or bush."

In the fall season a scattered flock of turkeys will respond to the calling of a hunter and work to re-congregate by listening for calls from other birds. It was then, observed Henry, "The time comes, and the hunter begins to call the birds. But he must be sure he makes no errors. One false call and the turkeys will be off in the other direction. No man can tell another how to work a turkey call. Nor can one man learn much by watching another work a call. It is an art that each must learn for himself. It takes much patience and much practice."

Another way to hunt at Woodmont were the "annual turkey drives [where] the gunners are stationed along the bottom of a ravine and the birds are driven from one ridge, across the ravine, to the next ridge. It is wing shooting at its best....On the other side of the ridge, the drivers walk through the brush talking, singing, making all available noise. And then suddenly there is a roar of wings and many turkeys take wing at once – a flock that all but darkens the sky."

MARRIAGE, WOODMONT AND BUSINESS

In 1922, Bridges fell under the spell of the young Cornelia Shelby Thomas of Washington County, Johnson City, Tennessee. Henry's dentist introduced him to Shelby; he was forty-four and she was twenty. Shelby was born on May 7, 1902 in Big Stone Gap, Virginia to Vint Thomas and Minnie Patton Thomas. Shelby was one of three children and accompanied the family on their move to Watauga Avenue in Johnson City, Tennessee. She first attended The Maryland College for Women in Baltimore before transferring to the Peabody Conservatory of Music to study piano. "The pupil is [a] sweet amiable girl, doing the best of which she is capable. Will never be able to do anything beyond playing a few pieces for her own pleasure." This rather harsh report came from her teacher, Miss Coulson, for the season 1920-1921.

Cornelia Shelby Bridges, 1922.

On May 22, 1922, Reverend Harris Elliot Kirk married them at the Franklin Street Presbyterian Church, where Bridges served as a trustee. The couple lived at the Washington Apartments by The Washington Monument Square in Mt. Vernon. Just twelve days before his wedding, Henry wrote a poem, which he dedicated "to my sweetheart to be my bride on May the 22, 1922. The sweetest girl on earth. And no love could be as great for a girl as mine."

It was in the springtime that I met you, as the flowers and buds began to unfold, In the bright glad days of spring time, Wandering over field and mountains.

And your dainty face before me, Lifting up a rosy mouth to kiss, Sweetness like unto no other pleasure, Oh, I'd give you all other joy for this.

Again I look into your eyes so tender, and their spell is on me still, Who can look into their depths ever, and yield not your will.

I've gone with marry woman, I've seen a scare or two, But I never thought I'd love a woman, as truly as I love you.

That night I opened my heart to you, and took you in forever, a permanent guest forever my darling, If there you are willing ever to stay.

Sweet idol of my dreams, Companion of my waking hours, Thou art as dear to me

as dew drop unto flowers.

But, oh: that voice of thine, It set my very soul on fire, and bade me linger by thy side

and thee my own, my all, desire.

Dast know thy voice's power, Its charm and sweetness rare! So full of soul and heart

and love beyond compare.

Again I see thy glorious eyes, So tender and true, That beam on me, Ere thy found love I know.

And the vision never fadeth, and my heart is warm and true, and the current of my being

Fondly leads the way to you.

Bridges and Shelby were now listed in the *Baltimore Society Visting List* or Blue Book. They attended all the social events in Baltimore while Henry continued entertaining the elite of Baltimore at the Woodmont Club. He was doing well financially and now had a life companion. Husband and wife complemented each other to the point of making a beautiful couple together.

In the 1920s, Henry found that conservation work included the task of game breeder. Bridges installed fourteen miles of fencing--two and a half inch mesh Elwood Diamond Lawn fence measuring nine and a half feet high--around the preserve. Fifteen men built the fence over a year and a half. Twenty-five carloads of wire were used at a total cost of $30,000; a breeding pen covering an area of 500 acres, or three miles, was enclosed with the same kind of fencing for $6,000. Brood pens and equipment on the club grounds cost $12,000. The brood stock had their wings clipped; however, the gobblers from the natural flocks of Woodmont were able to fly into the enclosure to breed with the brood stock. Bridges traveled hundreds of miles to locate wild turkey eggs. He would collect them and introduce the genes of these birds to his flock, ensuring a constant renewal of the wild genes.

In 1923, Paul A. Curtis wrote an article on hunting turkey at Woodmont in *Field & Stream.* The article noted that a movie, *"Turkey Hunt in Maryland,"* had been filmed by the magazine at Woodmont. Curtis wrote that the turkey hunter must be "a skilful tracker, versed in the ways of the woods, able to stalk his game with the stealth of a Red Indian and with the patience of a wooden one- quick and accurate both with the brain and rifle. Also, he must be able to 'talk turkey' as the turkey talks."

While staying at Woodmont, Curtis was awakened at the unholy hour of 4:30 AM by the chief guide Bill Elkins, and they were off to the preserve. Curtis described Elkins as "one of the passing race of Americans which one has to seek far from the beaten path--lean; gaunt, loose-jointed, a true son of the woods and hills, and as simple and generous as the country through which he had roamed all of his days." The sun was just peeking over the hill-tops on this November morning, and the ground was covered with frost.

Elkins instructed his group of five hunters to split up and surround a field planted with wheat feed for the turkeys. Other hunters from the night before had been successful in hunting this field. They spotted a gang of turkey in the field "but it was too late and even as I dropped to my knees, one huge gobbler stretched himself to the fullest extent- straight as a ram rod and stood looking in our direction." Before a shot could be fired the gobbler ran a couple of steps for a takeoff and jump, soaring high over the chestnuts and scaled to the other ridge, with the rest of the flock following. When they all sat down to discuss the matter Elkins complained, "we was wors'n a troop of cavalry and twice as noisy."

After their scolding, the group heard more yelping over the far ridge. Consequently, the hunters devised a plan to split the group in to two parties and outflank the turkeys by surrounding them and running them into the group that remained at the bottom of the ridge. Again Elkins responded "Them birds'll hear yo' all comin' a mile and no wise turkey is goin' to investigate. He'll just say to hisself....'I'm leavin'.'" Undaunted, they set out for the top of the ridge to secure a flanked position. It was not long before they heard a shot fired, followed by another.

They had set a rendezvous at a spring in the woods, and they climbed to this point and waited for their fellow hunters or turkey, whichever came first. It was one o'clock, and the other hunters finally appeared so they sat for lunch and heard a story. Jim, who had been out on his own, located a flock and began to call with his "wing bone" and got impatient as the turkey responded back to his calls. He slipped through heavy brush and got close to the flock when he made the mistake of calling once too often. But as that "last falsetto squeak resounded through the wood the turkey said 'One of us is wrong,' and lit out for farther fields of adventure." At the moment Jim realized he had called falsely. He immediately stood and fired at the flying turkey, only to wing it in the air. The distraught hunter ran after the bird, but to no avail, it was gone for the day.

After lunch the group headed for another opening in the woods where Elkins reported a covey of partridge. The hunters changed their ammunition and began to hunt the field. Elkins signaled to Curtis to "come quick!" As he moved forward through the brush, a turkey got up in front of him at about twenty yards. He quickly leveled his barrel and brought the bird down. Another of the hunters ran into a group of turkeys nestled in a hollow trying to hide. He fired his gun and took down one while wounding two others. As the wounded bird came toward him his gun was empty so he swung the stock of the gun at the bird and hit a stump, breaking his gun in two. When it was all over the party had brought down seven turkeys and lost one gun in the heat of *hor de combat.*

Elkins retrieved Curtis's gobbler, "which turned out to be a very young maiden turkey, and I will never hear the end of that gobbler." The author credited their hunting success to the inexperience of the young brood that they happened upon. They were eight- and ten-pound birds and "if they had been educated, they would have sneaked off ahead of us, and we would have never seen them, nor would they have hidden away in the trees so near by."

Guide William Elkins with Woodmont turkeys. The guide did not want hunters sounding like the Seventh Cavalry.

Curtis concluded his hunt with these words:

All of these birds are native to the district, but have been given every encouragement to breed and remain on the preserve. Grain is scattered through the woods for them when the snows are heavy in the winter, buckwheat and corn is sown in the patches in the clearings and left standing, and vermin (such as wild cats, skunks, etc.) are energetically hunted and trapped the year round by the keepers, with the result that the stock of game remains wild in its natural haunts. This has been done since the Club was organized about fifty-five years ago and speaks volumes for what preservation will do for our fast vanishing national game bird.

This experiment is of the utmost importance for it proves beyond a question of doubt that there is no legitimate excuse for the ultimate extinction of the wild turkey, such as is inevitable in the case of so much of the rest of our American game. Turkey can and do live and prosper on this large preserve- wake up and do as much for them in your section before it is too late, experiment on other game and also fish, you may come out ahead, and if you do you are sure to be paid ten-fold for your efforts.

Bridges' conservation work at Woodmont was proving itself. When Henry began his work, there were very few wild turkeys left in America. He had used the confines of the Woodmont preserve to breed the bird by the thousands. The bird was plentiful at Woodmont, and his brood stock produced disease-free birds that naturally assimilated back into the wild. Woodmont also featured a deer program. Bridges captured large white-tailed deer from Michigan and Wisconsin which he released into the fenced preserve. The offspring, weighing from 250 to 315 pounds, were the largest deer in the area. Bridges' pioneering conservation effort would serve as a model for other preserves in America.

Henry's friend Lee Harr from Johnson City wrote him in Baltimore the following letter on November 28, 1923, concerning a recent visit:

> *Dear commander-in chief of Billy and Jim:*
>
> *This is to notify you that you gave us the time of our lives. We arrived home Monday morning, sober, safe, and rejoicing. You should have seen Fred strut. And in a few days you will receive a handsome picture of Bro. Locket--all bedecked with his game.*
>
> *But speaking for myself. I enjoyed the trip. First, you and Shelby could not have treated us nicer while in Baltimore, and we enjoyed our stay there. Bob is still talking about Sallie Brown. And while we are all talking a great deal-all's mum about the other fellow's shortcomings-for fear that he also will be exposed. They haven't even told it on me about letting my gun accidentally go off.*
>
> *And then the hunt. Well-I am spoiled for the rest of the season. You can talk all you want to about roughing it while hunting etc., but I will take my hunts as easily as possible. And you sure have it down to a fine point. We enjoyed it all-including Harvey-and will always remember the entire trip as our best hunt-from all angles.*
>
> *Enclosed find clipping from Johnson City Staff. Give Shelby my best regards. Wish you two were going down to Nashville with Marie and I to see the Game. We are leaving this afternoon to be gone until Sunday. Some time-what says you to all going up to New York for a few days together- to see the shows- etc.*
>
> *Again thanking you for your many courtesies shown to us on our wonderful hunt with you, and awaiting your hunt with us Xmas with the hope that we can in a small way show you our appreciation of our visit to Woodmont.*

Good times were the rule for Bridges' guests at Woodmont. It was different for Henry's professional and, to some degree, personal lives. In 1924, The Berkeley Glass Sand Company hit dry rock, an event that discouraged partner Nelson Perin. Bridges predicted they would be through the rock in a week, but Perin did not believe him. Consequently, Bridges offered to buyout Perin's interest in the company, and Perin accepted. Shortly thereafter, the company was back into silica sand, too late for Perin. This turn of events created a great deal of enmity between Bridges and Perin for years to come.

In 1924, Bridges also built Rock Hill, a stately mountain home above the city of Berkeley Springs. the home, built for Shelby and Henry, had been completed for just a few months before its destruction from a fire set, ironically, the arson was believed to be an employee of the local fire department.

Rock Hill above Berkeley Springs, West Virginia.
(Fred T. Newbraugh Collection)

In 1925, an enterprising young engineer by the name of Earl Andrews joined the ranks of the Pennsylvania Glass Sand Company. Andrews was instrumental in building more efficient crusers and mining techniques for the Warm Springs Valley operation. At the time Bridges was consolidating his mill with some of the other smaller operators in Warm Springs Valley. He also began buying narrow thirty-six foot gauge railroad equipment powered by gasoline Plymouth engines to replace the mule-drawn rail trucks.

The narrow gauge engines pulled cars loaded by huge "Lauren Steam Shovels" in the quarries and hauled sand rock to tipple crushers. There were eventually four Plymouth engines hauling rocks to the crushers. The engines ran to the Hancock Works plant where they unloaded into a crusher along the B & O tracks. The sand rocks were moved on a conveyor for pulverizing into a form that could be stored in silos and shipped to be melted into glass by manufacturers.

One of the largest buyers of Berkeley Works sand was the Pittsburgh Plate Glass Corporation. The raw material for windshields and binocular lenses for World War I originated from the Berkeley Works. The sand had to be extremely pure for these and other products.

Bridges continued to push for the consolidation of mines in the region. He joined Berkeley Glass Sand with West Virginia Glass Sand Company I and West Virginia Glass Sand Company II; Pittsburgh Glass Sand; Speer and White Sand Company; Duckwall; and Pennsylvania Glass Sand Company, Hancock Works. Henry had the vision and charisma to inspire three other investors into the consolidation: Addison Mulligan, his fraternity brother and a Baltimore lawyer; A.J. Fink, the owner of the Southern Hotel in Baltimore; and Pennsylvania Glass Sand competitor William J. Woods of Lewistown, Pennsylvania. The stock of the consolidated Berkeley Works was initially traded over the counter.

Narrow gauge train with Lauren steam shovel in the quarry, with nary a mule to be seen.

The new company was called Pennsylvania Glass Sand Company. Woods' father Samuel and a group of men from Lewistown had been mining Oriskany sand since 1894. They organized and incorporated the Pennsylvania Glass Sand Company in1902. The new firm grouped together various sand plants in Pennsylvania and Warm Springs Valley.

No matter how vexing, the need to protect riparian rights and to replace machinery was anything but dangerous. The actual work of mining the sand, however, was something else. A constant danger for miners was silicosis, or sand in the lung. The effects were similar to the black lung suffered by coal miners. The particles of silica sand entered the lungs of the miners, who did not wear protective masks. The fine particles were like a scissors edge that cut away at the lining of the lungs, resulting in diminished breathing capacity and, oftentimes, death.

Silicosis was one of the inherent dangers of mining. Another was accidents, such as those resulting from the use of explosives in quarry excavation. One such terrible accident occurred June 7, 1926. Killed immediately by an explosion were Berkeley Glass Sand workers Irvin Henry, 30; Emory Miller, 34; and head driller George Walls, 30. All were married. They had eleven children among them. Romanis Dawson, 30; Joseph Miller, 23; Oliver Moon, who had one adopted child, also died somewhat later. The sole survivor, Philmore Norris remembers being blown eight feet into the air as 3,000 tons of stone came tumbling down the mountainside late that afternoon.

Nine holes where drilled into the 100 foot face of the mountain and over 3,000 sticks of dynamite were rammed into the holes, nearly 1,200 pounds of 60 percent high-test dynamite filled the mountain. "With the dynamite 20 feet deep in these holes, no warning of the explosion was given. The stone bulged out first, with terrific force, and the warning crack came afterward. The men were killed or fatally crushed without the slightest warning. They were picked up by the force of the blast, as the face of the cliff erupted outward driven by the dynamite within, and carried with the hurtling stone as it showered down about them in boulders." It was never determined what caused the explosion that day. However, the way the dynamite was packed may have been the culprit.

The songwriter John Unger, a Berkeley Springs native, wrote the song "*The Miners Doom*" about this dark day in the history of sand mines,

All comrades, wives, and children,
Please listen what I say,
About your dearest loved ones
Who left their home one day;
They went to Berkeley sand mine,
Not very far away.
But they will not return
Until the judgment day.
Early one Monday morning,
A warm June summer day,
They bade farewell to loved ones
And started on their way;
They all were gay and happy
And joked with every one,
But none of them were thinking
That death was soon to come.
Then side by side they started
In mine to do their work.
But still they were not thinking
That they would soon be hurt;
But on that Monday evening,
Something past four o'clock,
There was a great explosion
Which covered them with rock.
Then friends and comrades struggled
To save them from their doom,
But six young men lie sleeping
Beneath the sand and stone;
Now miners all take warning,
From these six young men's fate,
And get right with your Maker,
Before it is too late.
Dear mothers do not worry,
Wives and children don't cry,
But try to meet your loved ones
In that sweet bye and bye;
There is a home in Heaven,
Where there's no tears and pain,
There is no death nor sorrow,
And they will live again.

In 1924, Bridges was more fortunate at Woodmont, where in an ambitious project went to completion without a problem. The club engineered two man-made lakes from a natural spring that flowed into a pristine valley in the preserve. The Potomac River had become so polluted that the fish populations were either destroyed or inedible. According to Bridges, the lakes "fit so naturally into the lay of the land that they seemed to have been glistening forever in that wooded and hill-shaded solitude."

A fifty-foot high dam was constructed at the end of a valley in the preserve. The natural stream flooded an upper lake, called Lake Nesbit, and then flowed over a spillway to a lake named Lanahan. Both bodies of water were named after prominent club members. The upper lake was stocked with trout, the lower lake with bass. Camp Cleveland, consisting of a log cabin, sat between the lakes. There, hunters were fed garlic venison, spiced apples and potatoes for lunch.

Bridges invited Lee LeCompte, the state game warden, to lunch at Woodmont in the fall of 1927. While there on game inspections he visited "an artificial lake, which is being built on said Club's property for the purpose of attracting wild fowl. This lake covers an area of about twenty-five acres. The Club established a lake about the same some three years ago on which they have prohibited the Club members to hunt or pursue wild fowl. The establishment of this new lake will be used as a hunting ground for the members of the Club and the old lake will be reserved as a resting ground." The lakes reflected Henry's Bridges' commitment to fishing. If the Potomac was no longer a refuge for black bass, which it had always been, then he would create a haven for the fish at Woodmont.

Bridges fishing the Potomac River, undated.

In 1927, Bridges began construction on the third and final clubhouse, a project which took three years to complete. All the construction materials came from the property. The final clubhouse cost the forty members $80,000 to build. Once finished, it offered comfortable sleeping accommodations for as many as fifty-five men. Adorning the walls was artwork depicting wildlife and hunting scenes; this art included two engravings and a sketch by James Audubon. A pipe owned by Sitting Bull and a dinner bell used by George Washington's slaves were among the clubhouse artifacts.

When hunters entered the 18,000 square foot clubhouse after a long day of hunting, they literally confronted a menagerie of stuffed animals and pelts mounted on the walls, standing alongside the furniture or lying on the floor. It was reportedly the finest collection of mounts in the world. An enormous turkey and a variety of vermin occupied two glass cases in the hallway. A bison head, an elk head and a cape water buffalo were each mounted above the three downstairs fireplaces. Throughout the building were hundreds of wild cats, deer, birds, and other animals, large and small, totaling some 600 pieces.

The clubhouse grand-opening dinner took place in the spring of 1931. A conservation magazine of the time reported:

John B. Ferguson and W. H. Green, of the Hagerstown engineering firm of John B. Ferguson & Co., builders of the Clubhouse [were honored]. Henry P. Bridges, secretary and treasurer of the Club, was host and toastmaster. The building was erected under Mr. Bridges' personal direction. The dinner came as an appreciation of what is regarded as an architectural triumph. The structure was completed in record time, being reared of stone taken from the mountain within a radius of half a mile of the Club with the interior done in rough-hewn timber, cut and sawed in the immediate vicinity.

List of Guests:

Among those present were: Vernon E. Johnson, chairman of the State Game and Fish Commission of West Virginia; J. Hammond Siler and Charles B. Ismond, Berkeley Springs, W. VA; Dr. J. M. Drumm, Mercersburg Academy; Robert L. Troxell and Frank Lee Carl, Cumberland; State Game Warden E. Lee LeCompte, State Conservation Commissioner Swepson Earle and Harold S. Kolmer, secretary of the State Game Department, Baltimore; Reuben Musey, mayor; Elmer B. Carl, president of the Hagerstown Chapter, Izaak Walton League, Frank L. Bentz, C. F. Strole, R. Q. Cook, H. R. Reisner, Charles Cromer, W. S. Green, John Fiery, E. A. Lakin, A. H. Onderdonk, J. B. Ferguson, Dr. E. A. Wareham, Samuel E. Phillips, William T. Hamilton, Dr. P. N. Fleming, Col. John Carmichael, F. Wilbur Bridges, Charles E. Hilliard, president of the Nicodemus Bank; Dr. Peregrine Wroth, J. Garvin Hager, Abel Miller, Kenneth

Bonner, Guy Gantz, Hagerstown; County Commissioners John B. Beard, Williamsport; Frank R. Beard, Hancock, and Dallas L. Ward, Albert Cordeman and W. H. Cunningham, Hagerstown; Maxwell Richards, president of the Hancock Bank, Dr. P. Elwood Stigers, John Page Caspar, Dr. Homer E. Tabler, Lee McCullough, deputy game warden, Earl Andrews, Harry Exline, Walter M. Widmeyer, R. Samuel Dillon, John A. Trostle, Jr., Harry McKinley, Hancock; Robert Willis Bridges, Barnard, MO, and Robert Bridges, Jr., Coraopolis, PA; Albert Crampton, deputy game warden, Sharpsburg.

The Woodmont Rod and Gun Club in 1930. The building combined a sense of nature together with modern amenities for members and guests.

On March 13, 1928, Bridges paid $42,500 for a home located on six acres in Johnson City Tennessee. The home had been commissioned by Roswell H. Spears on July 31, 1920. Speers, a wholesale lumber dealer, had D.R. Beeson, a local architect build the "Virginia Colonial Home" which he then occupied in 1921. It was first named Sunset Hill and later was called Shelbridge, a combination of Henry's and his wife's names. The property was a beautiful homestead complete with vegetable gardens, rose gardens, lily pools designed by LeLand Cardwell and a swimming pool and tennis court. Henry and Shelby loved to entertain their local friends and did so frequently in grand fashion at Shelbridge.

Shelbridge. It was more than a little bit Southern.

Shelbridge marked the beginning of a new chapter in the Bridges' life. On July 22, 1927, their first son, Henry Percival Bridges Jr., was born. The parents needed a suitable home to raise their son. Although Shelbridge more than provided that, it could not protect young Henry from a childhood disease like diphtheria. John Siler wrote the elder Bridges on May 15, 1928, from Berkeley Springs:

> *I am just in receipt of your telegram advising me of the condition of your dear boy, and I appreciate your thought of me during such a strenuous ordeal as you are going through. I heard on Saturday that you had called to Johnson City by the illness of your boy, and have been calling the office to enquire if they had any news concerning his condition.*
>
> *Mrs. Siler and I are both very glad to learn that the chances are very good for the recovery of the boy, and we hope soon to hear that he is out of danger. I know this is a trying ordeal to your wife, and you both have our sympathy.*

Luckily, a specialist brought in from Baltimore was able to save the infant's life. Young Henry would grow up to learn that he was descended on his mother's side from Captain James Gaines, who fought in the Revolutionary War. In fact, Shelby belonged to the Daughters of the American Revolution and even dedicated a Revolutionary War monument at King's Mountain, North Carolina. Her namesake--Evan Shelby, Jr. was one of many heroes at the Battle of King's Mountain during the Revolutionary War. Young Henry would be raised in a family that was not lacking in tradition.

Shelby and Henry, Jr. at Shelbridge, ca. 1929.

Shelby loved this "*Southern Home,*" as her husband referred to it, in Johnson City. The one great disappointing aspect of her new home was that she could not enjoy it full-time with her husband, who was busy attending to business and conservation in Berkeley Springs. Bridges made the trip home about every six weeks.

In 1927, Pennsylvania Glass Sand Company was incorporated in Pennsylvania under the leadership of Henry Bridges as Vice President and William Woods as President and General Manager working out of Lewistown. Bridges attended board meetings in Philadelphia with the other three major shareholders--A.J. Fink, Addison Mullikin and William Woods. Much confusion arose out of the consolidation due to sorting out which companies owned which land deeds. The unenviable task of sorting everything out fell to attorney J. Hammond Siler, who somehow managed to cut through the confusion.

On March 24, 1927, the *Morgan Messenger* reported:

> *While the matter of consolidating the several sand plants in this vicinity has been under advisement for some weeks and it is apparently certain that a combination will be formed, yet at this time, The Messenger is informed, it has not yet been consummated. This action has been practically forced upon our local operators by the low price of sand mined in Illinois that can be produced much cheaper than can be done here. Our workmen and businessmen are naturally uneasy because of the likelihood of some of the mines here being closed which means a number of men thrown out of employment. In face of this possibility it behooves our people to [avail] themselves*

through the Chamber of Commerce and see if some other industries cannot be secured for Berkeley Springs.

In the midst of the consolidation Bridges continued his conservation efforts. His personal log book listed the following people and organizations buying Woodmont wild turkeys in 1928 at the cost of $15 for a Tom and $12 for a Hen, "Mrs. M. Mayuard- Monclair, N.J.- 1 Tom, H.C. Lewis, Roslyn, N.Y.- 2 Hens, F.L. Jenckes, Pawtucket, R.I.—1 Gobbler, 2 Hens, Paul C. Edmunds, South Boston, VA- 1 Hen, 1 Gobbler, W. F. Buckley, Sharron Station, N.Y.- 4 Gobblers, 6 Hens, B.K. Leach, St. Louis, Missouri- 10 Hens, 2 Gobblers." Such was the detail work of conservation. In addition Henry shipped turkeys to Washington, D.C.; Mauhasset, and South Hampton on Long Island; Cincinnati; Brunswick Maine; Portsmouth Ohio; Springfield Illinois; Lincoln Nebraska; York Pennsylvania; Portland Maine; Oakland Maryland; Trenton New Jersey; Stanford Kentucky; Slonington Connecticut; Detroit Bayside in Queen County, New York; Richmond Virginia; Boston; and Berlin Maryland. For the year, Bridges shipped out 309 wild turkeys to game farms and individuals. The next year, Henry shipped nine deer and 671 turkeys to buyers in eighteen states. One of the major recipients was the state of Pennsylvania, which took 160 birds.

But no matter how busy conservation kept him, Henry still had to attend to matters of business. By June 1928 Pennsylvania Glass Sand was building a large new mill 80 by 240 feet, together with a large crusher house at the lower plant, the Noel mill. At the same time, West Virginia was working to pass a five percent tax on sand coming from the new consolidated works. This demanded Henry's attention, as did the rumored startup of yet another competitor. Although he did the work required of him, Henry found his interest more drawn to matters of family and conservation.

The four major Pennsylvania Glass Sand investors Henry P. Bridges, A. J. Fink, Addison Mullikin and William Woods-absent, in Atlantic City, New Jersey, ca. 1930. Bridges would soon play a far less active role in the company.

Bridges found more satisfaction in garnering publicity for Woodmont than taking sand out of his quarries. No doubt, he enjoyed the Winter 1929 issue of *Maryland Conservationist* with its article, *"The Woodmont Rod And Gun Club - - A Famous Shooting Preserve."*

> *Mr. William Elkins, one of the famous guides of the Club, had died three years ago, and he was connected with the Club since a year after its organization. The chair in the reception room of the Club-house, known as the President's chair, was made by Mr. Elkins and presented to the Club. On the arm of this chair [are silver plates] engraved with the names of all the Presidents who occupied it and the dates.*

> *Harvey Van Goshen became a guide at the Club twenty-three years ago, and he and the late William Elkins were selected by Admiral Carey Grayson to entertain President Wilson and Mrs. Wilson at the White House, with violin and accordion, during the administration of the late President. Mr. Van Goshen at present acts as entertainer for the Club members and their guests and possesses a violin, which bears the inscription, "1700" and is said to have been made by the famous Stradivarius. He was offered $5,000 for the instrument a short time ago and declined the offer.*

Harvey Van Goshen and William Elkins, Woodmont musicians and White House performers.

Fifteen years ago, Bridges purchased and liberated on the Woodmont property thirteen Michigan white-tailed deer. From this small nucleus there is at present a herd of 300 deer. There is an open season for the hunting of bucks (only) at Woodmont from December 1 to 15, and during the hunting season of 1927 the following kills were made,

December 3 – Loyal Crawford of Pittsburgh, killed an 8-prong buck, weighing 250 pounds.

December 8 – B.D. Phillips, Butler, Pa., killed an 8-prong buck, weighing 214 pounds.

December 11 – H. P. Bridges killed an 8-prong buck, weighing 218 pounds.

December 12, Frank Henderson of Johnson County, Tenn., killed an 8 prong buck, weighing 219 pounds.

December 14 – A. B. Knight of Fairmont, W. Va., killed an 18-prong buck, weighing 315 pounds.

In addition to these five deer killed during the hunting season of 1927, 315 wild turkeys, 3 Chinese pheasants, 40 bobwhite quail,

88 cottontail rabbits and 42 squirrels were shot by the members and their guests on the Club property. Bridges, through the employment of expert trappers, woodsmen, etc., carries on a very aggressive campaign against vermin, the following vermin were destroyed in this year: 1 catamount, 1 mink, 30 ground hogs, 21 opossums, 27 pole cats, 9 weasels, 9 foxes, 19 hawks, 10 cats and 28 horned owls.

Hunting at Woodmont was as a rule excellent each season, as the area is well stocked, vermin controlled, and numerous species of game propagated in captivity on the property. Bridges unquestionably knows more about the propagation of wild turkey than any man in the country, and has secured better results. During the season of 1928 he raised at the game farm, 2,000 wild turkeys, which he liberated and which soon become wild in this mountainous region.

On November 19, of last year, there were twenty sportsmen hunting on the Club property, including the following: B. K. Leach, Kirkwood, Mo.; F. G. McIntosh, Franklin, Pa.; F. S. Love, Pittsburgh; W. S. Findlay Jr., Pittsburgh; Dr. W. W. Lermann, Pittsburgh; J. M. Succoup, Pittsburgh; W. W. Keefer, Pittsburgh; Judge Reid Kennedy, Pittsburgh; H. L. Henitzlman, Fairmount, W. Va.; A. B. Knight, Fairmount; L. B. Darby, Fairmount; T. W. Phillips and D. B. Phillips, Judge A. E. Raiber, George Howard, Ross McCafferty, George C. Stewart and F. R. Hildebrand, all of Butler, Pa., and Talbott Denmead and E. Lee LeCompte of Baltimore, Md.

Each hunter, with the exception of one, bagged two wild turkeys, which is not only the bag limit according to the State law but also the rule of the Club. The State law and the Club regulations provide that no person shall kill more than two wild turkeys per day nor more than four during the entire season.

Bridges has attempted to increase the variety of game by the importation of the Maine snow-shoe hare, English hare, sage grouse, Hungarian partridge, jack rabbit and English ring-neck pheasant, but very little success has attended these efforts. He is to be congratulated for maintaining the present high standard of the club. The members, who are mostly millionaires, are ready and willing to furnish funds at all times to maintain this area, which is the natural habitat of the wild turkey, and which we hope will long furnish the members of the Club and their guests good hunting for this species *of game bird. It is estimated that the aggregate wealth of the sixty members of the Club is at least $800,000,000. The dues and initiation fee are $1,360.00 annually, and in becoming a member of the Club, one is also a stockholder in the property.*

The demands of business again asserted themselves in the early 1930s, when Bridges discovered that the sale of stock in his consolidated sand company was being suppressed by hostile banking interests. His enemies were attempting to drive the fledgling company out of business. Henry and company executives were forced to find ways to keep the stock viable. Pennsylvania Glass Sand survived the Great Depression because its assets were not leveraged. It was the banks that fell victim to bad business practices.

Sand mine workers pictured on September 25, 1931 are as follows: T. McKinley Smith, Tom Shade, Grover Hiles, 'Potie' Levi Henry, Jessie Farris, Fonza Breig, Pete Divelbliss, Bill Weber, Velvet Easton, Sherman Pennert, Web Parlett, Roscoe Spring, Smith Spring, Joe Sharon, Lawrence Youngblood, Brook Peck, Roy Smith, Scott Holliday, Hobert Farris, George Clingerman, Harry Spriggs, Pete Betts and Bill Divelbliss standing in Sand Mine #6. (Fred T. Newbraugh Collection)

CONSERVATION, RELIGION AND *A WOODLAND IDYLL*

Bridges was a profoundly spiritual man. While living at Woodmont, he attended the Hancock Presbyterian Church. In Tennessee he attended the First Presbyterian Church of Johnson City. But matters of faith were not confined to Sunday, as shown in the poem *"Life's Farewell"* that Henry wrote in his diary:

> *The average family is like unto a rose bush; each brother and sister represented by a bloom that through the mercy and kindness of a God of the Universe, has matured from the bloom of infancy to the bud of youth: then unfolded as the rose in its perfection to manhood and womanhood, and each one has hung on the green bush of existence like the radiant flowers of nature and enjoyed the warm and gentle kiss of many summers, but like the superb flowers of nature, each rose must wither and die and return again to the Mother Earth and become as the dust of the field, but unlike the rose of the plant creation, the rose of beauty and color and fragrance, the flower of humanity has a soul, a something that is transplanted in the realms of eternity that lives again and flourishes in another world not made and embellished with human hands, but prepared in all its grandeur by one who loves and gathers His children together, like a good shepherd, gathers each lamb to the fold as the sun sinks below the horizon and the shades of night endanger and compass his flock. Were it not for the sweet hope and consolation, the heart of man would grow faint with despair, as each loved one would pass the verge of human existence and step over the chasm that exists between time and eternity. It is contrary to nature of humanity to say farewell, often the saddest word that is ever spoken.*

> *It is best to lend the heart and bow the head in humble submission for the mortal cannot assume the role of immortality. Man must die to live again. The transformation is but the natural sequence of life. The mere fact of birth ensures death of the physical and a continued life of the soul through the ages of eternity.*

> *The infirmities of this life often cause the heart of man to long and pine for something better, for a haven of rest and purity. It is but natural for the human part of man's nature to fear and shrink at the thought of the dissolution of the soul from the body, yet the hope of the immortal part of man is a sweet comfort and solace that bears*

as if supported by a strong arm all through the deepest sorrows and afflictions of this life.

The infirmities of the body will often exempt a man from service in the wars of humanity, but all who are born of woman are at once soldiers in the battle of life and must fight with valor of bravery if they expect to join the legend of the great army who have passed along the same road. Life is an empty dream and but a bubble of existence unless one has the faith and sweet hope that proves a lotion to sooth the pangs and pain of existence.

We cannot lay our weary head on down pillows of sweet scented roses in this life because of the sin in the world that is born with us at the dawn of life. The babe of humanity is a weakling and experiences the pangs and pains of life from the time of its first gasp for breath, and its initial heartthrob. It comes into the world in all its innocence from its mother's womb, condemned and sentenced by a just God: though the hour of death is withheld through compassion and mercy, yet the climax of life which is death is inevitable. Man who is born of woman lives but to die.

The tears that flow at the passing of man are but natural and availeth nothing. Sorrow is only calmed and soothed by a clinging hope for the future that some day, somewhere, there will be a family reunion. The suddenness of death is compatible with the love of man: the object of his love must live again. We mourn but to rejoice; we say farewell for a time only and give to the grave our loved one, buoyed by the hope of meeting them again in a haven of rest or on the shores of eternal peace.

We exist in the present but many of us actually live in the future: in other words, if our hope and mind-view of the future were cut off and the sun of our existence would fail to shine, we would pine and die.

The earth is but a hotbed for Heaven. The flowers that are started here will be transplanted in the realms of perfection to breathe the air of purity all down through the ages. While it is hard to say, it is better to murmur words of resignation and say are well to our loved one as each one answers the summons of the messenger of death, and with submissive reverence, bend over their lifeless forms and say, "Eyes, take your last look; lips, take your last kiss; arms, take your last embrace, feelings as we step aside that there is a sweet hope and solace even in death and an earthly farewell.

Henry kept the poem in his diary. But his first book, *A Woodland Idyll* (1922), was intended for a wider audience. In it, Bridges wrote about his love for Ella Vaughn Patterson (the woman he dated before Shelby), Woodmont and Creation. "Love of nature is the measure of the heart's kinship with God: for there is no breast that loves nature that does not sometimes rise to God." Henry believed that caring for the creatures in God's creation was one and the same as loving God. As for Woodmont, Henry believed the "country atmosphere at Woodmont is man's greatest blessing; we get more good out of a pint of God's fresh air than we would from fifty gallons of the finest patent medicine, or any other kind of medicine that ever was poured in a bottle."

During the late nineteenth century wilderness regions like western Maryland attracted elite urbanites looking for recreation and health. While more glamorous resort hotels provided relaxation and family entertainment, the sporting clubs offered a chance to match one's hunting skills against an untamed nature "without molestation by the general public," as one participant put it. In the early years of the wilderness craze, from 1870 to 1900, the well-to-do were generally the only group having the time and finances to afford hunting clubs.

Woodmont provided an opportunity for men of means to act out wilderness fantasies they had read about, then return with relative ease to their lives in the city. A site plan of the property shows roads, game fields, and hunting grounds thoughtfully arranged to create and sustain a feeling of vastness and solitude. Even when a hundred members and guests were present at the club, there was little sense of Baltimore-like crowding. Forty game fields, ranging in size from one to six acres, provided ready targets for hunters.

And there was no lack of game. Bridges crossbred whitetail deer with the breed purchased from Michigan and Wisconsin to produce the largest bucks in the vicinity; the animals ranged from two to three hundred pounds. Bridges also raised pheasants, mallard ducks, and quail. His most active breeding program, of course, was with the wild turkey. He reintroduced a turkey without any strain of domesticated bloodlines. He trapped adult birds, collected eggs from local nests, and imported other eggs in order to infuse wild genes into the flock. His hobby was expensive, and he paid more than a hundred dollars apiece for some birds while selling thousands across the country.

In the fenced preserve, guides flushed out deer and game birds toward the hunters. During the turkey drives, as many as one hundred birds would shoot up into the air. The birds were taken from the breeding grounds and set free into the area of the shoot. Hunters knelt at the edge of the woods on the side of the field as the guides moved the birds toward them. Even now, the genetic makeup of Bridges' wild turkey can be found across the country.

The Woodmont wild turkey, whose preservation Henry Bridges did so much to ensure.

CHAPTER 5

NURTURING CONSERVATION AT WOODMONT, 1931-1940:
The Personal and Professional Growth of One Man

OUTDOORSMEN'S PHILOSOPHY

"Fishermen, hunters, woodchoppers, and others, spending their lives in the fields and woods, in a peculiar sense a part of Nature themselves, are often in a more favorable mood for observing her, in the intervals of their pursuits, than philosophers or poets even, who approach her with expectation. She is not afraid to exhibit herself to them."

So wrote Henry David Thoreau (born 1817) during his celebrated stay at Walden Pond.

John Muir (born 1821) also was profoundly influenced by nature, "Oh, these forest gardens of our Father! What perfection, what divinity, in their architecture! What simplicity and mysterious complexity of detail! Who shall read the teaching of these sylvan pages, the glad brotherhood of rills that sing in the valleys, and all the happy creatures that dwell in them under the tender keeping of a Father's care?" A Presbyterian-rooted faith led the Scots-born Muir to credit the God of Creation for the beauty he experienced in nature. The mountains held a special allure for Muir, and he dedicated much of his adult life letting the mountains teach him what they could about the tranquility, power and beauty.

Aldo Leopold (born 1887) encountered nature a good deal after Thoreau and Muir. According to scholars Curt Meine and Richard Knight, Leopold believed that "for humans hunting is 'almost a physiological characteristic' and a wellspring for our sense of affiliation with the natural world. At one point he concludes, 'the man who does not like to see, hunt, photograph, or otherwise outwit birds or animals is hardly normal. He is supercivilized, and I for one do not know how to deal with him.'" For Leopold, "Physical combat between men and beasts was, in like manner, an economic fact, now preserved as hunting and fishing for sport. Public wilderness areas are, first of all, a means of perpetuating, in sport form, the more virile and primitive skills in pioneering travel and subsistence."

Thoreau framed the same notion this way:

Our village life would stagnate if it were not for the unexplored forests and meadows which surround it. We need the tonic of wild-

ness, to wade sometimes in marshes where the bittern and the mead-ow-hen lurk, and hear the booming of the snipe; to smell the whis-pering sedge where only some wilder and more solitary fowl builds her nest, and the mink crawls with its belly close to the ground. At the same time that we are earnest to explore and learn all things, we require that all things be mysterious and unexplorable, that land and sea be infinitely wild, unsurveyed and unfathomed by us become unfathomable. We can never have enough of Nature.

Archibald Rutledge was a close friend of Henry Bridges and was some-thing of a Southern-born Thoreau:

I know not a pleasanter thing than thus to walk at dawn through sweet chill woods, with nature's nameless fragrances awaft in the mountain air. There is a "country where men are men," but it isn't found in any particular place. Rather it is on the bosom of Nature, for there a man is essentially at home. There he was cradled, and there he shall sleep at last. Most people who are sick are heartsick. They ought to go back to the woods and the fields; there they'll find man's ancient home. And just as a man can lay aside his business cares when he gets home, so life's cares can be laid away as we ap-proach Nature's old hearthstone.

These views would have appealed to Henry for obvious reasons, along with Leopold's contention, "Poets sing and hunters scale the mountains pri-marily for one and the same reason--the thrill to beauty." It was Bridges love of nature, the companionship he experienced while hunting with friends and the beauty of the whole outdoor life that led him to mix the visions of Tho-reau, Muir and Leopold at Woodmont.

WOODMONT: A HUNTER'S PARADISE

If it had not been for Henry's conservation efforts, the wild turkey of North America might have been hunted to extinction. Over the course of sixty years, Bridges raised turkeys by the thousand for purposes of repopu-lating and sport. In 1934 Aldo Leopold wrote, "To be a practitioner of con-servation on a piece of land takes more brains" than could be found "in a college or a conservation bureau." Henry Bridges the lawyer and business-man felt the need to prove himself in all the ways that Leopold thought important.

Bridges was not alone in his love of Woodmont and the outdoor life. He had inspired a group of men who supported his work. Their names appeared in national newspapers on a regular basis because of their obvious power and wealth. The active governors of the club in 1931 were, "Harrison Nesbit, president of the Bank of Pittsburgh and president of the Woodmont Club; Nelson E. Perin, Washington, DC; Eugene DuPont, Wilmington Delaware; Dr. Thomas S. Cullen, Baltimore; Stuart Oliver, Baltimore; Homes D. Baker, Fredrick Maryland; Dr. W.W. Lermann, Pittsburgh; E. Bartlett Hayward, Baltimore; Emil Winters, Pittsburgh; and Henry P. Bridges, secretary/treasurer of the Club." There wasn't a turkey in the bunch.

On July 22, 1931, the family celebrated Henry, Jr.'s fourth birthday at Shelbridge. Many of the influential members of Woodmont Club were also close family friends with the Bridges of Johnson City. Henry P. Bridges, Addison Mulligan (Addison was Henry, Jr.'s Godfather), A.J. Fink and Harrison Nesbit traveled to Shelbridge for the birthday occasion. There was a big party on the Shelbridge lawn with all Henry, Jr.'s young friends. The showstopper was when a house on a truck came up the driveway. The truck proceeded to the lower yard and unloaded the playhouse that became a Shelbridge trademark. The day after the party the caravan of cars drove to the edge of the Blowing Rock in North Carolina. Stories were told about hats being thrown over the hanging bridge and lifted by the wind the hats were blown back. A. J. Fink, owner of The Southern Hotel in Baltimore City, loved to sing, and he continued even though Henry repeatedly said, "Mr. Fink, please don't sing." It was on that day that A. J. Fink coined the name Shelbridge for the Bridges' home in Johnson City.

Henry, Jr.'s fourth birthday party on the lawn at Shelbridge.
Many club members were also close friends of the Bridges.

Back at the Woodmont Club, in November, Mr. Edward Jenkins, sixteen year member of Woodmont, from Warrenton, Virginia, was elected president of the Club. Previous presidents of the Club from its inception included: Rear-Admiral Robley D. Evans, founder of the Club, Judge Jeremiah M. Wilson, Washington, D.C., Dr. Walter S. Harban, Washington, DC, Nelson Perin, Baltimore City and Harrison Nesbit, Pittsburgh. Mr. Harrison Nesbit and his daughter had been killed in a car accident this same year. Consequently, after the members lamented the death of Harrison Nesbit, they elected Edward Jenkins the Club's sixth president.

In the fall of 1931, Peter Chambliss of *The Baltimore Sun* wrote an article, *"Stalking the Wild Turkey at Woodmont, A Famous Old Hunting Preserve Yields a Day of Sport."* Chambliss offered a detailed account of Henry's work and his world:

> *Far back in fastness of Washington County, on a lofty wooded plateau blocked in by the towering slopes of Sideling Hill Mountain to the west and Tonoloway ridge to the east, with the Potomac winding along the south, is located one of the oldest and certainly one of the most unusual of hunting and fishing preserves.*

> *...Today it is as rich in tradition as its membership of sixty is in dollars – and that membership is said to be worth a matter of $800,000,000....Statesmen, ranking officers of the army and navy, diplomats and financiers have inscribed their names as members or guests in the club's annals and a glance at the register reveals the signatures of many leaders in their various fields of endeavor over a period of a half century. Today Woodmont stands not alone as a place of recreation for its membership and their friends but a veritable monument in the conservation of America's greatest gamebird, the wild turkey.*

> *Under the guidance of Henry P. Bridges, secretary of the club, known throughout the United States as an authority on the propagation of the wild turkey, and the sanction of President Harrison Nesbitt, Pittsburgh, and the board of governors, Woodmont has earned a reputation among hunters and conservationists. From its brood stock, a flock that numbers about 175 hens and 25 gobblers, whose strain is untainted by the barnyard fowl, thousands of thoroughbred wild turkeys have been distributed to conservation departments in Maryland, Virginia, Tennessee, Florida, Pennsylvania, West Virginia, and every other state that is making an effort to bring back what some have held should be our national bird.*

> *Brood stock from Woodmont has been shipped, too, to England and Japan. This brood produced 3,000 eggs last year, from which*

*approximately 1,400 turkeys were dispensed....But it is of the wild-
ness of the wild turkeys that range the hills of Woodmont that we
would sing. Some of the uninitiated who have not had the privilege
of tramping the hills of Woodmont in search of the fleet-footed, fleet-
winged birds have cast aspersions on the wildness of Woodmont wild
turkeys. They have been wont to raise their eyebrows, turn up their
noses and cast glances of amusement at the efforts of Woodmont's
Nimrod in bagging their quota of the noble game.*

*"Huh! Goin to Woodmont to hunt wild turkeys, eh?" one re-
marked. "That'll be easy. They tell me those wild turkeys are so
tame that anybody could kill 'em with a stick. You don't need a
gun!" And so it was that we started on our trip to Woodmont with
misgivings mingled with great expectations. Three miles outside of
Hancock we turned from the State highway into the road carrying us
the remaining six miles to Woodmont and shortly afterward began
mounting until we entered the preserves through a gate in the nine-
foot wire-mesh fence that entirely encompasses the 5,000 acres of
the Woodmont area (5,000 acres included some Pennsylvania Glass
Sand Company land adjacent to Woodmont which was not fenced-
the fenced area was only the preserve).*

*That fence is sunk eighteen inches in the ground. Its purposes
are to keep the club's deer herd from wandering, to warn poachers
away and to prevent such game destroyers as foxes, bob-cats, stray
house cats, dogs, etc., from entering the enclosure and preying on
the game. The wild turkeys and pheasants of Woodmont can, and
frequently do, fly at will from the preserves, but the promise of a
square meal in any one of the 30 fields of the club that have been
sown with their favorite feeds and left unharvested is enough to coax
them back.*

*Entering the enclosure one arrives finally on a roadway that, atop
a tablelike hill, parallels Sideling Hill mountain on the right and
Tonoloway ridge on the left, separated by about four or five miles of
virgin forest covering hill and valley. On the left away over on a hill
was pointed out the first clubhouse of Woodmont – a log cabin, which
has been standing more than 100 years, and is now occupied by the
chief gamekeeper (reference to original clubhouse). A bit farther on
we passed the recent and more pretentious home of Woodmont, the
rooms of which, inhabited by the memories of the great and near-
great who have been the club's guests, are now being converted into*

a great hatchery for pheasants, quail, and ruffed grouse to stock the covers of the preserve. A little later and the green-tile roof of the new Woodmont Club, just finished in time for the opening of the hunting season, hove into view. ...

Old Clubhouse on the hill transformed into a game farm.

More than a score from Baltimore, Pittsburgh, and Fairmont gathered that night at a table for a dinner of roast wild turkey, pursued by entertainment of a sort that could be produced only by Harvey Van Goshen, for years as much of a fixture at Woodmont as are the very rocks of the hills. Harvey is officially known as the "Walking Directory" for his store of knowledge on all subjects; "General Utility Man" for his uses in any phase of the club life, and as 'Entertainer Extraordinary' for his talents in recitation and the tunes he can wrest from a violin, his most prized possession. His fiddling fame has spread far from Woodmont, for he has the winning of two old-time fiddling contests to this credit; has broadcast over the radio and was summoned to play at the White House before President Wilson. On his return from that Washington trip the crack Capitol Limited, which acknowledges few stops in its hurried flight, halted at Woodmont long enough to allow the famous Harvey to alight. It was the first and last time that the flyer's amazed engineer ever even slowed up at the tiny mountain station.

And then to be in preparation for the hunt on the morrow. Sleeping quarters at Woodmont are on the second floor of the clubhouse, with accommodations for twosome or more of guests. It fell to the lot of the two Presbyterian ministers and a brother cleric of the Catholic Church and our own party to share a large room containing six beds.

The clergy elected to occupy the three beds lining one side of the big room and we of the laity chose the other side, admitting a suggestion that thus were divided 'the sheep and the goats' but politely declining to identify which was which. We saw instantly that one of the clerics was a fundamentalist, for he provided our wondering eyes with their first glimpse of an old-fashioned nightshirt, the kind grandpa used to wear. Another perhaps was even prefundamentalist, for he wooed slumber au naturel. Pondering on these evidences of schism in the faith we fell asleep. And the next thing we knew it was morning and high time to be up and at the chase. Breakfast was of venison, killed by special permit in Woodmont forests; sausage of the kind you hear about but seldom meet, and buckwheat cakes of a size and lightness that only a hunting lodge can turn out. It was a feast to linger over, but the turkeys were calling.

Four buckboards, drawn by sturdy horses, were waiting to carry the score plus two of eager Nimrods to the hunting fields. There are 30 of these fields, each named for some prominent member of the club and arranged on seven well-defined routes, separated one from the other by distances of a half mile or more of woodland. The fields, sown in corn, wheat, barley, millet, Kaffir corn, and other grains, which have been left standing, are the magnets that hold the wild turkeys, pheasants, quail, and other game close to Woodmont. Not only do they return, even should they wander to far distant ranges, but those who flee the fold undoubtedly do bring others of their kind back with them. What is more enticing to a hungry bird than the promise of a square meal and the knowledge that the table is always set?

Other than this arrangement of grain fields and the blessed buckboards to transport one from the hunting lodge to the fields, the physical task of hunting at Woodmont differs little from that on public lands on the other side of Sideling Hill over which we tramped last year in earnest but futile chase for wild turkeys. Near the first of the game fields the party alights and, accompanied by a guide, scatters and hunts the field, as one would any other field. Then on to the next, taking briars, underbrush, hills, and valleys as they come.

Of course, there is a better chance of getting game at Woodmont, for there is more game in the preserve to give the opportunity. Yet over a range of 5,000 acres, much of which is deeply wooded, hundreds of wild turkeys and pheasants may scurry out of the way. For instance, we tramped throughout the day, and came up with but one flock of wild turkeys, and saw but one pheasant. Though there were plenty of signs of deer, of which there are said to be over 600 on the reservation, we saw not a single one. In other words, even though there is game a plenty at Woodmont, it has to be hunted and hunted hard. I haven't yet seen a wild turkey or a pheasant that appears to have a longing to look inquiringly into the muzzle of a 12-gauge. Another thing that helps conserve the game is that those who shoot with pump-guns and automatics are by club regulation allowed to carry only two shells in the chambers. That puts this type of gun on equal footing with the double-barrel firearms which predominate.

When one hears the explanation of Secretary Bridges one ceases to wonder at the plentifulness of game on the preserve. "When I re-organized the Woodmont Club in 1908," said Mr. Bridges, "we had only two pairs of natural wild turkeys. The first year those four birds raised 23 young ones. We did not allow any of them to be shot the first two years and by the third year we had over 300 turkeys on the place and began to shoot some of them. Gradually increasing year by year, we got up to 2,000 turkeys ranging on the reservation."

"And the same with deer. When we started we had about 10 deer on the place and about 11 years ago we put up the 14 miles of nine-foot special wire fence that surrounds the Woodmont Club and added 13 whitetail Michigan deer's to the native stock in the woods. The deer have increased rapidly, and at the rate they are multiplying I am sure that within five years we will have approximately 4,000."

"The club is now considering capturing 30 or 40 deer after January 1, which it plans to liberate on the adjoining State refuge. If the gunners in Washington County will take an interest in protecting the deer and wild turkeys this spring, these deer will be given as a present from the Woodmont Club. We also find that quail have increased, and we have prohibited the shooting of ruffed grouse on the preserve for the past 10 years and have been stocking them for the past four years. The club policy has been that if any class of game is not holding its own we at once stop shooting that particular species."

In our party that morning were seven, including the three parsons. A hundred yards or so from our first field we descended from the buckboard and with hopes high approached cautiously through the woodland. A glimpse at nearby territory revealed not a single feather, but the standing grain was high and we scattered to give it a thorough once-over in hopes of quail or pheasant. Two if the party promptly lost themselves from sight and that was the last seen of them for several hours, so then we were five. Of pheasants and quail there proved to be none in the field and we started through the woodland, but the driver of our buckboard, who had been doing a bit of scouting on his own account, came hurrying up with the news that turkeys were feeding on the next hill, and we hot-footed it – the parsons three, and the two laymen.

Two of the agile parsons decided a flank movement might prove effective and circled from a different angle. The rest of us were all for direct tactics and a saving of breath, and started in a beeline for where the turkeys had last been seen. Now, a wild turkey in addition to having wings with which to aid him has exceedingly long and powerful legs and he can use 'em. Those turkeys had not stayed put, but a quarter of an hour's scouting brought us our first glimpse, one which almost gave me turkey-fright, for they seemed to be as big as a horse and they showed no signs whatsoever of acting as our scoffing friends predicted Woodmont turkeys would behave.

The flock was probably a little more than a 100 yards off when we caught first sight, which didn't mean shooting range. As we saw them they saw us and off they went along a double-quick turkey trail through the underbrush. As my clerical comrade's congregation knows, he's a fast worker. When there's a job to be done he doesn't linger at it. When it comes to going through underbrush after turkeys he's as good as a beagle hound and his vocation of chasing the Unholy One out of his pastorate had put him in good trim for that turkey chase.

The leaves were dry, the going was hard and had it not been that two big old turkey gobblers got to fighting, probably over the affections of some demure henturk, this story might have been different. The 'battle' occurred during one of their rest periods when they were evidently waiting to see if they hadn't lost those pestiferous hunters back on the last ridge. So interested did the birds become in the fight that they lost sight of us. My comrade says the two gobblers were locked hard and fast and he could have killed both, but waited for me to come up. By that time the flock had discovered us. Even the battlers lost interest in their private feud and off they made with the others. It was a case of now or never, and at a distance of about 65 yards we fired. The underbrush was thick, but there was one slightly cleared place and three turkeys fell before they took wing. As they rose my parson fired again and another dropped, recovered and sailed to the top of a big tree. Another shot brought him down and our turkey hunting was over, for the limit at Woodmont is two a day or four to the season.

The birds proved to be three medium-sized hens and one young gobbler. We shouldered them and started for Camp Cleveland, a big log hut deep in the woods about a mile away, where all the hunters were to assemble for lunch. There we learned that the two other parsons had not been so fortunate at catching turkey as they are at the business of catching the sinners. And they were not alone. Out of the score of hunters only several others had bagged their limit. So it was a case of continue to hunt and find, if they could. The club's president, Harrison Nesbitt, showed his right to the presidency, for he had two fine gobblers to his credit.

Bridges on the far right with his dog Billy at Original Camp Cleveland. While the outfits worn while hunting turkeys have changed, the tactics have not.

Camp Cleveland gave up a delectable lunch of thick slices of sugar-cured ham, fried apples, apple butter and coffee, after which we were ready for the chase to begin anew. A canvas of those who had not bagged their turkeys was taken by Mr. Bridges, and the lot

127

divided into two parties. One under the guidance of veteran Guide Booth took one route, the other with Mr. Bridges and Bill and Fritz, the wild turkey dogs, took another.

Now the method of hunting with Fritz and Bill is both novel and efficacious. A canine genealogist would have quite a time tracing the family tree of either of those dogs, but they are worth their weight in gold when it comes to getting turkeys. While Mr. Bridges makes weird "kelping" sounds of turkey calling, so plaintively that the most hard-boiled gobbler is moved, Fritz and Bill hie themselves to the hillsides and down the deep valleys in search of flocks of birds. They know the turkey scent and once on the trail the turkeys might just as well heave-to and take a dose of hot shot. The flock located, Bill and Fritz charge with all the fury of four-legged demons. The turkeys take to wing, settling nine times out of ten in the tall tree tops, while the two dogs keep us an incessant yelping and barking below. Their chorus serves a double purposes. It notifies the waiting hunters that the game is treed and it so occupies the attention of the turkeys that they take no cognizance of mere human beings.

It is almost a simple matter to pick them from the tree tops or bag them as they go sailing to other trees in an attempt to rejoin their scattered comrades. With Fritz and Bill on the job the shotguns sounded far more frequently than they did in the morning, and only one hunter failed to get his pair. Finally the autumn sun sank behind the hogback of Sideling Hill Mountain. The western sky took on hues of gold and pink, against which were sharply outlined the smallest branches of Sideling's topmost sentinels. The glow faded, and a chill wind came stirring from the heights to mark the end of another hunting day – with plenty of those wild turkeys still safe in the wilds of Woodmont.

The preserve at Woodmont teamed with wild turkeys. Bridges and his well trained dogs and guides were expert at finding the birds for the guests and members alike. The hunting was not always as easy as it appeared, and on occasion hunters would share much the same experience as Aldo Leopold had while hunting turkey:

Rounding the point of a little bench, I suddenly felt a shock that seemed to freeze my feet to the ground. (I'm sure I felt that turkey in my knees quite as soon as I saw him!) There he was, right over the

*point of the bench, a big hump-backed gobbler, clipping the seeds
off a stalk of wild oats.*

*I knew there must be more behind the point. My plan was to slip
forward a few steps to a little oak tree and get a rest for the first
shot. But I couldn't make my knees behave! I freely confess it, they
were wobbling – wobbling like a reed shaken in the wind. I can look
the biggest blacktail buck in the face without a tremor, but turkey?
Never!"*

It took an experienced turkey hunter like Archibald Rutledge to put the
illusive bird in perspective:

*Successful hunting of this great bird calls for an almost perfect
knowledge of its habits, and requires also a high degree of individual
initiative. As a rule, the deeper you go into the wilderness, the better
your chance of success will be. Nor is the hunting standardized as
is the case with practically all other game. It takes a lot of personal
scheming and hard work. For it is to be remembered that this bird
has legs that enable it to outdistance a good horse; he has wings
that can carry him a mile or more out of danger; his eyes and ears
are among the most perfect in all nature; his behavior is as unpre-
dictable as his mentality is high. As a general rule, if you move, he
will see you and hear you long before you are aware of his presence.
"Not many hunters can kill a turkey," as an old friend, Phineas
McConnor, says. And that remark makes you realize the difference
between the ordinary variety of hunter and the turkey-loving tribe.*

The Maryland Conservationist reported that:

*The Woodmont Rod & Gun Club breed in captivity annually, thou-
sands of pieces of game, the majority of which belong to the feath-
ered tribe. Even though this property is fenced with a nine-foot fencing, thousands of pieces of game fly over the fence annually and
supply the surrounding territory with brood stock and furnish the
sportsmen who hunt in that section excellent hunting.*

*During the hunting season which opened on November 15, 1931,
there were approximately 1,400 wild turkeys, 600 deer, 200 Chinese
ring-necked pheasants and at least eight bevies of bob-whites running from 14 to 24 to the bevy, as well as hundreds upon hundreds
of rabbits and squirrels in the woods on this area and at least 900
mallard ducks on an artificial lake which Mr. Henry P. Bridges, secretary and treasurer, caused to be built for the attraction of wild*

129

fowl. A very small percentage of this game was killed. Therefore, what was left at the end of the hunting season will naturally supply brood stock, not only for the club property, but for the entire area surrounding it.

The following is a list of game killed on the club property during the hunting season of 1931: 24 buck deer, 571 wild turkeys, 100 Chinese ring-necked cock pheasants, 479 mallard ducks, 57 cottontail rabbits and 7 squirrels total 1,238 pieces of game. The old adage of 'Sow that you may reap' is followed out by the management of the Woodmont Rod & Gun Club.

They have efficient employees, whose duties are at all times to control the vermin on this property, in charge of this work, reports that from January 1, 1932, to March 1, 1932, he has trapped and killed on the club property the following vermin: 32 opossum, 1 catamount, 4 house cats, 4 raccoons, 4 owls, 4 hawks, 2 weasels and 10 skunks, total 61 pieces. Mr. Henry P. Bridges reports that the lynx or catamount killed this past winter weighs 35 pounds. This animal is considered one of the worst enemies of game, especially deer and wild turkey. There was one killed on the property last year that had destroyed 22 wild turkeys in the breeding pens, killing the birds on their nests during the incubation period. It was estimated this animal weighed about 35 pounds. We congratulate Mr. Bridges on the great work which he has done in conservation and I am sure as long as his club continues in the propagation of game as they have in the past, that section of Maryland will not have a scarcity of wildlife.

Henry's good friend State Game Warden Lee LeCompte offered this evaluation of Bridges' conservation efforts in 1932:

The Propagation of Game in captivity has made rapid strides in the last few years and remarkable progress has been shown. Today, all thinking sportsmen are concerned about tomorrow. Yesterday's conservation program of constructive restriction has borne fruit scarcely sufficient for its own day and certainly not in keeping with the present demand. In this real emergency, when energetic leaders are thoughtfully feeling their way to more substantial ground, scientific game management is acquiring a new and encouraging significance.

No matter how efficient our game breeders may be, scientific knowledge is necessary and has rendered great assistance in game management. Facts are the only basis on which an adequate plan of propagation of any species of game may be based. Facts are based on experiences. Tuned is the heart of every true sportsmen to their thrill. The hunting tales told around flickering firelight, homes and clubhouses, are wonderful stories, but not the type on which to base a sound plan of game protection, propagation, perpetuation, and increase.

The Woodmont turkey flock in fenced breeding pen. The fencing could not prevent midnight visits from amorous toms.

Aldo Leopold agreed with LeCompte on the need to propagate game species for release into the forests of America:

There are still those who shy at this prospect of a man-made game crop as at something artificial and therefore repugnant. This attitude shows good taste but poor insight. Every head of wild life still alive in this country is already artificialized, in that its existence is conditioned by economic forces. Game management merely proposes that their impact shall not remain wholly fortuitous. The hope of the future lies not in curbing the influence of human occupancy-it is already too late for that-but in creating a better understanding of the extent of that influence and a new ethic for its governance.

In 1919, Russell O'Rourke started raising birds at Woodmont while Walter Exline worked at Woodmont and another site off the mountain to raise the birds. Upon the completion of the new clubhouse the old facility was turned into a turkey, quail, duck and pheasant breeding location. The birds were hatched by electrical and hard-coal incubators and reared under great brooders at the game farms. The birds had limited contact with humans and for this reason they stayed wild. When released, Bridges believed that the turkey reverted to its wild status after two weeks in the woods. Bridges also thought that turkeys with "tame" blood would migrate to a local farm yard

131

or would be easily captured by predators. Bridges took a great deal of pride in raising wild birds, and he worked diligently to keep them that way.

Woodmont was also self sufficient by way of fruits and vegetables. The Woodmont Fruit Company operated with financial assistance from Eugene DuPont, Nelson Perin and Bridges. Apples constituted the major crop, for butter and other products. Fruits and vegetables were harvested and canned (or jarred), to be used later for dinner at the club. The fresh mountain air together with the Woodmont scenery and food could put a person in the mood for a little Thoreau, "Morning air! If men will not drink of this at the fountain-head of the day, why, then, we must even bottle up some and sell it in the shops, for the benefit of those who have lost their subscription ticket to morning time in this world."

The ducks at Woodmont appear to have learned more than a few survival skills from the turkeys. Bridges had a conversation with a guest from Colorado who was a passionate duck hunter:

> *The man-let us call him Fred-was staring at the flames that danced over the five-foot log in the lounge fireplace. "Bridges," he said carelessly, "I daresay I'll get a duck with every shell tomorrow." "Well, now, Fred," I said, "you probably would, if you were hunting anywhere other than at Woodmont. But you won't get a duck with every shell here."*

> *He rose to the lure. "Oh, yes, I will," he said confidently. "I can kill a duck with every shell. I don't care whether I'm in a rocking boat or freezing in a blind." I said, "I'll bet, say, fifty dollars that you can't kill six ducks with fifteen shells tomorrow." He sat up and slapped his knees. "You're on!" "And just to make it easy," I said, "you can pick your ducks. You don't have to shoot at any you think are poor shots."*

> *His look told me he thought I had a few slates loose in the belfry region. Poor fellow, he didn't know what I knew. If he had, he'd likely not have made that bet. For at Woodmont, duck hunting is conducted in this manner: The ducks are taken from the lakes to a mountain about one-half mile away. The duck blinds are in a ravine that stretches from the lake to the mountain. At a signal, the game-keeper releases the ducks from the mountain, two at a time, where-upon the ducks fly down the ravine, back to the lake.*

> *Trouble is, the ducks are not decoying, but are flying at about sixty-five miles per hour back to the lake. More than one hunter at Wood-*

132

mont has shot until his gun all but glowed red and hit not one duck. Invariably the hunter leads the speeding ducks too far, or does not lead them enough, and in either instance the result is a clean miss.

Back to Fred, the Colorado duck hunter. Next morning we went to the blinds. Fred readied himself to begin. Far away, on top of the mountain, the gamekeeper began releasing ducks, two at a time. Down the ravine came the mallards, flying swift as arrows from a bow. "Watch this," said Fred. "Here's a good pair," And as two ducks winged over he rose, shouldered his gun and fired twice. A look of surprise came to his face. The ducks were still on their way to the lake. "Huh," said Fred weakly, "that's a funny one." More ducks came highballing down the ravine; more gunshots boomed out. The mallards continued safely on their way. The upshot of the hunt was that Fred got only three ducks with his fifteen shells. "Bridges," he said, breaking his gun, shucking out the last two empty cases, "that's the hardest duck shooting I ever had in my life."

Duck hunting party with Bridges second on left. Many were shot at, but relatively few fell from the sky.

Fred's arduous hunt was no accident. Henry designed Woodmont with the same care that Claude Monet painted his lilies. Above all, Bridges wanted sportsmanship and wing shooting. He crafted his setting with a master's touch. Every hunter had ample opportunity to kill the duck, pheasant, quail, turkey or deer that passed by a gunner's position. It was left up to the hunter to bring down the game while not faltering to buck-ague or miss leading the flying bird. Those who talked the biggest game were the best targets for Bridges' light-hearted fun and wagers.

BECOMING A BUSINESSMAN EMERITUS

In 1931, at the age of fifty-three, Bridges was devoting most of his time to family and Woodmont. Whenever possible, he minimized his involvement with Pennsylvania Glass Sand. Ironically, both work and Woodmont could take on political in the 1930s: West Virginia tried to increase the tax on sand while White House visitors dropped by from time to time. Henry preferred the latter by far.

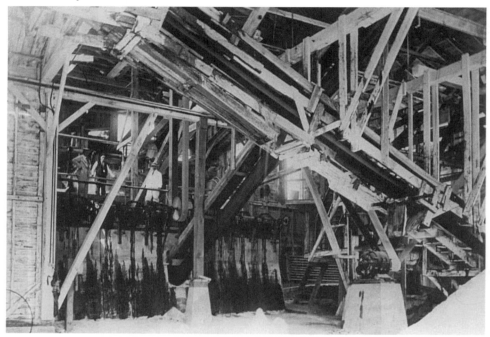

Bridges on the left inspecting part of the Pennsylvania Glass Sand operation. His father would have been hard-pressed to recognize the business given the extent of modernization.

In December of 1931 two members of Herbert Hoover's cabinet--Attorney General William D. Mitchell and Secretary of the Interior Ray Lyman Wilbur--came out to hunt Woodmont with Bridges, as did Hoover assistant Lawrence Richey. *The Baltimore Sun* of December 13,1931, reported the trio shot one eight point buck at 200 pounds, six wild turkeys, eighteen pheasants, and fourteen mallard ducks. Bridges loaded the hunters into a buckboard and planted them one mile into the preserve. Fritz and Billy, Bridges' turkey dogs, did a wonderful job when they scattered a flock of fifty turkeys. The hunters then each went after there own birds and brought home fourteen-pound birds. Bridges himself shot two immense gobblers that he sent to President Hoover at the White House. The ducks were shot as they flew over the lower lake and the hunters lined the valley waiting for the high flyers to land on the upper lake. General Mitchell was credited with the kill on the buck, one shot to the heart and the buck went down 100 yards from where it was hit. Bridges had pointers and setters that he called either Jim or Dick that he used for quail and pheasant hunts. The quail shooting was excellent at Woodmont and grouse were found naturally and very sporty shooting.

Bridges continued to worship at Hancock Presbyterian Church, which had been founded by his grandfather. Henry had much to be thankful for—his investments survived the Depression, and he was blessed with a second son, Shelby Powell Bridges, born April 29, 1932. Bridges was old enough to be a grandfather to Henry Jr. and Shelby, but the love and wisdom shown was that of a parent.

In February 1933, outgoing President Herbert Hoover made a visit to Woodmont and sat in the President's chair carved by the legendary William Elkins. Hoover made the fifth United States President to occupy the chair. Henry had gone personally to the White House to extend the invitation.

President Herbert Hoover. Franklin Roosevelt would follow him into the White House and the President's Chair at Woodmont.

In 1934, Pennsylvania Glass Sand took the company public with $8.3 million in bonds and $3.16 million in preferred stock. Bridges became Vice President and Director. Debuting on Wall Street in the midst of a depression was no easy task, but Henry pulled it off. He was aided in his efforts by friends who bought enough shares to make the company look a winner. However, the Depression did make itself felt. In August 1930, the company shut down the Hazel Atlas Sand Plant at Great Cacapon West Virginia. The Morgan Messenger reported, "It is little short of a calamity that the Hazel-Atlas Glass Sand Company, for seventeen years operating a sand plant at Great Cacapon, this county, has definitely decided to discontinue operations at that place. By its closing 90 men, nearly all of who are married and each have several in family are thrown out of employment. Approximately 359 people depended largely upon this labor for support, and the loss of it cannot but prove a hardship. Fortunately for nearly all of the men, they have small farms or gardens from which much sustenance is derived."

WOODMONT RESPLENDENT

On November 15, 1934, Henry was above Preachers Hollow in the Woodmont preserve to flush out turkeys for a hunt. He fired his twelve-gauge shotgun randomly into the air to move the birds to the forty or so hunters below the ridge. He had driven turkey in this fashion for many years and it was routine for him on any given hunt.

Suddenly, there was a very loud explosion on the ridge top, and Bridges crumpled over in agonizing pain. He had mistaken a twenty-gauge shotgun shell, which a guest may have mistakenly placed in his shell box, for a twelve-gauge shell which he then loaded into the second gun barrel. In his haste to keep the birds moving for the hunters, Henry fired, only to assume the shell had misfired. Consequently, he loaded another twelve-gauge shell into the barrel and pulled the trigger again. But the smaller twenty-gauge shell had slid half way through the barrel of the gun. When the gun fired, the twelve-gauge load caused the other shell in the barrel to explode. Henry's left hand was shattered. "I lay on the ground a moment. There was no pain. There was only shock. Then I looked at my hand. Mangled beyond recognition. Well, I thought, this is it!"

His favorite guide, Ott Booth, was driving the car they used to get to Preachers Hollow, and he sprang out to wrap up what remained of the hand. Booth rushed Bridges to a Hagerstown hospital, forty-five minutes away. The doctors considered surgery to repair the hand, but they concluded the damage was too great to attempt reconstructive surgery. Instead, surgeons fashioned a rounded end to the limb. Bridges spent considerable time in the hospital recovering from the accident. For a year he struggled with depression. He was, after all, the primary shareholder and Secretary Manager of the finest hunting operation in North America. Among those sending their sympathy was the new President of the United States.

On December 20, 1934, Franklin Delano Roosevelt wrote Bridges from The White House, "My dear Mr. Bridges: That fine buck deer arrived yesterday. I know that it will add flavor and variety to the Christmas table. It was kind of you to remember me and I appreciate your thoughtfulness. I hope very much that yours will be a Merry Christmas and that you have by now entirely recovered from that very unfortunate accident." A month later, Bridges and his wife visited the White House. Henry had supported FDR's election in 1932. He and Mrs. Bridges attended the Gridiron Dinner and then visited the President at 9 PM.

The President and Mrs. Roosevelt

request the pleasure of the company of

Mr. and Mrs. Bridges

at a reception to be held at

The White House

Thursday evening, January the seventeenth

nineteen hundred and thirty-five

at nine o'clock

Invitation to the Roosevelt White House.
It was an offer hard to refuse.

Ultimately, Henry came to terms with his misfortune. "So I lost my left hand. But it did not stop me from hunting. In fact, I am a better shot without the hand than I was with it, for I am now a more deliberate shot." In fact Bridges shot hundreds whitetail deer with his .351 repeater rifle. He rested the rifle on his arm and could knock down two and three deer at a dead run. On one hunt he shot five deer with four shoots, as one deer ran beside another. Bridges orchestrated deer drives for his guests, and he amazed them with his deadly aim despite his handicap.

This is how Henry came to view his altered life:

For in the later years of my life, angling has been a means of demonstrating that a man with a handicap need not quit and retire from life but may instead employ ingenuity and determination and continue to live as before. What I am getting at here is the loss of my left hand in the hunting accident. When this happened, many of my friends expected me to leave Woodmont. Surely, they thought, Henry will no longer hunt and certainly he will no longer fish, for how is a man to handle pole and net with but one hand? Well, I believe that I shoot as well today as I ever did, and I fish as well as before.

While I require no special equipment for hunting, there is one device I employ while fishing. It is a strong belt with a small socket affixed to the center of the belt. I place the butt of the rod in the socket and, with this arrangement, can fish with the best of them! To reel, I simply place the rod in the crook of my left arm and reel with my right hand. Nor do I require assistance with the net. Now, anyone could have done this, could have overcome this handicap had he so desired it. This reflects no special credit upon myself, but I mention it because I want to emphasize the human spirit, the soul, that indomitable reality which can, when buttressed with faith and determination, overcome any and all obstacles.

Why did Bridges bother? No doubt he agreed with Aldo Leopold, who described this trout fishing adventure:

For the duration of a cigarette I sit on a rock midstream-and watch my trout rise under his guardian bush, while my rod and line hang drying on the alders of the sunny bank. Then-for prudence' sake-a little longer. What pool is too smooth up there. A breeze is stirring and may shortly ruffle it for an instant, and thus make more deadly that perfect cast I shall shortly lay upon its bosom. It will come-a puff strong enough to shake a brown miller off the laughing alder, and cast it upon the pool.

Ready now! Coil up the dry line and stand midstream, rod in instant readiness. It's coming-a little premonitory and shiver in that aspen on the hill lets me get out half a case, and swish it gently back and forth, ready for the main puff to hit the pool. No more than half a line, mind you! The sun is high now, and any flicking shadow overhead would forewarn my hunker of his impending fate. Now! The last three yards shoot out, the fly falls gracefully at the feet of the laughing alder-he has it! I set hard to hold him out of the jungle beyond. He rushes downstream. In a few minutes he, too, is kicking in the creel.

I sit in happy meditation on my rock, pondering, while my line dries again, upon the ways of trout and men. How like fish we are: ready, nay eager, to seize upon whatever new thing some wind of circumstance shakes down upon the river of time! And how we rue our haste, finding the gilded morsel to contain a hook. Even so, I think there is some virtue in eagerness, whether its object prove true or false. How utterly dull would be a wholly prudent man, or trout, or world! Did I say a while ago that I waited 'for prudence sake'? That was not so. The only prudence in fishermen is that designed to set the stage for taking yet another, and perhaps a longer, chance."

On May 11, 1935, President Roosevelt fished Woodmont. The Presidential entourage moved through Hancock on the road leading to Woodmont. An eyewitness reported, "People from miles around came to see their President. It was easy to recognize the President with his cigarette holder in his mouth cocked at an angle. Big Jim Farley, the Post Master General, was riding with him." Among those with FDR were Vice President John Nance Garner, Speaker of the House Joseph W. Byrnes and Democratic leader Senator Joseph T. Robinson.

President Roosevelt and friends coming through Hancock on the way to Woodmont. A member of the Secret Serviceman took a camera for a gun.

When the President arrived at Woodmont, he had a supper of wild pheasant and venison. Bridges asked the President if he'd like to try a bit of trout fishing. "He rubbed his hands together and smiled, 'That's what I came here for.'" So after supper he was driven to Camp Cleveland to fish for speckled trout from the earthen dam between the two lakes. Bridges suggested a wet fly at first; when they didn't bite he became worried. He then switched the President to a worm, and he caught his limit of ten.

They returned to the clubhouse for dinner. After dinner Bridges first called on Vice President Garner for a few words and then on other of the seventeen guests assembled. Finally, Henry asked FDR to speak. "Mr. President, I've hesitated to call on you because I know that you came up here for a rest. I know you must be tired of making speeches. But, if it suits you, I know everyone here would like very much to hear from you." FDR did not disappoint. Later, Harvey Van Goshen, the violinist who preformed for President Wilson at the White House, played his [alleged] Stradivarius for President Roosevelt.

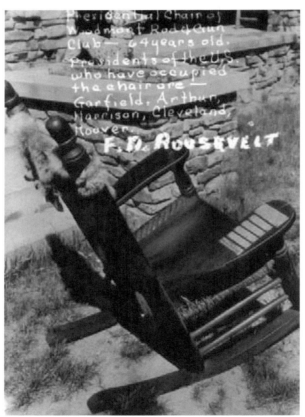

The Woodmont Presidential Chair. Franklin Delano Roosevelt was the sixth chief executive to avail himself of it.

Bridges used the President's visit to lobby on behalf of the turkey as America's national symbol. While driving in the preserve the next morning Henry presented the President with his proposal. The President replied, "Bridges, you may well be right, but, man, do you have an idea of what it would take to bring about such a change? I'd need an act of Congress to do it and I've enough trouble with congress as it is."

Bridges reflected:

> *Our jaunt around the preserve was soon over. It was a journey that afforded me a certain insight into the man whom so many millions seemed to love outright and whom so many millions repeatedly elected to serve as President. He was, it seemed to me, a type of man who, although weighed down with grave responsibilities, would yet always wear a cheerful countenance. He was a man who emanated hope and encouragement no matter what the odds. And he seemed to be a man who, if he exhibited irritation at all, would vent it only towards the minor problems about him.*

After leaving Woodmont, the President drove to The West Virginia Crippled Children's Foundation in Berkeley Springs for a surprise visit to seventeen children stricken with infantile paralysis. The President said, "Seeing these children is even more wonderful than my fishing trip, and I am glad I went out of my way to do it." Polio was never far from FDR's thoughts.

On May 16, 1935, the President wrote Bridges this letter of thanks:

THE WHITE HOUSE
WASHINGTON

May 16, 1935.

Dear Mr. Bridges:-

      I cannot tell you how much I enjoyed every minute of my stay at the Club. It is a delightful spot and I hereby accept your invitation to come again! All of us had a wonderful time and a real rest. Will you also thank Mr. Jenkins? I would write him but I do not know his address.

      Thank you for your nice letter about the crippled children and the highway. As you know, both of these subjects are of tremendous interest to me. I hope that before I get through in Washington we can do something about a Parkway from here all the way to Cumberland.

Always sincerely,

Franklin D Roosevelt

Henry P. Bridges, Esq.,
Berkeley Springs,
West Virginia.

President Roosevelt's thank-you to Henry.

The parkway referred to was a proposal to fill in old C & O Canal.

On November 21, 1935, Freeman Gosden and Charles Correll, the two comedians know as "Amos and Andy" hunted Woodmont with Lawrence Richey, former secretary to Herbert Hoover. Bridges was talking with them outside the Clubhouse where they said to him:

We'll call you "Henry," and you call us "Amos and Andy".... "All right," I said, "and I'll also call you up some prime wild turkeys as soon as you're ready." In a short while, Amos, Andy, myself and my turkey dog Billy were out in the deep woods. Billy found a flock of turkeys and, barking, scattered them. I put Amos and Andy behind two white oak trees.

"Now, Amos," I said, "I'll call you up a turkey first." I turned to Andy. "And, Andy, you stay hidden," I said. "Don't show yourself.

If you do, the turkey will fly away." Then I began calling. Amos watched me intently. Andy looked at both of us as if he wanted to laugh. Soon a gobbler answered the call and then a big bird came towards us. I could see Amos tense, ready to shoot. Slowly the big bird came forward. It was just about within range of Amos's gun.

And then Andy stuck his head around the tree and peered, grinning, at the bird. Instantly the turkey saw him and flew away. Amos looked disgusted. "Andy," he snapped, "why in the world did you do that? Henry told you to keep yourself out of sight!" Andy looked sheepishly at the ground. Amos went on, "Here we are, missing our first broadcast in…years just to hunt with Henry – and you have to stick your head around the tree!" "Listen, Andy," I said, laughing, "next time keep your head out of sight!"

**Amos & Andy with Bridges calling turkey,
none of whom were much impressed.**

They were each able to bag two wild turkeys, and their limit in ducks and pheasants. They reported it was "the grandest hunting" they had ever seen. The comedians were unable to depart on time due to a snowstorm and they missed their 7 PM radio broadcast for the first time. They wrote Bridges on November 25, 1935:

Frankly, I think that our day with you was one of the high spots of our outdoor life, of which we have had considerable. I think we enjoyed the day at Woodmont more than any other thing of that kind

*that we have ever experienced. We want to thank you for your kind-
ness to us in sending us the invitation. We are sending you a little
package which should reach you the latter part of this week. A du-
plicate of this package also is going to your wife at Johnson City. If
we can ever be of any service to you in Chicago or entertain you in
any way, we would be very happy to do so.*

On December 22, 1935, Bridges hunted Woodmont for the bounty which
he planned to send FDR. He shot two wild turkeys, one deer, six plump
Chinese ring neck pheasant, and eight wild mallard ducks for the White
House Christmas dinner. Guide Ott Booth and turkey dog Billy, responsible
for over 2,000 turkey kills, took to the woods with Bridges to provide the
piece de resistance for the President's Christmas dinner from the Woodmont
preserve. Despite the loss of his left hand, Henry still welded his favorite
28-gauge shotgun and automatic rifle with deadly accuracy.

At the close of the 1935 season at Woodmont *Maryland Conservationist*
reported the game killed and who killed bucks from the preserve.

*Mr. Henry P. Bridges, secretary-treasurer of the club reports a kill
of game at Woodmont during the hunting season of 1935 as follows:
Deer 60, Wild Turkeys 779, Mallard Ducks 1635, Mutant Pheasants 669, Bob-White 96, Cottontail Rabbits 100....The bucks killed
by gunners, 50 deer, killed for table 10 deer, Total - 60 deer. Mr.
Bridges also reports that the club is keeping for brood stock in 1936:
200 Wild Turkeys, 300 Mutant Pheasants, 300 Wild Mallard Ducks,
60 Bobwhite and we hope the club will have a successful propagating season and a bountiful supply of game for the hunting season of
1936.*

In February 1936, Bridges was at home in Johnson City when he received
news that the earthen dam at Woodmont had washed out. Henry blamed
Arby Hoover, one of the guides, who was supposed to keep the leaves
cleaned out of the spillway. The clogged spillway caused the dam's failure.
By August the structure was rebuilt and another added. This fifty-foot tall
stone dam at the end of the valley created a lake for bass. The upper spring-
fed lake, formed many years earlier, was stocked with trout. The rains not
only knocked out the dam at Woodmont, but they soon descended on the
town of Hancock itself. On March 18, the Potomac flooded Main Street and
destroyed the Hancock bridge over the river.

**The Flood of '36 in downtown Hancock. Flooding
was one aspect of nature Thoreau and other writers
largely ignored, for obvious reasons.**

In April another calamity befell Henry with the death of his ninety-four year old mother, Priscilla Breathed Bridges. She had been born in 1842 in Berkeley Springs, Virginia, (now West Virginia) and to the end maintained the matronly charm of a woman of the old school. Priscilla gave birth to thirteen children, eleven of whom lived to adulthood. And one of them was intent on persevering in matters of conservation.

Henry especially wanted genuine Eastern wild turkeys to breed with his flock. On April 22, 1936, he wrote E.E. Strickland of The Strickland Game Farms in Kosciusko, Mississippi, requesting birds, "If you have some 100 per cent genuine wild turkeys this coming Fall, I would like to get half a dozen hens and half a dozen gobblers. I do not care to have any with Mexican or Texas blood in them. Will send some pictures of what I want in the next few days, which I consider genuine wild." Strickland responded, "With the exception of eggs taken from next of wild turkeys my stock is made up of wild trapped birds. Except few of my select youngsters last year. I have a friend in this county who has been protecting feeding thru' Fall and Winter the genuine wild turkeys. Been doing this for thirty odd years. Turkeys come and go from his place from miles around." Bridges made sure not to mix any tame blood with his flock in order to guarantee the 100 per cent wild-turkey genes in his birds.

**Woodmont's Whitetail deer, at one point hunted
to exhaustion. Henry Bridges sought to increase
their number as he did that of the wild turkey.**

It was inevitable that someone so interested with flying creatures should turn his attention to flying machines. In 1936 Henry undertook the construction of an airstrip at Woodmont with funds given by Henry A. Roemer of Sharon Steel Corporation. The strip, known as Roemer Field, enabled hunters to fly to a secluded landing stripe deep in the preserve and hunt for a weekend and then fly back to their homes. On November 20, the airstrip was completed and Lorenz Iverson, President of the Mesta Machine Company, loaded a group of hunters and took them to Pittsburgh with their turkey bag limits. The roundtrip was completed without incident.

**Passengers boarding Mr. Lorenz Iverson's plane at Roemer
Air Field. Takeoffs and landings were anything but smooth.**

Later that month Henry wrote his brother, attorney F. Wilbur Bridges of
Hagerstown, a quick note about conditions at Woodmont and the prospect
of a new member from Baltimore, "After the big rush is over I will ask
you to come to the Club with Dr. Fleming and Dr. Poole. Last week was
a busy one for me and Mr. Osmond [Henry P.'s personal secretary], as we
had 66 gunners out the first day, and the balance of the week we averaged
about 29 gunners a day. Another big crowd came in yesterday to shoot today
and tomorrow. Be sure to write me giving me the man's name, and I will
find if he is suitable for membership through some of our Baltimore members." Bridges was constantly searching for and inviting new members to
join Woodmont. The club had a waiting list of prospective members. After
an individual made it to the top of the list, the board of governors voted on
membership.

When the immediate family came to Woodmont, the days were lonely for
Mrs. Bridges. Henry P., Henry, Jr. and Powell were on the go all day keeping
busy attending to the tasks of operating the club. Henry P. followed a routine
in which he drove to the game farm to check on his turkeys. Then he drove
through the preserve to check on the game fields. Walking outside the car,
he always carried a large stick for any chance encounters with rattlesnakes

or copperheads. Young Powell was always ready, at his father's request, to jump out of the car and remove sticks and rocks from the roadway. Shelby remained at the clubhouse and worked on needle point until her husband and boys returned to have lunch with her. She would sometimes visit her only close friends Suella and Jack Casper of Hancock or Mabelyn and Bill Hamilton of Hagerstown. Shelby did not socialize much with Henry P.'s family in Hancock and Hagerstown primarily because they were so much older. The family visited Woodmont every August to spend time together.

Henry and wife Shelby hunting at Woodmont.

On December 15, 1936, Bridges wrote Dr. Louis F. Knoll of Brooklyn, N.Y. who was interested in membership at Woodmont the following letter:

Your letter of 8th received. We have a 5000 acre preserve and a fine stone Clubhouse, and wonderful shooting for deer, wild turkeys, mallard ducks, pheasants and quail. The Clubhouse contains about 600 mountings of birds and animals from all over the world. A United States Senator told me that he had traveled all over the world, and that he considered we had the finest club he had ever seen. The preserve is enclosed with a nine-foot fence, 14 miles in length. We also have a lake for trout and also one for bass. The trout fishing opens April 1st and closes July 1st. The bass fishing opens July 1st and closes November 15th. The hunting season is from November 15th to January 1st, so there is something doing at the Club for nine months in the year.

We have entertained six Presidents of the United States and people from all over the world. The membership is limited to sixty members. We have about $615,000.00 invested in the Club and the actual value of a membership is about $8,000.00 The Board of Directors however, decided that on account of the depression, to make the cost of a membership $3,500.00, the initiation fee being $1,500.00 and 40 shares of the Club stock at $50.00 per share, $2,000.00, total $3,500.00. The dues are $150.00 per year plus tax of $15.00. New members coming in are usually proposed by one of the Club members and their names put up before our Board of Governors for election to membership. Should you wish to apply for membership, if you do not know any of our present members, I would suggest that you send us some reference so that your name could be put up before our Board. After getting this reference I would be glad to have you put on the waiting list, and use my influence with the President of our Club and the Board to have you elected as quickly as possible.

This was the process which all new members went through and there was no assurance of membership. No market existed for Woodmont stock, and the by-laws provided that any retiring member could sell their stock to any individual that the board of governors approved. The individual would be approved by the board before the transfer took place.

On January 29, 1937, Bridges wrote Mr. Frank Hall Fraysur, his first contact with *LIFE Magazine* of New York City, trying to get the magazine to come out to Woodmont for a photo shoot. Bridges constantly promoted the club and did what he could to put it in the spot light. The magazine at first turned him down. But Henry got his way in the end.

Bridges had the same zeal for wild turkeys, and he enjoyed showing them off to the public whenever possible. In February 1937, he wrote C.J. McPhail, superintendent of Gwynnbrook State Game Farm in Owings Mills Maryland, about some turkeys he was to ship for the *Outdoor Life Show*:

We will ship you on Tuesday morning, Feb. 9th, one wild turkey gobbler and two hens to be exhibited in the Outdoor Life Show which opens on Feb. 11th. After the exhibition is over, these wild turkeys are to go back to your farm, and Mr. LeCompte said he would put six additional hens with them so you can get sufficient eggs to *raise some fine breeders for another year. We are shipping you very fine birds, which are out of some birds for which we paid $100.00 each. Do not cut the gobbler's wing, as they are cut from the inside, and we always leave two or three flight feathers so the gobbler can balance himself when he struts and treads. We do all our breeding gobblers this way.*

The birds will be shipped by express on Western Maryland Railway from Pearre, Md., about one o'clock on Tuesday so you should receive them at your station, Glyndon, about four or five o'clock. I expect you know the time the train gets to your station. I hope you will have good luck with these birds.

The Western Maryland Pearre Station was directly below the old Clubhouse and was very convenient for the shipping of Bridges' wild game. Turkey and deer were shipped in creates specially built for the animals. The sale of wild game produced a strong revenue stream for the Club as well as repopulating the game in areas of the country it was delivered. Bridges contended that these birds will not visit farms and homes. The gunners at the Club were complaining about the turkeys being so wild that they were hard to shoot.

When Henry's boys were growing up at Shelbridge he had picked out the Blackard girls for his two sons to marry before they even understood courtship. Their father, Dr. William Blackard a minister at the Munsey Memorial Methodist Church in Johnson City, was hunting turkey with Bridges at Woodmont one trip. On the hunt William was in a blind with a guide, that Henry had placed him with, poised to shot an approaching turkey. Bridges had told him to "shoot the turkey with both barrels." The turkey came closer and he pulled both triggers at once and knocked himself over in the blind. The guide later reported to Bridges that Dr. Blackard missed the turkey and ended up flat on his back in the blind. Henry got a great laugh from the tale.

**Shelby, Henry Jr. and Powell with family
friends Edith and Louise Blackard.**

Henry often thought of his family when at Woodmont. His conservation and business interests kept him away from his wife and children more than he liked. In the early summer of 1937 Bridges had a swimming pool installed at Shelbridge. The pool provided hours of fun and amusement for the children and Shelby, who had frequent pool parties. She also invited friends to enjoy the gardens, the lily pools and the beautiful grounds surrounding Shelbridge.

**The Bridges boys and their friends at the
Shelbridge pool, which did not lack for users.**

In July of 1937, Henry's first cousin John Breathed wrote him from New York about a prospective club member:

The other day I had luncheon with a very good friend of mine in New York who apparently has acquired the hunting fever. He mentioned to me that he had done some hunting last fall and liked it tremendously and thought he was going in for it for a fall diversion. He has heard of Woodmont and I told him that I thought it might barely be possible that I could arrange to have him go down and see Woodmont this fall and, if he liked it, it might be arranged to get him a membership although I could not guarantee it. The reason for this note now is merely to find out if you are still building up your membership or if you have obtained a sufficient number of members and have closed your list again.

Bridges wrote back:

Shelby and I went to the DuPont-Roosevelt [DuPont heiress Ethel and FDR Jr]. wedding, and we had a wonderful time. Shelby enjoys these affairs, and I go on that account. She enjoyed her trip to New York, and often speaks of you and Rae. I am always glad to get any friend of yours as a member of the club. Your friend Shields is one of our best members, and is a fine fellow. It may be possible he would not want to bring your friend to the club, so why don't you bring him down. Do you think he would like to do some bass fishing, and if so you and Rae could come down with him....I feel that we have enough Pittsburgh and Baltimore members, and any new members coming in we would like them from New York or Philadelphia.

In turn John, a meatpacking executive, wrote his cousin:

"Thanks for your letter of the 13th. Your estimation of my friends in New York is quite flattering and I appreciate your sentiments very much."

The man I have in mind I am sure would not be able to come down to Woodmont this summer as I believe he and his wife are planning an ocean cruise, but, now that I know of your willingness to consider additional members for Woodmont, I will start soon to lay the foundation for trying to get him down during the hunting season this fall. He has only met Bob Shields once but is a bosom friend of Fred Griffiths who likewise is a close friend of Bob Shields. As a matter of fact, I believe you will recall it was with Fred Griffiths' aid that I was able to line up Bob Shields for Woodmont. Fred will do almost anything I ask and I will get him to work on this fellow so we can have him lined up for the fall if possible.

I got quite a kick out of your comment regarding your attendance at the DuPont-Roosevelt wedding, especially the part where you say that Shelby enjoys those affairs and you go only on her account. You cannot convince me of that as I know you are such an ardent New Dealer you would go many, many miles to be with President Roosevelt. It must have been tough on you New Dealers to accept the hospitality and break bread in the throne room of the Liberty League. I am saving some of my best political arguments until I see you next as you are the only New Dealer with whom I can argue who doesn't want to get mad and kill me before the argument ends. Give our best regards to Shelby the family and, with best to you.

**The Great Room with members lounging
around the Washington Fireplace.**

CONSERVATION AND WOODMONT AS A MODEL SPORTING PRESERVE

Jas. T. Begg a member of Woodmont worried about the state of the club without the presence of Henry Bridges. Begg wrote Henry in August 1937, "In reading of the many things you have done to make the club more attractive for its members, the thought strikes me as it often has done before: What would Woodmont be like if anything happened to you? Mrs. Begg often speaks of your fine wife and wants to join me in being remembered to you and your fine family." Bridges worked to make possible the conservation efforts and advances described here by Lee LeCompte:

Among the several duties of the State Game Warden of Maryland is the propagation of game birds and game animals in captivity which are released in the covers of this State for propagation in the natural state. The State Game Department of Maryland operates two state-owned game farms, namely Gwynnbrook State Game Farm, No. 1, located at Gwynnbrook, Baltimore County, where we propagate in captivity principally bob-white, Chinese and melanistic mutant pheasants (Silver, golden, Reeves and Lady Amherst pheasants, used as show birds), wild turkey, Egyptian partridge (chukar), California quail, ruffed grouse, wild mallard ducks, Canadian geese (honker) and Virginia white-tailed deer; and, the Wicomico State Game Farm No. 2, Salisbury, Wicomico County, Maryland, where we propagate bob-white exclusively.

In addition to these two farms, we operate a wild turkey propagating plant on the Washington County Game Refuge at Pearre, Washington County. At the Montgomery County Game Refuge we propagate bobwhite, pheasants and wild mallard ducks. From these plants we are liberating in the covers thousands of pieces of broodstock annually. When the department purchased the Gwynnbrook property, the first game farm established in Maryland, there were only a few states in the Union owning and operating state-owned game propagation plants. In 1937 the majority of the states of the Union are operating plants for propagating game birds and game animals in captivity to replenish the covers of their state.

Advantage of Game Farms:

From these farms and from leased areas known as State Game Refuges, many thousands of game birds have been distributed to each and every county of this State annually for a number of years past. Thousands of bobwhite and large numbers of pheasants and pheasant eggs have been distributed through sportsmen's clubs in cooperation with the department and the District Deputy Game Wardens. By owning the State Game farms, the department has maintained better control of its supply of sound, healthy birds which are required for liberation annually due to the severe winters taking a heavy toll and summer floods drowning thousands of ground-nesting birds and game animals.

Wild Turkey:

From 1927 to 1930 we imported wild turkeys from North Dakota, Pennsylvania, and Virginia. Prior to these importation's there were very few wild turkeys found in the coverts of Maryland. In 1930 we started the propagation of wild turkeys at the Gwynnbrook State Game Farm and at the Washington County Game Refuge and the report of kill in 1936 was 1,217 birds in Garrett and Allegany Counties, 67 in Washington County. Therefore, without a doubt, our plantings of wild turkeys and especially those which were raised at the state-owned farms have been very beneficial in increasing the supply of this wonderful game bird.

Pheasants:

We established the Gwynnbrook Plant for the purpose of raising Chinese ring-necked pheasants which were becoming popular in some of the states of the Union at that time. We have planted annually from 1921 to 1936 from 2,000 to 4,000 birds. In 1930 we introduce into Maryland the melanistic mutant pheasant, which is a bird of not as high plumage as the Chinese ring-necked and not as easily distinguished in the coverts as the highly-colored ring-neck. However, these birds have only established themselves in a few sections of our State and we came to the conclusion there was some cause for it.

Virginia White-Tailed Deer:

The deer has shown a great increase in Maryland during the past few years. We raise these animals in captivity in a wild state at the Gwynnbrook State Game Farm, and also have a corral comprised of a 100-acre area on the Meadow Mountain Game Refuge in Garrett County. Our policy is to liberate the surplus from this corral as they show an increase and we have released 120 deer from this refuge within the past few years. These releases showed excellent results as the kill of deer in Garrett and Allegany Counties has shown an increase annually.

Bridges' work at Woodmont provided many of the wild turkey that made possible the state's operation. The key to success was insuring that the gene pool stayed one-hundred percent wild. This standard proved easier to meet with deer than fowl. In September 1937, Bridges invited governors from thirty states to visit Woodmont after a luncheon at The White House and a speech at Antietam Battlefield given by President Roosevelt. This was how Henry spread his gospel--the message of conservation wrapped around fine dining and fellowship.

A month later, Robert Bridges of Charles Scribners Sons Publishers in New York City wrote his cousin, "Dear Cousin Harry: I shall be glad to be at your party on November 14th at the Club, 7 o'clock. Don't ask the Roosevelts [members of Teddy's family] to bring me, as I expect to stop home first. I'll think about a speech – short if I make it." Henry replied:

I received your letter of the 14th, and I am certainly delighted that we are going to have you at our opening dinner. I will not ask Colo-nel Roosevelt [Theodore Jr.] to bring you down, but would like you to let him know you are coming, as you know him well. We expect to have about seventy-five men at this dinner and I am sure you will enjoy it. I know you are not a gunner, but if you would like to try out the bass fishing in the lake, I will get a guide to take you. I do not know if it will be too late for the bass to bite, but you might try it out. I have been toastmaster for the past thirty years, and always call on our prominent guests to make a speech. I know all my friends will enjoy hearing from you. PS: Do not bring dinner coat, as we never wear them at the Club. All dinners are informal.

Editors, presidents, titans of business and industry—these were the kind of people Henry wanted to see Woodmont. And he had no problems with any royals who wanted to visit. In writing Charles E. Bedeaux, of Fifth Av-enue in New York City, Henry offered:

It would give me great pleasure and also our Club, to entertain the Duke and Duchess of Windsor and yourself at the Woodmont Rod & Gun Club to shoot wild turkeys, ducks and pheasants. If you all could arrange it I would like your party to come and spend the night at the Club and shoot the following day. I could show you some wonderful shooting.

We have more wild turkeys on our preserve than any preserve in the United States, and also large numbers of pheasants and ducks. An Attorney General of the United States and a U. S. Senator, whom I entertained at the Club as my guests, stated that they had traveled all over the world, and that they considered the Woodmont Club and preserve the finest they had ever seen. We have over 600 mountings of birds and animals, and I am sure the Duke and Duchess would enjoy their visit. I think it is one place in the United States that they should see on their trip. We have a "Presidential Chair," 70 years old, and six presidents of the United States have occupied this chair. We have their names engraved on silver plates and placed on the chair. I am anxious for the Duke to occupy this chair, so we can also put his name on the chair with the six Presidents.

We have an opening dinner at the Club on November 14th, at which dinner we are expecting about 75 men. Among the guests will be Theodore Roosevelt, Jr., Richard Cleveland, son of Grover Cleveland, Robert Bridges, the author, editor of Scribner's Magazine and my first cousin, the Governor of Maryland and some U.S. Senators and Congressmen. I do not know if you all would like to attend this opening dinner, or come afterwards when there will not be such a crowd. I am anxious to take you all shooting with my trained wild turkey dog, and also call up some wild turkeys for you to shoot. All the shooting is wing shooting.

Honorable S. Davies Warfield and his famous guide Phil Thompson at Woodmont. Warfield was related to the woman who became the Duchess of Windsor and a friend of Henry's from early days in Baltimore City.

157

This time the famous Bridges' charm failed to carry the day, even though the Duchess, Wallis Warfield Simpson, was from a wealthy Baltimore family. Had they come the royal couple would have witnessed the dedication of a new lunch-lodge at Camp Cleveland. The ceremony included the son of the former president. "A lake is the landscape's most beautiful and expressive feature," wrote Thoreau. "It is earth's eye; looking into which the beholder measures the depth of his own nature. The fluviatile trees next the shore are the slender eyelashes which fringe it, and the wooded hills and cliffs around are its overhanging brows." The House of Windsor did not agree, at least on this day in 1937.

**The new Camp Cleveland. The son of a former president
came for the dedication, but a former king did not.**

Two letters give a sense of Woodmont in the late 1930s. Henry wrote his friend E. Lee LeCompte:

"I forgot to advise you regarding the number of deer killed at Woodmont during the 1937 season."

The number killed was twenty-one and we also killed the following game: 1,200 wild turkeys, 1,425 Mutant pheasants, 1,500 Mallard ducks and that the Club was keeping in the breeding pens the following game: 200 wild turkey hens, 30 wild turkey gobblers, 85 Mutant pheasant hens, 25 Mutant pheasant cocks, 90 Mallard ducks hens, 25 Mallard ducks drakes, 40 pair American Bob Whites to be liberated in the Spring.

Bridges reported to the state of Maryland for regulatory reasons because Woodmont had a special State Preserve permit to raise the birds and to shoot deer for the purpose of serving the members and guests at the Wood-mont table.

In February 1938, Bridges wrote James O. Watson of Cleveland:

You can tell him [a former member] that since you were a member of the Club we have built a beautiful new Clubhouse, also two fine lakes costing $31,000.00, and also have many many other improvements. We have also converted the old Clubhouse into a hatchery for small game, where we raise pheasants, quail and ducks. We also have a large wild turkey hatchery in another part of the preserve. As we have spent about $700,000.00 on the property and made so many improvements, we had to increase the cost of membership.

We also have a lake stocked with bass, the bass fishing opening July 1st and running to November 14th, at which time the hunting season opens and continues to January 1st. You will see that we now have something going on at the Club for nine months in the year. During January, February and March, when the weather is bad, we close up the Clubhouse, or rather the main part of it, and the Booths' stay there during those months and look after it. I go over to the Club about March 10th and get everything ready for the opening on April 1st.

**The Parkview Inn in Berkeley Springs. Bridges
stayed here when not at the club or Shelbridge.**

Yet a third piece of correspondence illustrates another Bridges' interest, deer conservation. In April of 1938, Frank Betz of the Maryland Conservation Department in Baltimore wrote to Bridges about acquiring some

Woodmont deer for the Baltimore City Park, "The herd of deer in the Balto. City Park has become much depleted and an effort is going to be made by a number of interested people to bring back the zoo to its former good standing. Knowing of your interest in such things, the thought occurred to me you might have a surplus of deer that you may contribute a pair to this worthy project. The City will take care of the delivery and will give full to the donor."

Bridges' deer program at Woodmont was as productive as the turkey program. Trapping pens were located throughout the preserve, allowing for the easy capture of animals. The traps were baited with corn; when a deer entered, the doors fell shut behind it. Animals were crated and shipped on the Western Maryland Railroad to buyers. Bridges himself went out into the preserve and shot the venison for the tables of Woodmont. By culling the herd Henry was able to leave the best animals for members and guests.

Happy hunters and fishermen at Camp Cleveland for lunch.

Bridges did not even mind about helping a start-up competitor, provided, of course, it was not in the sand business. In September 1938, Max McGraw of Chicago wrote Bridges for some turkeys. Born in 1883 in Clear Lake Iowa, McGraw started out as a paper delivery boy; by 1900 he was an electrical contractor. An interest in electricity led him to start the McGraw-Edison Company, a manufacturer and supplier of electrical and mechanical products which would eventually have sales in excess of $1 billion.

McGraw wrote Bridges:

I would like to have you send me at whatever you think is the proper time ten hens and two gobblers, so that I can start raising wild turkeys. Would also appreciate any instructions you may care to give me regarding their care, which I may pass on to my game-keeper. I have one man who is an expert on poultry and another who is an expert on pheasants. It looks like our pheasant crop this year will turn out about the same as yours, except that ours are mostly English ring neck pheasants, although we have a few mutants. Recently we chased a wild deer out of our place....We had a lot of doves on our place this year, and I have had quite a little fun shooting them and at them.

McGraw was starting his own Club north of Chicago and buying Woodmont turkeys to start his flock. Bridges replied:

Your letter received, and we will arrange to ship you two wild turkey gobblers and ten hens as soon as the weather gets cooler, as it is a little too warm to ship now. The writer will personally select these wild turkeys, and you will get some fine birds....You should get from these hens next Spring 200 to 250 eggs....About an acre of ground is sufficient for a dozen turkeys. I am enclosing a formula of the grain feed we use. In cold weather feed this mixture in the morning and corn in the evening, also give them some cut up apples.

Colonel Richard K. Mellon, a banker, friend and fellow hunter.

In November, Henry wrote Hiedwohl's Studio in Hagerstown concerning a movie being filmed at Woodmont. "When will you have the titling of the new movie picture completed? Let me know, as I am anxious to have same ready before our opening dinner at the Club on November 14th. When I walk up the steps to the monument at 'Lake Jenkins,' let the title read 'Henry P. Bridges, Secretary of the Club.'" The local production highlighted the many aspects of Woodmont and was shown to the members. It included a piece on the final completion of the Roemer Airstrip.

That same month Bridges wrote Steve Early, Secretary to the President:

I have been greatly interested in the raising of wild turkeys for the past forty years. When I started raising them they were about extinct, and since I started I have raised from 25,000 to 30,000 wild turkeys at my private farm and at the Woodmont Club. What I would like to see would be for the Government to have a wild turkey farm for the purpose of stocking the parks and other land owned by the Government, and also give each State so many wild turkeys each Spring to stock the woods and bring back this wild bird. I consider the wild turkey the most valuable game bird we have in the United States. I conceived this idea when I was in Johnson City, Tennessee. My friend Joe Summers took me down to the State Game Farm at Rutledge, Tennessee, where the Government has spent a considerable sum of money on the quail farm to raise 10,000 quail per year.

A splendid turkey outfit could be installed, with a cost of $25,000.00, and with this equipment 3,500 to 4,000 wild turkeys could be raised each season. The Government has a CCC [Civilian Conservation Corps] Camp in Morgan County, West Virginia, about ten miles from Berkeley Springs, and considerable money has been spent on 5,000 acres there. It might be arranged that they would set apart about 200 acres for the wild turkey farm, and as I am so much interested in the raising of wild turkeys, I would be glad to frequently inspect the turkey farm, and advise the Government how it is progressing. I feel sure if the President would see the Senate Committee on Wild Life Conservation, the funds could be provided from the Federal Excise Tax on fire-arms and ammunition to equip this wild turkey farm and run the same. I would say that with a good wild turkey man to run it, the expenses, including cost of feed, would be about $8,000.00 to $10,000.00 per year. I have in mind a man who had secured some of the finest turkeys I have ever seen from the Santee River in South Carolina, and whom I am sure could be gotten to take charge of the *farm and raise the wild turkeys. He would also be willing to take the trapped birds he has to the said farm and raise the wild turkeys for the Government.*

Realizing that the President is a very busy man, I decided to ask you as a favor to present this matter to him to see if you could not get him interested in making a request to the Senate Committee on Wild Life Conservation, so that sufficient funds could be supplied and the wild turkey farm could be started.

While President Roosevelt declined, the proposal shows again the depth of Henry's commitment to the challenge of repopulating the wild turkey in North America.

Eugene DuPont after Woodmont hunt.

Henry's other conservation interest focused on the white tailed deer, and his mixing the gene pool with Michigan bucks added to the number and strength of the herd. The driven deer drives took place in the preserve. Hunters were strategically placed up and down a valley so that they were not in danger of shooting each other. When they were ready, Bridges signaled the guides to start walking down the valley. The deer stuck together and the big bucks typically came behind a herd of does. The hunters, as if in a shooting gallery, patiently sighted down their rifles looking for the antlers. The challenge came when the does passed at a dead run--many hunters were over come with "buck-ague" and could not pull the trigger amidst the panic of deer running pell-mell in all directions. Only the experienced hunter could hold steady on the moving targets and drop a prize buck.

A driven deer hunt at Woodmont was a great sporting experience for the members and Bridges himself:

My companions were Congressman John Cooper of Youngstown and James T. Begg of Cleveland, Ohio, but only the latter had a license to shoot deer. The guide stationed Cooper and myself at points where deer were likely to pass when the drive got underway. We stood for perhaps an hour when there was a disturbance in the brush nearby and a big buck crossed in the open directly in front of us.

From our vantage point we could see Mr. Begg taking careful aim, but before he pulled the trigger, the buck was out of sight. I looked at the Congressman but before I could say a word, there came sounds of a hurricane sweeping through the leaves and several deer appeared in the open place. This time our friend with the gun blazed away without stopping the hurried exit of the fleeing quarry. Mr. Begg turned around and looked at us for almost five minutes, too stunned, surprised or disgusted to utter a sound, but finally he did speak this one sentence, "A whole trainload of deer and only one shot-a miss!" The deer hunting was sporty and there was never a guarantee that the hunters could get their deer.

Left to Right (Standing, from left): G. Tyler Smith; John Kennedy; Judge Thad A. Cox; Dr. James A. Lyon; Dr. Walker A. Denny; ex-Congressman James T. Begg; and F.S. Henderson. (Sitting, from left): Henry B. Mann; Ott Booth; Henry P. Bridges; Otis R. Johnson; and Dr. U. G. Jones.

November 1938, was an exceptionally busy month for Bridges at Wood-mont. Somehow, he found the time to write Archibald Rutledge, poet laureate of South Carolina at his Hampton Plantation in McClellanville:

> *Your letter of the 20th received. I am enclosing herewith a few pictures I have of wild turkeys. They are on postal cards, but I hope they will serve your purpose. I have greatly enjoyed your articles that have appeared in different magazines. I also appreciate your interest in trying to get me some wild turkeys. If you are able to trap the gobblers in time to send them in December or January it would give them time to get used to our pens so they would breed this coming Spring. When you get them shipped, ship them by express collect to Woodmont Rod & Gun Club, Pearre, Maryland. I am anxious to know if you can come to the Woodmont Club and spend a week or ten days with me. I would like you to come as soon after December 1st as possible. We have more wild turkeys, pheasants and ducks than we have ever had, and the shooting is excellent. I am sorry I have delayed answering your letter, but we have been rushed at the Club for the past two weeks. We had 62 men at the opening Dinner.*

Rutledge was a prolific outdoor writer who did much of his hunting at Hampton Plantation. Bridges was interested in getting some turkeys from the Low Country of South Carolina to add to his flock. Rutledge wrote many turkey hunting stories. This one told the story of his 339th gobbler killed.

> *Suddenly, close to me but off to my right and behind a dense screen of pine needles, I heard the strident call of a gobbler. It surprised me, and for a moment I thought it might be another hunter touching his call. But then I heard a short soft note. That was unmistakable. At least one gobbler, possibly more, was within easy range. I couldn't see him, and I dared not move. Would he pass behind me out of range? Would the rain turn him back? Or would he walk out into the open woods in front of me?*

> *I waited. The rain continued and thunder rolled through the misty forest. I was in a position that seemed to call for breaking all hunting rules, and this I decided to do, for sometimes it's the only way to win. Getting my gun ready for instant action, I simply stepped out of my ambush. The rain hid a good deal from view, but what I saw was enough. A small flock of gobblers was huddled droopingly under some jasmine vines about 30 yards to my right. Apparently they*

were more interested in trying to keep dry than in breakfasting on the dogwood berries.

The instant I appeared, they were galvanized into action. Some dashed through the thickets, two took wing away from me and through dense timber, but a third rose across the open woods and headed for the swamp. As my gun spoke, he dropped like a plummet. It was my 339th gobbler, killed under circumstances I'd never encountered before. A regal bird he was, weighting, as I found later, 21 pounds. A pure wild turkey gobbler rarely exceeds that.

Had he gotten that gobbler at Woodmont, Rutledge no doubt would have used one of the guides who tended to every need of members and guests. Bridges knew he was fortunate to have so many dedicated men at the club's service. He wrote in *The Woodmont Story*:

No, what I am trying to do here is to give the feeling of the rich humor and hilarity bequeathed the club by many of its guides during their long years of service. Of course, they gave more than humor. They gave of their special woodsman's knowledge, they gave of their time and energy. Season after season they served at the club, and although well paid for their services there was really no way to pay them for the zest they added to the lives of those busy men who came to Woodmont for a few day's relaxation and hunting. Then, as now, Woodmont's guides served not only as woodsmen but also as porters and, sometimes, cooks. They were and are men who know the woods, the ways of the animals and fish in forest and lake.

A partial list of the guides in the late 1930's included: Frank Clay, Raymond McCusker, Arby Hoover, Charles Robey, Oscar Bishop, Lester McCuster, Harry Booth, Wilbur McCusker, Allen McCusker, Tom Donegan, Ike Norris, Lou McKnight, Roy Munson, Ott Booth, Edward Exline, Austin McCusker, Allen Booth, Reed Booth, Sunny Ziest and Bitts Exline.

In particular there was Harvey Van Goshen. Bridges described him in this way:

Harvey was a tall, apple-faced man with the loose-limbed appearance of a marionette. He was a man with a phenomenal memory and much musical talent. He was quick witted and had a sharp tongue. He was a man who drank liquor continuously and copiously. The personality that resulted from the combination of these qualities was one that few men were able to forget. Harvey was a favorite of two

United Sates Presidents and scores of other notables including both club members and guests.

Harvey greeted newcomers to the club by handing them a post-card which bore a picture of himself and the legend, "Harvey Van Goshen, General Utility Man and Walking Directory." It was a caption that summed up only part of Harvey's contribution to the club. Officially, Harvey tended Woodmont's furnace, helped gather and saw firewood and, in general acted as clubhouse handyman for everyone.

Harvey was a walking political encyclopedia and could trace the history of both political parties back to their inception. The source of this knowledge was not books, but the Baltimore Sun newspaper which he read cover to cover everyday. Harvey claimed his fiddle was a genuine Stradivarius, but Bridges knew that it was a fiddle that came from the Ashkittles family deep in the West Virginia Mountains.

Harvey was a man of irrepressible wit, and he loved to impress the guests of the club and use words like "disempandimonbility" to impress guests. When asked why he used such big words he would reply, "Why, Judge, I did that because I wanted to talk to you personally. I knew you were the only one who could understand them." Keeping Harvey sober was a Herculean task, Bridges knew, and he struggled to do so the three months of the year he was at the Club.

Henry reported:

One year when he came to the club it soon became apparent that my efforts to keep him sober were of less avail than they had ever been. It was Harvey's custom to sleep on a bunk down by the furnace – he would not sleep upstairs in a room – and, this year, he was spending most of his time on his cellar bunk, too intoxicated to stand. His source of supply was a mystery. So far as I knew he had no means of obtaining liquor at the club.

One morning I went down in the basement to see him. But his bunk was empty. "He's gone," I thought. Then I heard a hoarse whisper. "Shhhhh" a spectral voice said, and then I saw Harvey, not on his bunk, but under it, his eyes rolling wildly. He gestured feebly to the chimney that rose alongside his head. "Hear the music?" he gasped. "It's coming down the chimney. Someone's playing 'Turkey in the Straw' on the violin – just for me. Hear it?"

167

I tried to convince him there was no music. And I also looked about to see if I could find his liquor. All in vain. I could find nothing. It was baffling....Obviously the time had come to take corrective action in Harvey's behalf. So we bundled Harvey off to Mount Hope, a state asylum. It was not until Harvey had gone that I discovered where he had been getting his liquor. I had a large barrel of cider in the cellar. I was letting it get hard to make vinegar. It got hard all right, but it was never served for vinegar. For Harvey had come upon the barrel and, in a short time, had consumed it all.

Harvey came back to serve the club after his institutionalization, but he never gave up the bottle. Many years later, Bridges saw Harvey at age seventy-one walking down a street in Hancock with a bottle in his hand. "'Harvey,' I said, 'why not give me that and let me throw it away!' A look of horror crossed his lined, seventy-one-year-old face. 'Oh , no,' he snapped. 'Why, the doctor told me gin is good for the kidneys!'"

Henry employed the same open manner with guides and members alike. In January 1939, he wrote banker Richard K. Mellon:

I received your letter, and I am delighted to know that you and Mrs. Mellon enjoyed the wild turkeys. I went to my Southern home for the Holidays on December 22nd, and while there went shooting with my friend Haynes Miller. We got up ten coveys of quail and bagged 32 birds.

Eugene DuPont shot with me at the Club this Fall, and he invited me to come to Charleston, S.C. and bring Mrs. Bridges and some of my friends. I was however busy with matters at the Club and could not get away. He has 20,000 acres near Charleston, and the shooting is fine. He has some excellent dogs. Another year, if you and Mrs. Mellon can join us, we will arrange a trip and go down to shoot with Eugene. He has invited me several times to spend a week with him, but it has been at a time when I have been busy at Woodmont. If I can get an invitation to go down in January or February, it would make a nice trip. We all could motor to Johnson City and spend the night at my home, and motor to Eugene's place at Charleston, S.C.

If Mrs. Bridges comes up to the Club this Spring, we will let you and Mrs. Mellon know and motor up to Rolling Rock. I know we will enjoy the trout fishing and going over the breeding pens. Be sure you and Mrs. Mellon come to the Club in April to fish for trout. A friend gave us 150 trout, three to seven pounds, and we are also stocking the lake with other trout. The season opens April 1st, and I am anxious for you to catch some of the seven pounders.

The shooting at the Club the past season was the finest we have ever had. One gunner told me he never saw so many wild turkeys fly over his head, and we had more wing shooting than ever before. We are keeping 200 hens and 30 gobblers for breeders, and expect to get more than 4,000 eggs this Spring. I am anxious to see what results you have with Chukars. I understand you expect to turn out 400 of these birds in the fields and woods. If you are having good results we will try to raise some at the Woodmont Club.

Mellon replied:

"I received your letter and we would like very much to accompany Mrs. Bridges and you to Eugene DuPont's in Charleston, but the additional duties I have now will prevent me from leaving Pittsburgh for sometime. We are both interested in trout fishing and will try to make arrangements to come down the early part of the season."

By the way, you know we have been attempting to have trout fishing at Rolling Rock and last year was quite successful; I was wondering if you could give me some figures as to what trout cost you, what you charge individuals, and what your fish limit is per day; also any other information you are willing to disclose. Our charge last year was $10.00 for the season and $3.50 per day for a guide who must accompany each fishing party or individual. The limit was ten trout per day. Of course, all fishing parties are made up of members of Rolling Rock Club or their guests.

Bridges did as requested:

The Government delivered to me 150 trout. They had promised to give me trout weighing from three to seven pounds, but last summer on account of low water we could not receive them, so they disposed of them to someone else. Those they brought us weighed from one pound to one and one-half pounds. I am trying to get the State to give us 500 to 600 so we will not have to buy any for the Club this coming season. We have been buying our trout from the Paradise Brook Trout Co., Cresco, Pennsylvania. They formerly charged us 80¢ per pound delivered at our lake, but last year they charged $1.00 per pound, so this year we do not want to buy any as we consider this price too high. I will try to get enough trout from the Government and State without cost if possible.

We last year allowed a member with one or more guests to catch 15 trout on the trip, which would amount to $16.00 or $17.00. The Club would only receive from member and one guest $16.00 per day for one day's fishing if they spent the night at the Club so we were losing money. One member would drive from Baltimore and bring his lunch, and as he made five such trips during the season he took away 15 trout. The price of $1.00 per pound we think is unreasonable. We did think of assessing members 50¢ per fish on all trout caught, but the Board of Governors thought it better not to do this. We will therefore only charge members for their accommodations at the Club, so if I can get the trout for nothing, it will be beneficial to our Club.

Fishing was a great part of Woodmont, as this poem indicates:

OUT FISHING

A feller isn't thinking mean, Out fishing, His thoughts are mostly good and clean, Out fishing, He doesn't knock his fellow-men, Or harbor any grudges then; A feller's at his finest when, Out fishing, The rich are comrades to the poor, Out fishing, All are brothers of a common lure, Out fishing, The urchin, with his pin and string, Can chum with millionaire or king;
Vain pride is a forgotten thing, Out fishing,
A feller gets a chance to dream, Out fishing, He learns the beauties of the stream,
Out fishing, And he can wash his soul in air, That isn't foul with selfish care, And relish plain and simple fare, Out fishing.
A feller has not time for hate, Out fishing, He isn't eager to be great, Out fishing,
He isn't thinking thoughts of self, Or goods stacked high upon his shelf; But he is always just himself, Out fishing.
A feller's glad to be a friend, Out fishing, A helping hand he'll always lend, Out fishing, The brotherhood of rod and line, An' sky and stream always fine; Men come real close to God's design, Out fishing.

Edgar A. Guest

ONE DAY TROUT FISHING IN LAKE NESBIT-LANAHAN AT WOODMONT ROD & GUN CLUB, HANCOCK, MD., BY A.B.KNIGHT AND ONE GUEST.

Happy angler after day of fishing at the Woodmont lakes.

Henry may have been too busy to offer a definition of wildlife management. Aldo Leopold did it for him:

> *It is clear by now that there is no short cut to wildlife conservation. Neither laws, nor appropriations, nor bureaus, nor the training of technical men, nor popular agitation of the subject is going to accomplish much until there exists: (a) A critical judgment in the average citizen as to what wildlife conservation is, what methods are sound or unsound, what worthwhile or trivial. (b) A personal enthusiasm for and enjoyment of wildlife in a high proportion of citizens, especially landowners. (c) A much deeper knowledge of natural mechanisms, and a correspondingly sounder technique. To bring these three things into existence is a job requiring generations rather than years.*

When a move for curbing hunting at Woodmont began, Henry applied Leopold to remedy the situation. He wrote the Hancock News on March 13, 1939:

> *"I notice in your paper an account in reference to a bill filed by Mr. S. Ninehart Cohill to prohibit the Woodmont Rod & Gun Club from hunting game except during the regular hunting season."*

> *The present law, which allows Clubs to raise game and kill same, also provides that none of this game shall be shot or hunted outside of regular hunting season, but that the owner has the right to have*

the gamekeeper go to the pens and cut off the heads of turkeys and pheasants, same as chickens, for table use. Members of our Club have never hunted or killed any game outside of the regular hunting season, but when the Club was giving a dinner to distinguished guests we have had the gamekeeper go to the pens and cut off the heads of game needed to serve at the table. This game being purchased by the Club, hatched in incubators and raised in brooder houses and kept in breeding pens, with a feed bill amounting to $5,200.00 per year and with the expense of salary paid to two gamekeepers. I see no reason why the Club should not have the privilege of serving this game on table whenever they so desire.

Also under the law, any individual, club or corporation in the State of Maryland who entirely encloses a preserve and stocks same with deer or elk have the right to kill the deer or elk any time they so desire. The deer in our preserve were purchases by the Club at a cost of $70.00 each, and were released in the enclosure 22 years ago, and the members of our Club and guests have never shot or hunted any deer except in the regular open season. The Secretary of the Club before the hunting season opens in November kills some deer and hangs them in cold storage so that we will have venison to serve to members and guests at our camp during the hunting season.

I do not know of any organization which has done more to protect, raise and increase game in the State of Maryland and any number of other states than the Woodmont Rod & Gun Club. We have turned out of our preserve deer, wild turkeys and other game for a number of years, and any property owner in our vicinity will state that they never had any deer or wild turkeys until the Woodmont Club started. We raise from 5,000 to 6,000 wild turkeys, pheasants, ducks and quail, and any amount of this game goes over the fence and stocks the surrounding country for miles. We have had wild turkeys, ring-neck pheasants and mutant pheasants with bands on killed on Town Hill, Green Ridge, Fulton County, Va. and Morgan County, W. Va. We have shipped the wild turkey and Michigan white tail deer to every state which formerly had the wild turkey which was about exterminated, also to the English, Japanese and Cuban Governments.

Occasionally during the past eight years we have found it necessary to kill does during the deer hunting season instead of bucks, as bucks had become scarce and we had 20 or more does to a buck, and we found it necessary to save our bucks for breeders. Last Fall *during the deer season we killed does, as we had purchased a number of bucks from Michigan the previous March at $70.00 each and released in our preserve. To keep these bucks for breeders, we could not shoot bucks last Fall.*

Mr. LeCompte states that there are 56 individuals, clubs and corporations in Maryland operating under this law, which raise any amount of game to increase the supply of game in the State of Maryland. A number of other States have the same law, and are only too glad to encourage their citizens to invest their money in raising a large amount of game which increases the supply of breeders. A large amount of the game we raise is released in Maryland and some is shipped to the other States for breeders where the wild turkey was about extinct.

The Woodmont Dining Hall.

The controversy also caught the attention of E. Lee LeCompte, who wrote Bridges in April, "I am sure it is gratifying to you to learn that H.B.477, introduced by Mr. Cohill relative to repealing the law regarding game in captivity, received an unfavorable report, which report was accepted by the House, therefore, killing the Bill. I ran into Mr. Cohill on Wednesday last and he informed me I had killed his Bill; but my shoulders are broad, Big Boy, and I can still take it. I am very glad he did not secure the enactment of this legislation." Bridges responded, "I myself and the Club greatly appreciate the fine work you did and also what Harvey Miller did in killing Cohill's bill, and we wish to thank you as it would have injured the Club greatly. Miller said that Cohill jumped on him and told him that he killed the

173

bill, so I expect he blames both of you. Miller said that all the Committee reported unfavorably against Cohill's bill. It seems that Cohill was about the only one in favor of it."

In June 1936, Bridges wrote Maryland Game Commissioner James H. Gambrill, Jr.:

> *As I understand the law The Commission has the right to shorten the hunting season on game birds or animals or entirely close it whenever a petition is filed by so many signers in any county. I wish you would bear in mind that if any petition should be filed in Washington County, I would appreciate it if you would see that the season would not be closed or shortened on any game birds or animals inside the Woodmont Rod & Gun Club fence. As you are aware, we stock our preserve with all kinds of game, and each season we have a big supply. We have been stocking with quail this year, and I feel sure we will have a large amount of quail in addition to deer, wild turkeys, pheasants, ducks, squirrels and rabbits. It would therefore injure the Club if the season should be shortened or closed as the members of our Club come from distant points at considerable expense to shoot the game. Our feed bill in raising game runs as high as $5,100.00 per year and our total expense in running the Club ranges from $15,000.00 to $18,000.00 per year. I am writing this in case any petition should be filed in Washington County, that the Commission would not close or shorten the season on game raised inside our fence.*

Henry was fortunate Gambrill belonged to Woodmont.

Another situation bothered Henry enough to write the White House in July. He wrote the White House:

> *There is a fellow named Ted ------ who occupies the Lock House at Dam No. 6. The C. & O. Canal is now owned by the United States Government including this house. This fellow is the biggest thief in the neighborhood, stealing chickens and other things. Last year we had 1200 pheasants in our pen, and I am sure he stole about 200 of them. I am writing to see if you could get Mr. Delano, President of the Park Board, to notify this man to get out of the house. If we could get him out, it would be a big relief to the Woodmont Club and to the other citizens. He also shoots wild turkeys and deer at nights. If you can arrange to see that we are guaranteed this protection, there will be some game left for you to shoot when you next visit Woodmont. I*

will ask you to keep this confidential, as he is a bad character and would not hesitate to try to burn our Clubhouse down. He does not work and makes his living stealing. I will appreciate anything you can do in this matter. I hope to have the pleasure next Fall for you to come to the Club to shoot some of our blind turkeys. I understand the President accused you of shooting blind ones. If a notice is sent to this man, I would suggest that you have same sent by registered mail, requesting a return card, so the Government will know he got the notice. He is smart enough to tear it up and swear that he did not receive any notice, and remain in the house.

Bridges struggled constantly with the local population, especially a few cantankerous mountain men who constantly poached game at Woodmont. They would cut holes in the fence and enter the preserve to shoot game. And Bridges had good reason to worry about the club burning down. One year Arby Hoover stood by a burning house on the property and watched it burn. Henry happened by and asked who started the blaze. Hoover smiled and said he had no idea. Some people around Woodmont did not mind partici- pating in a little vandalism or poaching. On July 7, 1939, Brigadier General Edwin M. Watson wrote Bridges, "I have your letter of July third and shall be glad to bring the matter to Mr. Delano's attention. It would be a real plea- sure to come up to the Club and shoot turkeys next Fall and I would love to do it, but I can never make any definite commitments while I am on this job." The problem was addressed as Henry hoped.

Still, he worried constantly. Poachers posed a danger both to members and guests as well as themselves. A gun did not care what target it hit. Henry felt no qualms in making sure that an invader who shot a bear on Woodmont property received six months in the house of corrections and a $125 fine. Bridges repeatedly warned the locals to stay off club property. It reached a point where he thought that deer and turkey breeding operations might be poached into oblivion.

Also that July Bridges wrote Vincent Bendix of New York City on capital improvements and club membership.

When we built the new Clubhouse and furnished same, we solicit- ed the Club members asking them to take 40 additional shares of the Club stock at $50.00 per share, which would cost them $2,000.00. Out of our membership of sixty, we got about thirty of them to sub- scribe and take these additional 40 shares. The others did not care to put up $2,000.00 for the additional stock. We however went ahead *with the proposition and finished the Clubhouse in 1930. The depression came, so Mr. Jenkins, President of the Club, put up $33,000.00 and I put up $150,000.00 to pay for these improvements. We both took notes of the Club, on which so far we have waived interest. The amount invested in the Club is about $600,000.00, which includes the original cost plus improvements. During the past 31 years we have purchased eight farms out of money derived from the sale of game and other income. We afterwards built the new Clubhouse, and the Board of Governors then decided that new members coming in should pay an initiation fee of $1,500.00 and purchase forty shares of stock at $50.00 per share, $2,000.00, the total cost of membership being $3,500.00. The dues were raised from $110.00 per year to $165.00 per year.*

Capital improvements were not the only plans to interest Henry. He wanted to write a book on Woodmont and sent along some materials that summer to Archibald Rutledge. The outdoors' writer liked what he saw. (*The Woodmont* story was finally published in 1953)

What a strange man you are! With all your other gifts!.....I have been greatly charmed by it [materials sent for review]. As to whether it would go with a group of other sketches, I think that cannot be decided until we see these later pieces. Shall I send the little book back now or will you send me the material for the new book while I still have your earlier volume? That was a fine afternoon I had with you. It was good of you to give me so much time, every minute of which I enjoyed. The beautiful rifle you gave me I shall always treasure; and I hope to be able to report to you something concerning its exceptions.

Henry wrote back:

I received your letter, and I was sorry you did not make me a visit at the Club while you were up here. Can I count on your coming to the Opening Dinner at the Club on November 14th, and spend a week or ten days with me. I expect it will be a stag dinner this time. I never before have seen so many wild turkeys and other game in the woods as we have this year so the shooting should be excellent. Now in reference to the book, I have been thinking that I would at various times dictate a lot of data to my secretary, and I was wondering if you could set this data up in book form. We could have same published, and if there were any profits we could divide same.

My idea would be to have one chapter regarding my fishing and hunting for 31 years with various people, many of them being very prominent, President Roosevelt, Amos and Andy, etc. I would have another chapter on wild turkeys and how we raise them, a chapter on pheasants, ducks, quail and other small game; a chapter on deer raising and shooting, and a chapter on vermin, how to trap and control same. I would also have a chapter on the Woodmont Club, preserve, giving a description of same. I have told a number of people some of my experiences, and several of them suggested that I write a book regarding same, one of them stating he would be glad to pay $3.00 for the book. Let me know about the matter, and I will get to work and get up the dates, and when you get this you can tell whether or not it will work in with the other book. I am glad you like the rifle, and I am sure that if you hit anything with it, it will be your bird or animal.

The Woodmont Club's game breeding program continued to produce on a large scale. Both wild turkey and deer were sold at a reasonable price. Bridges contacted *Game Breeder & Sportsman* in New York City, "Please advise me promptly if you can get the following ad in the September issue of your magazine, and what the cost will be per month. You can quote on your classified ad and also on various sizes of special ads, FOR SALE: 1,000 Genuine Wild Turkeys, October and November $10.00 each, December, $12.00, January and February, $15.00, March, $20.00. Also- 500 Mixed Breed Michigan and Virginia Deer, January, $75.00 each, February $100.00." This ad furthered Bridges' attempts to sell game across the country.

Meanwhile, Bridges corresponded with Max McGraw on the latter's starting a club in Illinois along the lines of Woodmont, without the deer. McGraw's creation, called the Fin'n Feather Club, proved a success. He had raised 500 turkeys from the stock Bridges sold him, and he was pleased with his flock. McGraw was also interested in the Woodmont by-laws along with Henry's ability to attract an upscale membership.

Henry wrote in September:

I have just returned from a visit to New York with Mrs. Bridges and my two boys, and on my return I find your letter of August 25. In regard to our duck shooting, we take the ducks from the lake to a point about half a mile from the lake, and release them from a hill in the woods, three or four at a time. We have a pen on the hill which will hold about six hundred ducks, and release whatever we think necessary according to the number of gunners. They come down by the blinds on their way to the lake where they have been fed. There is no trouble in getting them to fly as we try them out before the season opens. We have a number of blinds built so there is no danger of the gunners getting shot. As regards the pheasants we have blinds built below the Watson field. The gamekeepers release the birds from the Watson field back of the blinds in which the gunners are located. No gunner is allowed to turn around to shoot but shoots the birds after they fly over the blind going away. Now as to the wild turkeys, I do not think releasing them would be a success. I have never tried it, but during the past three or four years we have put on a turkey drive, using a dog and four guides. We place the gunners in a ravine, and they shoot them over their heads as they fly from one ridge to another, and sometimes from the tops of trees. We have a 500 acre enclosure with a nine foot fence inside our preserve in which is lo- cated our turkey breeding pens. All the turkeys roost in the woods near the gamekeeper's house. No one is allowed to hunt in this 500 acre pen.

Dealing with poachers and conservation programs was draining work. At the end of every summer, Henry tried to take the family on vacation, to someplace like Atlantic City. When New York held a World's Fair in 1939, they went there. A man interested in the future of some species could not help but want to visit The World of Tomorrow.

Bridges big and small atop the Empire State building during World's Fair vacation, 1939.

Back at work that autumn, Henry was busy planning the Opening Stag Dinner, to be held in mid-November. His invitation read:

For the past 31 years various Governors of Maryland have attended the annual opening dinner, which is a stag dinner, at the Woodmont Club. The dinner is given the night before the hunting season opens. This year the dinner will be held at seven p.m. the night of Tuesday, November 14th. It will be a great pleasure to us for you to attend this dinner and shoot with me the next day, November 15th, and we will send you back with your limit of wild game, being two wild turkeys, eight mallard ducks, six pheasants and other small game. Some of the Governors did not know much about shooting, but we supplied them with the game to take home. Each year we have distinguished guests from other States. We already have the acceptance of Babe Ruth and are expecting others. Last year we had 63 members and guests at the opening dinner, and the previous year we had 75. The rules of the Club provide that no dinner coats be worn at any of our dinners. Even when we entertained the six Presidents of the United States, dinner coats were not worn.

Although Woodmont was dedicated to the ideal of male bonding, the outside world could not help but intrude on occasion. By October, the war in Europe was making its presence felt in the clubhouse. Bridges had some choice words to share with his friend, John P. Hoelzel of the Pittsburgh Screw & Bolt Company:

It was a great pleasure to have you and your friend Mr. Wichert at the Club. You tell him that I read in the paper this morning that Hitler was getting ready to make an attack on Switzerland. Also tell him that he had better bridle the Jackass before he gets marching, because I am afraid the Jackass cannot be controlled, and will kick Switzerland off the map. You can tell him if this does happen, you and I will volunteer to help him out at once, and try to save his country....In reading the paper last night I notice that Hitler has quite a number of troops lined up on the Switzerland border, and it also said that he might make a drive through Switzerland, so it looks as though I may soon be able to send you a telegram that "The Jackass is moving." I hope he will have more regard for your country than to invade it.

Bridges did more than posture. Pennsylvania Glass Sand would contribute to the war effort with material to make vehicle windshields, binoculars, plane windows and other war-related glass needs. As a director and vice president of the company, Henry made sure to do his bit.

In October Bridges wrote club members updating them on the events and status of Woodmont.

The Club has been very successful in the propagation of game, and this year we will have more game than we have had for the past 31 years. We have 3,000 wild turkeys, 1,700 Mallard ducks, 1,600 Mutant pheasants, and any amount of small game. The opening stag dinner will be held at the Club on Tuesday evening, November 14th, at seven o'clock. We expect the Governor of Maryland to be present and some other distinguished guests from outside the State. The hunting season will open the next morning, November 15th, for wild turkeys, pheasants, ducks, quail and rabbits (no squirrels). The deer season will open December 15th and run to December 24th, inclusive, shooting bucks only with one or more points. For deer hunting only rifle must be used with soft nose bullets.

All arrangements have been made for shells for 12, 16 and 20 gauge guns, and same can be purchased from Mr. James Booth at the Club. He will also furnish shells at the duck and pheasant shoots, and you can purchase the shells at these shoots. You are entitled to bring three guests to the dinner and any time during the hunting season. During the hunting season the rates will be as follows: $8.00 per day for members, $8.00 per day for the first guest, $25.00 per day for the second guest and $25.00 for the third guest. You may come as many times as you please. The secretary will appreciate it if you will make your reservations as early as possible for the opening dinner, stating the number of guests you will bring, time of arrival and the number of guides you desire.

All this attention to Woodmont did not mean that Henry was slighting his family. Rather in October he contracted with Riley Daniels of M.P. Moller Pipe Organ Manufacturers on behalf of Henry, Jr. to install a three-manual, 1,700-pipe organ at Shelbridge. Henry Jr. was something of a prodigy on the instrument. Dr. Charles M. Courboin, a world renowned organist from the Peabody Conservatory in Baltimore, once heard a recital of young Henry and declared that but five other lads in the country could play as well.

The pipes were installed in the attic and the console in the living room two floors below. But the music led to a new family frustration at Shelbridge. The organ was too loud in the bedrooms and could hardly be heard at the console. So the basement was excavated to move the pipes below the organ. This way, the sound came out of the floor vents. Oftentimes, Henry P. Bridges requested to hear his four favorite hymns: *Nearer My God to Thee, Lead Kindly Light, Jesus Lover of My Soul* and *Silent Night*. There were frequent Music Club groups held at Shelbridge, and young Henry Jr. always played the organ.

Henry Jr. on new Moeller Pipe Organ at Shelbridge.

With the coming of the holidays 1939, Bridges kept busy reading this report from the United States Department of The Interior, Bureau of Biological Survey, Division of Information. It was part of his efforts at self-education in the field of conservation:

> *The wild turkey, symbol of Thanksgiving Day, has been on the road to becoming a vanishing bird, but effective efforts are now being taken to save the feathered American, according to the Bureau of Biological Survey of the Department of the Interior. Once common in favorable territory over most of the United States east of the Rocky Mountains and in the Southwest, the species rapidly disappeared from most of its favorite haunts and is now found only in restricted ranges. What is being done to save and restore the wild turkey was explained in Biological Survey report.*
>
> *The rapid depletion in numbers of the bird that was a common source of food supply for the pilgrims of New England is said by*

some observers to have been caused by various factors, the most im-portant of which probably was the influence of man. The wild turkey is still of some importance as food for residents of certain remote areas. Its greatest economic value today, however, is as an object of sport, though it is largely insectivorous in its feeding habits. Tur-keys, although nonmigratory, are wide-ranging birds, requiring a larger area on which to roam than do most resident species. Some gobblers have been known to travel 15 miles from their roosts. When submarginal lands and wooded areas were taken over for farms, the turkey was driven off its best nesting and feeding grounds.

The turkey derived its name by way of England from Africa. In the seventeenth century, guinea fowl were transported from the Dark Continent to the British Isles. These birds were shipped via Tur-key, for which country the English gave the name "turkey cocke" to the guinea fowl. When the American bird was shipped to England, people became confused and began calling this species the turkey also. The term became popular and has been used for the American bird ever since. The turkey was Benjamin Franklin's choice for the National emblem.

Overshooting did not help the turkey's situation, Survey officials commented. In fact, large takes by too many hunters are in great part responsible for the scarcity of the wild turkey today. Drawing a lesson from the past, when man carelessly permitted other species to die out, Federal agencies, State governments, private organizations, and individuals are taking steps to save the turkey. Fortunately, at-tempts to restore its habitat and increase its population are being made now, before the species comes too close to the danger point. On many of its original ranges throughout the country, however, it is already gone.

In the Ozark region of Missouri, it is pointed out, there is much excellent wild turkey range on which the bird once flourished. The species was nearly extirpated from this region. Now various orga-nizations are spending thousands of dollars in an attempt to restore the bird to the area. In Missouri, the Survey cooperates with the State college in its studies of the turkey's range, food habits, and other factors related to the management of the species. Since 1925, investigations have been conducted in counties where the bird is extinct or on the verge of being wiped out.

The Bureau of Biological Survey and other agencies are doing considerable work in other regions also. In South Carolina and other southeastern States, the Biological Survey has sent some of its best turkey experts to devise methods to protect the bird and increase its present population. Virginia, too, remembers when the gobblers were abundant. Today the Biological Survey and its cooperating State organizations are bending every effort to give the wild turkey sufficient living space in the Old Dominion and to encourage it to breed and raise its flocks in larger numbers.

State interest in the problem is shown by the type of Federal Aid projects that are being proposed by State Game Commissions and approved by the Biological Survey. Under the Federal Aid in Wildlife Restoration Act, Congress appropriates funds to be used by the States for projects designed to benefit their wildlife. Eleven States already are spending part of their allotments to study the turkey and methods of increasing its populations. Projects are under way in Alabama, Arizona, Kentucky, Maryland, Mississippi, North Carolina, Pennsylvania, Tennessee, Texas, Virginia, and West Virginia.

In some sections of the country, sportsmen, finding turkey hunting poor, have purchases lands upon which to conduct wild turkey management and do their hunting. Surplus stock may be liberated on club grounds and be hunted by members. Breeding and nesting studies also are being made to learn more about the turkey's habits. Wild turkeys prefer to breed in rather dense woodlands, usually near a swamp or stream. The birds nest on the ground and remain well concealed in tangled thickets. Even during other seasons of the year, the wild turkey is adept at hiding. Experts often are unable to find a flock of turkeys even when they know the birds are in a certain locality.

Formerly the gobbler was easy to approach, but experience apparently has taught it to be wary of man, for now it is suspicious and difficult to reach. That the wild turkey will ever be as numerous as it was in the early days is improbable, but certainly vigorous efforts are being made to preserve this important game bird. With Federal, State, and private resources available for wild turkey studies and management, the report concluded, the outlook for satisfactory return of the species is hopeful.

The Opening Dinner of November 14, 1939, included Babe Ruth along with such political luminaries as Ohio Senator Taft, Michigan Congressman Roy Woodruff and Maryland Governor Herbert R. O'Conor. The dinner at the Club had the largest gathering of guest in its history with 76 nimrods in attendance. The Babe spoke that night and hunted the next day. "The Governor and the Babe got their turkeys, ducks and their pheasants and there they both acquired sore shoulders and the sense of deep satisfaction that comes from a job well done," reported the Baltimore Sun. "It might be said that the Babe while justly being called the King of Swat, is just another gunner pretty much like the average. He can hit them upon occasion and he can miss them with equal facility. He laid his two turkeys low with a shot each, once he was able to get within range of them."

**Babe Ruth and Henry Bridges after Woodmont
hunt. Autographs were in order.**

Bridges wrote in *The Woodmont Story*:

> *I found Babe to be a man with a great appetite for life. He was the Sultan of Gusto as well as of Swat. One did not have to know him long in order to realize that his broad familiar face served to give expression to a heart as big as his shoulders were broad. Babe's shoulders! I cannot think of them without again feeling a deep momentary confusion. Babe began his day at Woodmont by shooting*

dozens of clay pigeons on the club's skeet field to sharpen his aim – an aim that was better than average – and then he gunned for turkeys and pheasants. By the time he came to the duck blinds he had shot at least one hundred rounds. In the blind, Babe's shotgun boomed for almost an hour as he tried again and again to bag his limit of speeding ducks. When at last he emerged I expected him to remark about the difficult shooting. But, instead, he grimaced and said, "Blast those ducks, Henry. I'm plenty sore now!" For an instant I was confused and deeply worried. What had so displeased my guest? But then he rubbed his shoulder and I understood.

Bridges also wrote Ruth in New York City that:

I am delighted to know you enjoyed your visit to the Club, and I hope to see you again next Fall. I greatly appreciate your sending my boys the autographed pictures, and you will certainly hear from both of them. Their mother is now in Baltimore doing some Christmas shopping, so they will probably await her return before writing. If I get up to New York I will arrange to see you. Tell Jack Matthews to practice up on ducks, so that when he comes to the Club next time, he will be able to get back his $50.00. I also bet Irvine Rutledge (Archibald's son) of Hagerstown, MD on the ducks, and he only got two ducks with 15 shells. Thanking you again for sending the pictures to the boys, I am enclosing letter from my seven year-old-boy, as it is so cute, I knew you would enjoy it. We are still having wonderful shooting for all kinds of game. Remember me to Bob Edge and Jack Matthews. Tell Matthews that since he left, I have won three bets on the ducks, $20,00, $5.00, and a $7.50 box of cigars.

AN AMERICAN CONSERVATIONIST AND HIS MISSION

In 1908, when Henry Bridges and his Baltimore friends reorganized Woodmont, they started out with nineteen members. Henry proceeded to secure members from Chicago, Cleveland, Pittsburgh, Baltimore, Wilmington, Philadelphia, New York and Boston. He personally entertained Maryland governors Warfield, Crothers, Harrington, O'Conor and Trumbull. As club secretary, he took it upon himself to raise thousands of turkey, pheasant, ducks, quail and deer in the preserve. Henry went into the mountains and trapped some wild turkeys to get started; he also paid as high as $150 each for birds when necessary. His mission to repopulate the wild turkey made him an expert in conservation circles throughout America.

The club was thriving and *"The Sage of Woodmont"* was the reason why.

Henry Bridges and the object of his devotion.

CHAPTER 6

THE "SAGE OF WOODMONT" AND HIS WILD TURKEYS: 1940-1957
A Noble Mission Reflecting an Accomplished Life

BEAR HUNTING AND MORE

"The hunt took place quite unexpectedly one day in late fall. It was the first and last time I ever hunted big game other than deer."

It began when Ott Booth came to me with news that a big black bear had been seen on the preserve. Immediately I organized a hunt. Soon a few members then at the clubhouse and myself were afield with rifles to bag the big bruin. We went to a far corner of the preserve, where the bear had been seen. We were standing in the center of an old grassy road, figuring out a strategy for the hunt when suddenly, to our consternation, someone called out, "Here comes the bear!"

And there, about three hundred yards away, was a big, shaggy black bear, and the beast was lumbering down the road straight at us. It was a sight to spur a man's feet into action, the action of running. And that is just what those about me did: they ran. And it is said, discretion is the better part of valor, even a bear hunter's valor. I however, stood my ground. It was the act of a confident man, not a brave one. For I had my rifle and I had a confidence in it that the others lacked in theirs. Any man who must carry a gun nearly the year around, as I must, gets to feel that way about the weapon he uses - he knows what it will do and because he knows this he is not easily frightened.

At any rate, I stood and waited as the bear lumbered nearer and nearer. The others were in a panic, yelling at me, "He'll kill you! Get away from him!" When he was within about seventy-five yards I lined up the sights on his body, just behind the shoulder, and squeezed the trigger. The great animal shuddered, tossed its head as the bullet slammed home, and went down heavily, struggled a few moments and then died. And, as it died, my hunting knife had its first taste of bear blood. He was a four hundred-pound male, a sizable brute, and today rests - or, at least his skin rests - on the floor of the clubhouse lounge.

Whoever said conservation was easy business? Mr. Frank Heller was a local mountain man who Bridges had heard about all his life. He was a legendary hunter and was know for his adventurous inclination to go into mountain caves armed with nothing but a knife. He wrestled black bear to the ground and killed them with his knife and bare hands. Bridges standing up to the bear was courageous, but nothing in comparison to the legendary mountain man Heller.

Bears, no matter how big, were not great consumers of venison and Woodmont's deer population had exploded in numbers. For that purpose, Henry contracted with his trapper and game keeper, Fillmore Bishop and Russell O'Rourke respectively, to trap 100 deer, crate them and deliver them to Pearre Station to be expressed to the State of Tennessee. The trappers would receive $5 for each and every deer that was trapped, crated and shipped. O'Rourke, both raised turkeys at Woodmont and lived on the grounds, could understand their behavior better than any man in the country; it was a skill he transferred to other animals as well. The deer trapping took place in late December 1940.

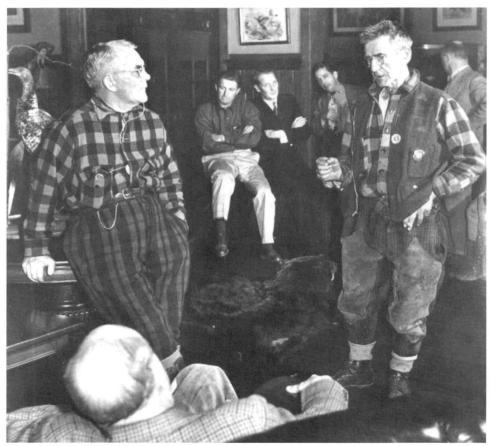

Talking turkey at Woodmont, "Mr. Fox" F. S. Ambrose.

The business of Woodmont continued despite the approach of war. There were orders to fill and preparations to make for different parts of the season, as Bridges explained to Henry Roemer:

For the past three years, after January 1, I come and stay at the Park View Inn at Berkeley Springs, and do not go back to stay at the Club until March 25 to get ready for the opening of the trout season on April 1. We drain the water from the main part of the Clubhouse, and the Booth family have their own section. We close the Clubhouse during January, February and March, as we do not have any members coming during these months and we get rid of running the furnace and fireplaces during those months. The trout fishing will be good this year, and also the bass fishing as we built a trap at the spillway to prevent the bass getting out.

Henry A. Roemer Jr. of Sharon Steel Corporation.

Henry was fortunate in having the Booths at Woodmont for a total of forty-two years. "First was James Booth and his wife, who served Woodmont for thirty-three years. Then James' oldest son, Ott, and his wife, took the places of James and Mrs. Booth. Now, Ott is dead, but Mrs. Ott Booth and her daughter, Nellie, serve the club, as does also Miss Ivy Weltech, Mrs. Booth's niece. It is due to the Booths that Woodmont members and guests have had such excellent food." In particular, Henry depended on Nellie Booth as his "left hand" at Woodmont.

Ms. Nellie Booth, who served Woodmont so well for so long.

The success of Woodmont depended no less on finances than it did game. In early 1940 Bridges worked with H. K. Holmes of First National Bank at Pittsburgh in Pittsburgh to get the interest on a club loan reduced. The collateral on the loan was 10,000 shares of Pennsylvania Glass Sand common stock with a value of $140,000. The appraised value of the assets of Woodmont stood at $581,000, consisting mostly of real estate, while the total indebtedness was $300,000. At times like this, Bridges acted as both Sage and Savior of Woodmont. While others may have asked to see the books, only Henry made sure they stayed balanced.

He also kept a hand in business. Woodmont helped as a kind of secret weapon for Pennsylvania Glass Sand: who could say No in such a setting? Company executive William Woods knew the drill when he wrote Henry in August 1940: A corporate executive wrote Bridges:

> *Mr. Matthews is planning to come to Woodmont on Wednesday evening, September 4 with three of our customers. He would like to have dinner at 7 o'clock, spend the night and breakfast the next morning. Send the bill for this to the Company here. If this is not convenient to you to have them at Woodmont on Wednesday night I wish you would please wire me upon receipt of this letter. The men he is bringing with him are from Fostoria Glass Company and have expressed a desire to stay at Woodmont and to look over our plants at Hancock and if you could have a real nice game dinner of some*

kind for them it would create a good impression and I am sure it will be much appreciated. I hope that it will be convenient.

Pennsylvania Glass Sand narrow gauge engine and cars loaded with sand.

In November, Henry wrote George Huber of the Hancock News with a list of guests and a list of the speakers, often times there were to many speakers, but none the less they were influential:

I am enclosing herewith the list of members and guests who will attend the opening stag dinner at the Woodmont Rod & Gun Club on November 14th. This is the 33rd dinner in the past 33 years that I have been toastmaster, having been secretary of the Club for that length of time. The after dinner speakers will be as follows: Edward E. Jenkins, President of the Woodmont Rod & Gun Club, Hon. Herbert R. O'Conor, Governor of Maryland, Gene Tunney of New York, retired Heavy weight Champion of the World, Bobby Jones, the famous golfer, General L. S. Campbell of the U.S. Army, Washington, D. C., Arthur J. Morris, President of the Morris Plan Corporation and Stuart Olivier of Baltimore, Chairman of the Equitable Trust Company.

This was a part of life that Henry thrived on. And it did not hurt when the man who beat Jack Dempsey in Chicago called the pheasant at Woodmont "anything but an easy shot for a gunner."

Aldo Leopold formulated a Golden Rule of Ecology, "A thing is right when it tends to preserve the integrity, stability, and beauty of the biotic community. It is wrong when it tends otherwise." Everything Henry did at Woodmont fell within the confines of Leopold. That, or he may have

191

been working out his faith and salvation by reestablishing the wild turkey in North America. After all, it was Thoreau who said, "In wildness is the salvation of the world."

Which is not to say Henry ignored more formal aspects of his faith. In 1941, he started a trust with Pennsylvania Glass Sand stock to pay salaries and help with the maintenance of Hancock Presbyterian, St. Thomas Episcopal and The Methodist Churches in Hancock. Henry felt a connection to the residents of Hancock because they were the people from which he had come from. For all his wealth and accomplishments, Henry maintained aspects of his strict Scottish Presbyterian upbringing. He never allowed playing a sport or game on Sunday at his home in Tennessee. And, when he retired for the night (usually at nine o'clock), he read one of his favorite Psalms and then knelt beside his bed to say his prayers. For a number of years Bridges even picked up several children living between Woodmont and Hancock and took them to the Hancock Presbyterian Church's Sunday school. When at Woodmont he always dressed up, went to Sunday school and church, and after church often had a milk shake at Heller's Drug Store near the church. Then he went to visit his brother Tol or his sister Reba, who lived in the old Bridges home on Main Street in Hancock.

A man of faith could not easily be a poor parent, as shown in this letter from Henry to his cousin John Breathed in May 1941:

Shelby and I are certainly proud of Henry. When I was in Johnson City at the recital given by Dr. Courboin and Henry, Henry said 'Daddy, when I am 15 years old, I would like to make a tour. I would have to have a manager, but you do not know enough about it to be my manager, but you would have to finance the trip for me.' I wrote to Dr. Courboin asking his advice, so Shelby and I will follow whatever he says. Dr. Courboin gave thirty recitals last winter and he received $400.00 for each recital. Give my best to Rae and the boy. Will the boy have to go in the draft. I think it is only a matter of time before we will be sending men over, as England will not lick Germany until the U.S. sends about 5,000,000 men.

In May 1941, Henry suffered a personal loss with the retirement of his friend Lee LeCompte from the Maryland State Game and Fish Protective Association. Over the course of twenty-five years' service as state game warden, LeCompte made possible many reforms in the area of game protection. LeCompte and Bridges had worked countless hours to reestablish game. The retirement served as a reminder that Henry's time at Woodmont would be coming to an end sooner than later.

If Henry came to that realization, Archibald Rutledge helped soften with an article he wrote for *FAUNA*, The Zoological Society of Philadelphia quarterly magazine. In *"Can the Wild Turkey Survive?"* Rutledge wrote, "At the great Woodmont Club, in Maryland, Henry Bridges, who knows more about this business than any other man in America, annually rears from two to three thousand pure bred wild turkeys. He has spent forty years in getting the finest strain obtainable. He knows turkeys and he has raised more wild ones than any man who ever lived."

"Did you see an article by me in a magazine called Fauna?" Rutledge wrote Henry in October, 1941. "It has an important reference to you. If you'd not seen it, I should be so glad to send you one. I believe you know how I feel about you and about Woodmont. Some of the very happiest hours of my life have been spent there. Because of your sensitive kindness, I have some memories that are dear to me. It is with real and deep regret that I cannot get up this year. I know you will have great fellowship and fine sport. I know what I shall be missing."

Even after Pearl Harbor, the deer breeding program continued to provide the club with income while giving state game operations strong deer. Nor did the war stop Woodmont's efforts on behalf of Henry's beloved turkey. In December 1942, club member T.W. Phillips of Phillips Petroleum wrote *Pittsburgh Press* columnist John Mock.

I was interested in reading your article a few days ago on the wild turkey and was especially glad to see you bring out the fact, which I have found very few people seem to know, and that is that the domestic turkey we have was taken from a warmer section of this country (Mexico) to Europe by the Spaniards and as a cultivated bird was reintroduced by the early settlers. In my opinion this southern origin largely accounts for the inability of the domestic turkey even when interbred with the wild turkey to survive in our climate when made to rely on their own resources.

The Woodmont Rod & Gun Club (near Hancock, Maryland) under the outstanding management of Mr. Henry P. Bridges is raising wild turkeys in quantities, which are being shipped to various parts of the country for restocking purposes. The turkeys he is now raising are the wildest of the wild. If you are not already acquainted with Mr. Bridges, I am sure you would be interested in meeting him and seeing what he is doing and how he is doing it. if the wild turkey survives it will, in my opinion, be due more to the efforts of Mr. Bridges and the Woodmont Rod & Gun Club than to any other individual or association. As you intimate, many of the so-called wild turkeys used to restock the mountains are part tame turkey stock, and do not seem to have the hardiness to withstand the winters, or sufficient cunning to avoid their natural enemies.

Henry could not have said it better himself.

Woodmont guests and members gather round Henry to behold a genuine wild turkey.

Here is "*Wild Turkey Is Rapidly Diminishing in Numbers; Tame Variety Is Offspring,*" John Mock's article:

"Tomorrow the turkey will replace, for one day, the bald eagle as the national bird. While the forebearers of the birds gracing the festive board were wild denizens of the North American continent, very, very few will have retained that status until served to joyful members of the household."

Years ago, this most magnificent of all American game birds ranged over what is now the eastern section of the United States. Western Pennsylvania was a part of its home. George Washington is said to have killed five of the birds while traveling down the Ohio River, between the mouth of the Beaver River and Mingo, Ohio. Today, the turkey still continues to exist in the wild state in the Keystone State, but far from its former abundance. It is also its probable extreme northern range, being entirely wiped out in the New England States. Since 1915, the earliest period which game kill estimates were gathered and on up to the season of 1941, a total of 108,253 of the birds were bagged. Hungtingdon, Blair, Bedford, Somerset, Fulton and others of the central section of the state supply most of the turkey hunting still to be had.

Numbers Diminish:

The Game Commission has tried valiantly to continue the bird on the game list, but its efforts appear to be an uphill struggle while the turkey population appears to be on the down grade. At least, so it seems when consulting the records of the past five years. In 1936 the bag numbered 5208, the following year it increased to 6619. The record kill was established in 1938, when 6766 of the birds fell to the gunner's aim. In 1939 the number taken was 5191. A year later, 4910 and last season the bag totaled 3484, a decrease of almost 50 per cent over that of four years previous....

Perpetuation Problem:

The most successful method yet devised is to enclose wing-clipped hens in open enclosures, permitting the wild toms to fly in and out at will. Established in wild and isolated mountain slopes, the method has produced birds, which retain some semblance of wildness. How this noble game bird may be perpetuated is still a problem. As far as the hunter is concerned, the bag limit is as low as it can be made, one bird per season being all the law permits. Closing the season always has been nothing more than a temporary protection. Only once has this been attempted – in 1926, when no hunting was permitted. More of the propagating pens and a shorter hunting season may be the solution.

Interesting background:

The domestic turkey, offspring of the wild turkey, has an interesting background. Its origin wasn't with Turkey, from which many believe it derived its name. It is purely a North American bird. When Cortez landed in Mexico, he found the Aztecs had domesticated this bird and he was so impressed with its qualities that, together with his cargoes of valuables, he included a number of turkeys to be shipped back to Spain. Later, Cabot sent some to England and Laudonniere forwarded several consignments to France. The Pilgrims re-imported the birds and in that manner established them on the Atlantic seaboard.

It always has seemed strange that the settlers shot untold numbers of the wild turkey, making no effort to domesticate them, yet their tame turkeys became common stock in every barnyard. The answer is in the act that the present-day tame species is the Mexican turkey, while the modern wild turkey is still the Eastern or bronze turkey, as the margins or their upper tail covers verify – white on the Mexican turkey, brown or chestnut on the northern wild turkey.

Henry also drafted Woodmont game into patriotic service. He sent birds to Secretary of War Frank Knox and FDR, although wartime restrictions kept them from getting to the president in anything but the most circuitous route. Presidential Secretary Stephen Early advised, "Because of certain very rigid restrictions imposed regarding the receipt of food stuff at the White House, I suggest that the turkeys be addressed to me and sent to my home address--7704 Morningside Dr., Washington, DC, and please do not put my title on the address label. In this way I can give them to the President and he is sure to get them. This is strictly confidential." The President was delighted and most appreciative of the game that Bridges sent to the White House. Roosevelt gave the housekeeper instructions in person telling her when he wanted table service of the varied assortment of Woodmont game. He also wanted to know when the game was being served.

In February 1943, President Roosevelt wrote Bridges from The White House, "This is the first opportunity I have had to send you a little line of thanks for that grand assortment of pheasants, wild turkey, Country sausage and venison which you sent to me for Christmas. I have had grand eating as a result and am deeply grateful to you for thinking of me. My best wishes to you for the New Year."

There is no hint of war in this July 1943 letter from Bridges to Eugene DuPont:

We will have plenty of wild turkeys, quail, and other game this year. I have been working on quail for three years, and have been quite successful. I bought two setters in Johnson City at $160.00 each, and I have never hunted over finer dogs in my life. I was hunting in a sage field where the sage was very high. A covey got up and I killed four birds with a 410, two with each barrel. My oldest dog went in the sage field four times, and brought out a bird each time. I thought it was wonderful. Mr. W. E. Wine says I should breed the *dog to some setter. I would like to breed him and get a dog pup out of him. I thought perhaps you might have a fine gyp English setter. All I would want would be a dog pup, and the balance you could have.*

Bridges with his bird dog "Dick." Henry kept setters and pointers at the Woodmont kennels.

Henry received another reminder of mortality in November 1943. He wrote Dr. Paul Fleming of Hagerstown:

Fillmore Bishop, has been warden and head of the deer drives at the Woodmont Club for the past 38 years. About three weeks ago he had a heart attack and a slight stroke of paralysis as per the diagnosis of Dr. Tobias of Hancock. I was out to see Fillmore this morning, and he is suffering with his eyes. About two years ago he went to see Dr. Mish of Hagertown, who said he could not cure his eyes, but could give him something to relieve them and make them look better. I told Fillmore to get his son in law Frank Brooks to take him to your office at 149 W. Washington Street. I wish you would examine his eyes, and see if you can give him some medicine to relieve them, also see if the glasses he is using at the present time are suitable. If he has to have a new pair, get them for him, and send the Woodmont Club a bill for them and also the charge for your examination. The Club will send you a check for same. I have told Fillmore that you will be in your office at 149 W. Washington Street every day except on Sundays and Thursdays from 2 p.m. to 5 p.m..

By way of compensation, there was home. In 1943, Henry Jr. entered the eleventh grade at Mercersburg Academy in Pennsylvania. His first visit away from The Academy came at Thanksgiving, and he went to Woodmont to be with his parents, brother and members of his extended family. Henry P. took his eldest son hunting turkey; after missing numerous turkeys one was finally killed by chance. Henry Jr. learned that day he was not a hunter, and this was the last time he ever hunted. He loved nature and the outdoors but preferred to see the creatures living rather than dead. Henry Jr. was more the musician and his brother Powell the natural hunter. Henry P. bought a 410-gauge Parker shotgun that helped turn Powell into a fine wing shot in the likeness of his father.

Young Powell Bridges with three turkeys killed at Woodmont. He was a natural.

In April 1946, E. F. Warner of *Field and Stream* wrote Bridges, "Don't think I have forgotten all about our correspondence and the idea about making a motion picture down at Woodmont but I have simply been swamped here for the last week or ten days. I am just as interested as ever. I want to run down over a weekend, if possible, and convenient for you, and take down one of the directors from Pathe to look the situation over and have a pow-wow with you. I could probably arrange to go down the twenty-sixth how would that suit you?" Bridges began the process of creating a short movie featuring Woodmont and the conservation of the game species at the club. The project would further his mission by sharing his dream with other sportsmen around the country.

PREDATOR CONTROL AND THE WILD TURKEY

Vermin were a constant concern for Bridges at Woodmont. Aldo Leopold believed, "The wildlife conservation movement is divided over several basic issues, one of which is control of predatory species. Many (but no means all) sportsmen set a higher value on game than on other forms of wildlife, and are willing to sacrifice non-game to game species on a large scale in the form of 'vermin control.'" In addition, Leopold wrote, "First of all, a refuge is not a refuge unless it is surrounded by hunting grounds. The purpose of a refuge is to overflow....Secondly, a refuse is not a refuge unless the closed area is freed from vermin and provided with the necessary food-plants, water, fences, salt, etc., to make the breeding stock as productive as possible." Those ideas changed.

According to Curt Meine and Richard Knight:

Leopold also understood the fundamental importance of predator-prey relationships, and how they had been widely misconstrued by wildlife managers (including himself at a younger age) intent on increasing game populations. After observing firsthand, in Mexico's Sierra Madre, "an abundant game population thriving in the midst of its natural enemies," he encouraged "those who habitually ascribe all game scarcity to predators or who prescribe predator control as the first and inevitable step in all game management" to reexamine their premises. Reflecting the rapidly changing state of ecological knowledge during his lifetime, Leopold hoped to see changes in the profession's views as more information became available on predator-prey relationships.

**Sign at crafted by Bridges at the Original Camp
Cleveland instructing hunters on predator control.
The mature Aldo Leopold did not agree.**

On this matter, Henry was definitely behind the curve. He believed all vermin had to be trapped, shot or poisoned in order to protect the game species at Woodmont. In 1946, he wrote:

> *In 40 years experience in operating the 5000 acre game preserve at the Woodmont Rod and Gun Club, Hancock, Maryland, I have been secretary of this Club and active manager of it, and my experience in raising all kinds of game on the preserve is that if you want good shooting you have to control the vermin, consisting of wild cats, red and gray fox, minks, weasels, skunks, hawk, crow, house cat and the great horn owl. I have known the wild cat to kill wild turkeys on the nest, one every night for 22 nights, destroying also the eggs. The 23rd night we put up a dead turkey on a tree with a #1 trap and caught this cat by the toes, the writer catching three wild cats by the toes in a #1 trap. ....I find that the house cats destroy much quail, young rabbits, squirrels, and songbirds. They become wild and stay in a hollow log during the day and hunt at night the same as other vermin. In these box traps you can get all the house cats, any number of pole cats and opossums but the wild cat and the fox will not go in them.*

> *Also, it is important to destroy the snakes on your preserve, including black snakes. Every nest they run across they destroy the eggs and many times kill the bird on the nest. We have killed black snakes that had swallowed a full grown gray squirrel. Now, to get the Horn Owl put a 4 ft. post in an open place in the woods or in a field at the highest point out in the field. Get a No. 1 trap and fasten the chain to the side of the post and fasten the other side of the trap with bail wire, so that when the hawk or the owl lights on this trap he will not knock it off but you will catch him by the feet. You will get all of them that way.*

> *We had a trapper for 38 years, Fillmore Bishop. We always started Fill trapping on January 1st the day after the hunting season and he trapped until March 15. Fill was very successful in getting all the vermin except the fox. The red and gray fox were too smart for Fill. He would only get one or two a season. Therefore, the fox increased in the past four or five years since the war to such an extent that they destroyed all the rabbits...and they also destroyed 1700 quail, 2000 pheasants and nearly all the ruffled grouse. They also destroyed the wild turkey in the spring when they were setting and a number of hens with young ones. We found out that the game in the preserve*

was being destroyed by the gray and red fox to such an extent that it became serious, so we employed a trapper who is an expert, to trap the foxes and all kinds of vermin. He began trapping the first of October and trapped until about the first of March.

If you allow the fox to increase you are not going to have any game and what is the use of the different States spending an enormous lot of money on raising quail, wild turkeys and other game to be turned out to feed the foxes and other vermin. The gunner who pays his license is not getting any benefit from this money spent. In Maryland, since the foxes have become so plentiful, a number of farmers have said to me, "I had plenty of rabbits and quail on my farm, but since the foxes have gotten so numerous, I have none of that game at all, and when the State puts out the game on my farm and the neighbors' farms, in a few weeks the foxes have destroyed it all."

Maryland, Pennsylvania and West Virginia are doing everything they possibly can to destroy the foxes and other vermin. They have all increased the bounty on the red and gray fox which will pay in the long run in giving the sportsmen plenty of game to shoot when they go hunting. The State of Pennsylvania in 1945 paid $160,000 bounty on red and gray foxes. I hope the States will increase their bounty on foxes, wild cats, and other vermin, so that the hunters who have paid the license, when they go into the woods will have some game to shoot. There are a few counties in Maryland, such as Baltimore, Howard, Montgomery and Kent Counties who have fox clubs, such as Elkridge Kennels, Green Spring Valley Kennels, and other Clubs in these counties.

If the sportsmen in these counties are willing to let these Clubs have foxes and turn them out for hunting that is a matter between themselves, but that is no reason why a number of counties who do not have fox clubs should be prohibited in their way from destroying the red and gray fox and other vermin, and I think it would be a wise decision for these Clubs not to try to prohibit counties that do not have these fox clubs from destroying the red and gray fox as I feel sure they will not be able to get anywhere by trying to prohibit the killing of the red and grey fox in the State of Maryland or any other State. To save the game on the 5,000 acre preserve we employed Mr. Ambrose to do the trapping for the Club from October first to March first.

The vermin extermination program was nothing if not effective at Woodmont. Bridges posted a sign that was at old Camp Cleveland encouraging hunters to shoot all vermin on sight in the preserve.

On the subject of game propagation Leopold wrote, "The wild-life conservation movement is an attempt to prevent our expanding population from destroying its own opportunities for sport. Management is a way to maintain a supply of game, and other wild life, in the face of that expansion." Bridges was aware of the exploding human population and its effect on game and game management. His mission reflected Leopold's 1925 observation that, "We have learned that game, to be successfully conserved, must be positively produced, rather than merely negatively protected." This Henry tried to do.

Leopold also wrote on The Goals of Wildlife Management. The wise manager "understood that wildlife management worked toward several goals. Today we generally recognize four basic objectives of wildlife management: (1) to produce sustainable yields of exploited wildlife populations; (2) to control overabundant wildlife populations; (3) to recover rare and declining wildlife populations; and (4) to maintain intact wildlife communities as essential components of healthy ecosystems." Here too Henry agreed, along with Leopold's notion about "the art of making land produce sustained annual crops of wild game for recreational use." When Leopold declared, "In short, we have learned that game is a crop, which Nature will grow and grow abundantly, provided only we furnish the seed and a suitable environment," he was preaching to a choir that included Henry Bridges among its foremost members.

Henry wrote an article, "*The Genuine Pure Wild Turkey*," reflecting his beliefs.

"For 48 years I have been raising wild turkeys. During this period I have raised over 30,000 of them, and have spent $150,000.00 in raising them."

**In front of the Clubhouse with turkeys from a day's hunt—
many drumsticks, even more feathers.**

I have read quite a number of articles about wild turkeys, and frequently see pictures of wild turkeys that have been published. A great many pictures show them not to be genuine wild turkeys but half-breeds, and some of them are tame turkeys with a small percentage of wild blood in them. Frequently the complaint is that these turkeys go to some farm house and are sold on the market. If you have the pure wild turkey, you will have no trouble with them going to some house or farm.

We have 130 wild turkey hens and 14 gobblers in four turkey pens, and their wings are clipped so they cannot fly over the fence. We will get about 3200 eggs from them, and expect to raise 2500 wild turkeys this year. We have shipped our wild turkeys to nearly every State in the Union that has wild turkeys, also to England and Cuba. The real wild turkey never becomes tame in the pens, and if anyone enters the pens they will try to fly out. The young ones which we release in October go right to the woods and are as wild as any wild turkey hatched and raised in the woods.

This year we secured 28 wild turkeys from North Carolina raised from eggs gotten out of the woods, and are breeding the gobblers to our hens. Next Fall we will have as fine wild turkeys as ever were raised in captivity. If you put out genuine wild turkeys, they soon return to their natural habits, and the gunners will have a hard time in shooting them. In a few years you would find your State stocked with wild turkeys. I have promised to send some of these birds to your wild turkey farm this year, so you can use the gobblers and cross them with your wild hens. We have never had any trouble in stocking our preserve, but the gunners claim that they are too hard to shoot. Most of our wild turkey shooting is wing shooting.

We hatch our eggs in incubator, and put little turkeys in brooder houses with a sun porch and roosting shed. We have taken a personal interest in your wild turkey farm in Tennessee, and I have endeavored to help your gamekeeper in every way possible to make it a success. I am sure if you continue to improve your stock until you have the genuine wild turkey to liberate in your preserve, you will not have any trouble in stocking your forest with wild turkeys, and will have no trouble with them going to people's houses and farms. In the past five years by carefully selecting our breeders, and getting wild turkeys from the woods, we have improved our wild turkeys so that at the present time I do not think there are any better wild turkeys in the forests than those we have in our breeding pens. When we send some of them to your turkey farm this year I am sure your gamekeeper will say that they are the finest he has ever had.

I have also frequently talked with your faithful and experienced Commissioner, Joe Summers of Johnson City, Tennessee, who is a lover of outdoor life and of fishing and hunting. He is also a great protector of game and fish in your State, and he is doing everything possible to make Tennessee one of the greatest fish and game States in the South.

In May 1946, Bridges wrote Harry Truman to see if he could get another chief executive to sit in the club's President's chair:

I realize at the present time it would be impossible for you to make this trip but hope that you will come up some time in July or August when the bass fishing is unusually good in our private lake. My friend, Ex-Senator Fred Wolcott of Connecticut, who at different times has been my guest at the Club, told me that he had traveled all over Europe and the United States and that he considered this the finest Club of its kind any place. We are anxious for you to visit the Club and to occupy the Woodmont Rod and Gun Club Presidential Chair. Since the Club was organized in 1870 by Admiral Bob Evans there have been six Presidents to occupy the chair and we put a silver plate on the chair with the name of the President and the date that he occupied the chair. Up to the present time we have had Gar-

field, Arthur, Benjamin Harrison, Cleveland, Hoover, and Franklin D. Roosevelt, and we hope to have you as the seventh President. My friend Mr. Frank Yates enclosed me some data about the Club, which he asked me to enclose with the invitation.

Truman wrote the following letter from The White House:

THE WHITE HOUSE
WASHINGTON

May 25, 1946

Dear Mr. Bridges:

I appreciated most highly your cordial invitation to visit the Woodmont Rod and Gun Club and I hope that conditions will settle down to a point where I can take advantage of your invitation.

Every time I make a firm commitment, however, it has to be cancelled because of conditions around the country.

Sincerely yours,

Harry S. Truman

Mr. Henry P. Bridges
Secretary and Treasurer
Woodmont Rod and Gun Club
Berkeley Springs, West Virginia

President Truman to Henry Bridges: "I hope that conditions will settle down."

The advent of the Cold War did not allow a man to slip away easily for a day of hunting or fishing, but Henry persisted. In June he wrote a follow-up,

I received your letter and am delighted to know that when things settle down you will accept my invitation to visit the Woodmont Club. I expect to give you and your friends a special dinner as I did

to President Delano Roosevelt. In my previous letter I stated that we would like you to come in July or August when the bass fishing is good. Also the bass fishing will be good in September and October and it will be perfectly agreeable for you to come up with your party of twelve friends any time between now and October 20th. After October 20 it is a little cold and the bass may not bite.

When I hear that you are coming I will make all arrangements to serve you all some wild game and try to make your trip to Woodmont a very pleasant one. I know of no other place in the United States where there is more beautiful scenery or a better place to rest and take a vacation.

Despite his best efforts, Henry could never show Truman enough reasons to visit Woodmont.

He had better luck writing. On June 10, 1946, Bridges informed. Hugh Grey of *Field and Stream*:

I received your letter enclosing check for $50.00 for my article. I did not expect anything for this but appreciate your sending the check. My two boys, Henry, Jr. who is at Princeton preparing for a Presbyterian preacher, and Powell, who is living at my southern home in Johnson City, Tennessee, have had a savings account ever since they were five or six years old and have each saved up to the present time $18,000. I endorsed this check and sent it to Powell telling him to cash it and put half in Henry, Jr.'s account and half in his own. I told them I had received it for an article which I wrote and sent to Field and Stream. Some time ago I sent an article to Outdoor Life telling them they could have it if they wanted it and they sent me a check for $35.00.

The members in the Woodmont Rod and Gun Club and some of the guests in the past number of years have been after me to write a book on my forty years' experience in the Club, our Club being the oldest hunting club in the U.S. We have entertained six Presidents and a number of attorney generals and senators, congressmen and governors in the U.S. Also some foreign ambassadors and generals of foreign armies. I would have a chapter on the Woodmont Club, another on Hunting Deer, another Hunting Wild Turkeys, another Raising Wild Turkeys and Other Small Game, another Trapping Predator Animals and Other Vemin Which Destroy the Game, and another chapter of my experiences in taking out a number of very prominent citizens hunting and fishing, such as President Delano Roosevelt, Amos and Andy, Babe Ruth, Gene Tunney, General Mow of the Chinese Army and any number of Senators and Governors and important business people. I have quite a number of pictures of hunting, etc. also of the old guide who made the Presidential Chair 76 years ago out of native hickory and of the six presidents who have occupied the chair. Also I have pictures of the old fiddler and of the guide who played the accordion for a number of years to members and guests. Both of them also played for President and Mrs. Wilson from Washington.

What do you think of my publishing the pictures along with the book of a number of hunters, guides, etc. A congressman and his wife were at the Club and I was telling them of the different experiences I had with the president of the Pittsburgh Steel Co., the Vice President of the Pennsylvania R. R. and a number of others in shooting with them, and they said "Mr. Bridges, if you would write a book it would be very interesting and we would be willing to pay $3.00 for the book any time." So I have about decided to go to work on it and finish it up next spring. I would appreciate it if you would talk it over with my friend Warner as I would like to get his views on the matter.

But then in September he received another disappointment when General Omar Bradley, declined Bridges' invitation to hunt Woodmont and attend the opening stag dinner on November 14. Admiral Chester Nimitz and General Dwight Eisenhower also sent their regrets. Instead, the speakers for the opening dinner included Senators Burton K. Wheeler of Montana, Harley M. Kilgore of West Virginia and Bourke Hickenlooper of Iowa.

The dinner was held at about the same time Bridges completed "*Wild Turkey*," an RKO Pathe short directed by Eltinge F. Warner and photographed by James C. Clark. The movie depicted the turkey farm where thousands had been raised; the club house turkey hunts; and Camp Cleveland at the Lakes. The film explained how Henry raised turkey and shipped them to states, individuals and clubs all over The United States. The governments of England, Japan and Cuba had received birds and Bridges expected to ship to Sweden and Italy. Bridges was certain of the wild turkey's extinction without his efforts. Each year, the club raised 1,500 to 2,000 wild turkeys and received 5,000 wild turkey eggs; of that number, Woodmont kept 3,000 and sent the remainder around the country. The movie was shown at the Majestic Theater in Johnson City. The marquis read "See Johnson City's own Henry P. Bridges." *Field and Stream* made sure the film was shown at a number of theaters.

In 1947, Henry gave the Hancock Presbyterian Church a set of chimes and a Wurlitzer Electric Organ. Several years later he replaced it with a Hammond Organ, which Henry Jr. gave a recital on. Among the guests was Ferguson Woods, senior minister of First Presbyterian Church in Johnson City. Young Powell was a mischievous lad, and on the trip from Woodmont to the Church he slipped an empty liquor bottle into Woods' coat pocket. When he was crossing Main Street in front of the church, Reverend Woods reached inside his pocket only to pull out the bottle. Bridges and all the church members got a laugh from the prank.

Henry and family at Hancock Presbyterian Church.

As a church elder, Henry often made decisions without consulting anyone in the family. One day he took Shelby, Henry Jr. and Powell to the Hancock Presbyterian Church to show them a newly installed stained glass window. The inscription read, "Given by Henry Percival Bridges Jr. and Shelby Powell Bridges in memory of their parents." Henry Jr. reported, "This was the first news that we had heard of our parents' demise or of our memorial window." Bridges also dedicated windows to his Sunday school teacher and his parents. The following year Bridges added a copper plaque to mark the place and date of the cannon ball hitting the church, courtesy of the battery under direction of General Stonewall Jackson.

Henry made a different kind of contribution in 1955 to the First Presbyterian Church of Johnson City—he had the pipe organ from Shelbridge disassembled and reinstalled in the church, at a cost in excess of $12,000. The organ was dedicated on September 12, and Dr. James L. Fowl of Chattanooga Tennessee gave the dedicatory sermon. Dr. Fowl praised Bridges as "a gentleman, a good Presbyterian and a friend to the church."

Pennsylvania Glass Sand expansion.
The company continued to grow in the post-war era.

Henry's passion for Woodmont and the wild turkey showed no sign of cooling as he reached the age of seventy. He was that individual described by Archibald Rutledge:

> *I admire a good turkey hunter chiefly because such a man displays patience, enthusiasm, acute woodscraft, game sense, and quiet hardihood undaunted by rain, by cold, by long tough miles, by disappointment; not turned from his fine grim purpose even by feminine sarcasms from his Lady, who may pour it on him for neglecting her and all else in life for what she, in her resentment, terms "a poor miserable bird in a god-forsaken mountain." But if he happens to bring home one of these bronzed kings of the wilderness, she has ways to make his long and arduous campaign seem worthwhile.*

**Archibald Rutledge, Poet Laurette of South
Carolina, outdoorsman and hunter. At his family home
Hampton House, McClellanville, S.C., 1948.**

But the hunt could not go on indefinitely. On December 4, 1950, Henry was operated on for colon cancer. (He was never told that the doctors had found cancer). He went to his home at Johnson City, Tennessee to complete his convalescence, only to be stricken with a serious case of pleurisy. His son Powell, a freshman at Davidson College, wrote letters for him, including one that his father was sick in bed with a trained nurse. Sometimes, laughter made the best medicine. Henry returned to Woodmont early in 1951.

A year later, Henry started the Bridges Ministers' Trust for the education of Presbyterian clergy at Hampton-Sydney and Davidson Colleges and at Union Seminary. He used 5,000 shares of Pennsylvania Glass Sand stock to set up the fund. His intention was to enable students to go to seminary and avoid debt. Students from either the First Presbyterian Church in Johnson City or Hancock Presbyterian Church were eligible. This was the same year Henry Jr. left Union Seminary to obtain his Masters in Sacred Music at Union Theological Seminary in New York City. After this he studied pipe organ in Paris before becoming Minister of Music at Westminster Presbyterian Church in Bluefield, West Virginia.

In 1953, Bridges finished *The Woodmont Story* and at age 74 continued to be the lifeblood of the club. He dictated the manuscript to Al Capon of Berkeley Springs, a writer for the *Morgan Messenger*. Archibald Rutledge, poet laureate of South Carolina, crafted the manuscript into a fine book. Some 2,165 copies of the book were produced by A.S. Barnes & Company of New York City. Henry explained in the forward that the purpose of his account of Woodmont was to assist interested conservationists in learning more about raising wild turkeys and to set a sort of guide for other sportsmen who might care to develop private hunting and fishing grounds. Bridges' fraternity brother and close friend Addison E. Mullikin remarked, "I have examined carefully *The Woodmont Story* and you are to be congratulated on a real accomplishment. It has added considerably to your stature as a hunter and a man of broad view. I think it has brought some distinction to western Maryland and has been a matter of satisfaction to all members of the Club and many of your friends who are not connected with it."

Bridges shares his literary venture with a club member.

But Henry was not finished writing. In 1954, he completed an article, "*Raising Wild Turkey*," which further reflected his thinking on conservation practices and the propagation of the American Wild Turkey. He was responding to other articles on the subject of raising wild turkey in pens for the purpose of hunting and releasing the bird back into the wilderness. The debate over the best way to achieve reintroduction into the natural environments prompted the article. Conservationists were beginning to trap wild turkey and relocate them as a better means of propagating the birds, Henry wrote:

In reading your Conservationist Magazine, I have noticed several articles written in reference to wild turkeys that are raised on wire or otherwise. These articles state that when they are released they never return to their native wildness but are semi-wild and can be easily shot and gotten by predatory animals. The writer (Henry P. Bridges) has been personally interested in trying to bring back the wild turkey in the United States, having shipped them to nearly every state in the Union that has wild turkeys, also to Clubs, individuals and to foreign countries.

I have been Secretary of the Woodmont Rod and Gun Club for 39 years. We have raised 33,000 wild turkeys and have spent $150,000 on raising them. Our experience, and the writer's personal experience, has been that you get a genuine 100% wild turkey out of the woods, cut its wing and put it in the breeding pen, the offspring of such turkeys never become tame. We have at the present 150 breeders with their wings cut, in our breeding pen, and even though we have some that have been there for a number of years, as a wild turkey lives fifteen years, we find that these birds have never become tame. They are as wild as the day we put them in there, and the offspring from these birds, after being liberated in the woods, return to their natural wildness in a few months. The ones that we liberated last year are as wild as any turkey you could find in the woods. As soon as they see you they either run or fly.

The reason why some people write articles about wild turkeys, complaining of their not being wild when liberated, is that they have run across turkeys which are half breeds or have tame blood in them, and should they have tame blood in them, I admit, they will not return to their original wild state. Some few wild turkey breeders in the United States have the genuine 100% wild birds. Two years ago we got 28 wild turkeys out of North Carolina. They were raised from the eggs of wild turkeys out of the woods. We crossed these with our wild turkeys and this summer we have raised 700 or more of the most beautiful wild turkeys I have ever seen. Everybody who sees them says they are certainly 100% wild. They have the shape, long legs, long necks, small blue heads, the brown tipped feathers and beautiful sheen. Although hatched in May the sheen is beautiful now. When they shed out next year the sheen will be much higher in color and more beautiful.

The writer has been doing everything possible to persuade the States on their wild turkey farms, also Clubs and individuals, to get some stock from the Woodmont Rod and Gun Club to put in their breeding pens, as we know when they raise young from this stock they will have no trouble about their returning to their natural state when liberated, and will make a great success in stocking the woods with wild turkeys.

In March 1954, Supreme Court Justice, William O. Douglas, stopped to say hello to Bridges and spend a night at Woodmont. The justice was determined to walk the entire length of the C & O Canal from Cumberland Maryland to Washington, a distance of 189 miles. Douglas's efforts were to publicize a proposal to have a parkway built along the government-owned Canal. A band of naturalists, newsmen and other companions set out from Cumberland on the expedition. Justice Douglas believed camps or shelters could be erected every ten miles for hikers and riders on horseback or cyclists. The justice was among those advocating integration of the canal into a wide-range recreational development. The nearby woods together with the Potomac would be made into a great hunting and fishing paradise for millions of area residents.

In November, the Duke of Windsor, Edward wrote Bridges from Paris, "I am interested to know about the Woodmont Rod and Gun Club, and the Duchesse of Windsor and I look forward to receiving a copy of your recent book *The Woodmont Story* as soon as it is forwarded from the British Embassy in Washington. Unfortunately we do not reach America until after the close of your hunting season which deprives me of the pleasure of partaking in the fine game shooting you so generously offer at your Club at Hancock Maryland."

Bridges responded:

I received your letter of November 25th and am sorry that you will not return to America until after our hunting season has closed. Next fall our season will open on November 15th and I will write you in sufficient time so that you perhaps can make plans to come to Woodmont and hunt with me. If you would like to bring the Duchess along with you I would be delighted to entertain her at the Club. I am sure she would enjoy Woodmont, particularly since her uncle, S. Davies Warfield, was one of its founders. We have quite a collection of antiques, mounted trophies of the hunt, and pictures that delight our visitors. We certainly hope that next Fall we will have the pleasure of entertaining both of you here at Woodmont.

Henry had long been interested in having Dwight Eisenhower visit Woodmont. Finally, in September 1955, President Eisenhower wrote him from Denver:

THE WHITE HOUSE
WASHINGTON

Denver, Colorado
September 7, 1955

Dear Mr. Bridges:

Governor McKeldin has transmitted to me your very kind invitation to hunt at the Woodmont Rod and Gun Club some weekend during November. I am most appreciative of your kind suggestion, but a look at my calendar for that period tells me that I cannot possibly accept. I have a number of guests from foreign countries coming to Washington in November, and a great deal of my otherwise free time is thereby committed.

Won't you please convey an expression of my thanks for your cordial invitation to the members of your Club?

With best wishes,

Sincerely,

Dwight D. Eisenhower

Mr. Henry P. Bridges
Woodmont Rod and Gun Club
Woodmont, Maryland

President Eisenhower's letter to Bridges.

Henry worked until the very end of his life to promote Woodmont. Alas, the tradition of presidential hunting parties ended with Franklin D. Roosevelt.

A LIFE'S ACCOMPLISMENTS

Henry sensed that his life was beginning to wind down. The correspondence he received seemed to confirm it. There were numerous letters from old friends praising his life as a worthy one, full of accomplishment and great deeds. In November 1955 Eugene O'Dunne wrote from Baltimore:

"I was much interested in the 'Brown Section' of the Sunday's Sun and in its account of your life's activity there."

It takes me back, fifty years or more, to when we had law offices together at 806 Fidelity Building [in the city]. You were then a sly, rosy cheeked young lawyer. I can imagine no more glorious and satisfactory life than you have had, and I congratulate you on the success you have made of it.

The shadows for me are lengthing. If "life begins at 80," as the program says, I am already on the way. I still summer at the Bingalow at Blue Ridge Summit Pa., but am no longer active, in any line, due to heart and sight. Disposed of the car, at the end of this summer. Will have to depend on taxi service next season. I have a vague recollection of visiting your Club, one afternoon in the summer, many many years ago, and of a porch on the west side, overlooking a river, but that is all I recall. With renewed congratulations on your work and your success in it.

In late 1955, former President Herbert Hoover wrote Bridges from The Waldorf Astoria in New York City, "That was a grand array of birds which you sent to me and a magnificent sight to see. Some friends shared the pheasant with me and we are all of one mind--that we have never tasted more delicious birds. We all offered grateful thanks to you. I do want to express my deep appreciation to you for your generous and friendly thought of me." Bridges loved to send Woodmont game to his friends, and this tradition continued up to the end of his life.

In December of 1955, Henry Jr. became engaged to a Bluefield girl, Daisy Caldwell Wade. The Bridges family arrived at the Wade home in two cars on the day of the wedding rehearsal Shelby drove from Tennessee in her Cadillac. She was elegantly dressed in jewels and furs. A few minutes later, a beat-up green Plymouth with smoke pouring out the tail pipe arrived from Maryland. Henry P. Bridges got out wearing a rumpled suit littered with turkey feathers. He opened the trunk and picked up a dead turkey by the neck. He handed it to Daisy's mother, Earnestine. She accepted it with a big smile, great charm and a kiss. Henry's pride and joy, the wild turkey, was perhaps the greatest gift he could give anyone.

Justice William Douglas wrote Bridges in the spring of 1956, "Those of us who hiked the C & O Canal in 1954, are having a reunion on April 28, 1956. We are going to have dinner that night at 6 o'clock at the Hilltop Hotel in Harpers Ferry. We would like very much to have you attend as our guest. We know that you are an ardent conservationist and we are anxious this year to celebrate the plans which the National Park Service has prepared for the preservation of the C & O Canal property as a National Historical Park." But Henry could not attend because of failing health.

Theodore Roosevelt's son Archibald Roosevelt wrote Bridges that April about a fishing trip to Woodmont that he would attend in June. He invited Bridges to the Boone and Crockett Club luncheon at Sagamore Hill; this was the oldest game, sportsman and conservation club in the United States, founded by Theodore Roosevelt. Again, Henry could not attend for health reasons. Prior to his hospitalization Bridges had been toastmaster at forty-nine consecutive opening Stag dinners at Woodmont. But this part of his life had come to an end.

Bridges at his 79th birthday celebration at Shelbridge.
Seated left to right, Hanes Lancaster Sr.; U.G. Jones; Henry
P. Bridges; William Tomlinson; and Irvine Rutledge. Standing
left to right, Allen Harris Sr.; Ward Freiberg; Leonard Hasche;
Lee Harr; Thad Herndon; Dan Wexler Sr.; Nat Winston; Fred
Lockett Sr.; Jack Cummings; Vint Thomas; Ferguson Wood;
Allen Wofford; Mac Boyer; Jim Preas; Dave Miller; Adam
Bowman; Ed Brading; Jim Epps; and Perry Hunter.

On December 4, 1956, Maryland Governor McKeldin, a former guest at Woodmont, wrote Henry that he was saddened to learn of Bridges recent hospitalization at Johns Hopkins in Baltimore. Herbert Hoover also wrote. Henry's son Powell, then in his final year at Vanderbilt University Law School, recalled conversations with his father about his illness. Although never told about the cancer, Henry knew that he had it. He died April 22, 1957 in Johnson City Hospital at the age of 79.

On April 23, Chairman A.J. Fink and President William J. Woods had a declaration approved by the Board of Directors of Pennsylvania Glass Sand Corporation:

WHERE-AS, the Board of Directors of THE PENNSYLVANIA GLASS SAND CORPORATION have lost in the death of the late HENRY P. BRIDGES a fellow member of exceptional ability, valued service and fidelity to the welfare of this corporation; and

WHERE-AS, the members of this Board have lost by his death an esteemed and able business associate and a congenial, admired and valued personal friend; and

WHERE-AS, the service of Mr. Bridges to this corporation during the last thirty years have been characterized by keen interest, the highest loyalty, superior judgment and notable ability; and

WHERE-AS, the high character and warmly attractive personality of Mr. Bridges have left a profound and lasting impression upon all the members of this organization and have won for him the respect and affectionate regard of a vast host of friends throughout the community;

NOW THEREFORE BE IT RESOLVED by the Board of Directors of THE PENNSYLVANIA GLASS SAND CORPORATION that we deplore with heartfelt sorrow the loss of our brother Director and commend his high character and integrity as an ideal of personal conduct and as an example in the management of this enterprise; and

BE IT FURTHER RESOLVED, that out of respect for the memory of our deceased friend and in recognition of his valued services to this corporation and to us, we do now stand for a moment of silence and that these resolutions be spread upon the minutes of this meeting and a copy of them be sent to the family of Mr. Bridges as a token of the sympathy of the members of this Board.

At the time of Bridges' death, the Pennsylvania Glass Sand Company owned and operated ten plants in six states. Such dominance was a testament to the skills Henry brought to the business. But it was not business that defined him. "Let me put it this way: for almost half a century I have been a full-time conservationist, hunter and fisherman, a man whose life has been dedicated to the health of our woodlands and the animals and birds that live in them." Bridges explained his motives, "Now, when I first took it into my head to save the wild turkey from what I believed was its imminent extinction I faced a challenge that seemed insurmountable. For one thing, wild turkeys were scarce (1897). They were difficult enough to hunt down and shoot, and they were still difficult to trap alive for breeding purposes. Furthermore, I wanted only completely genuine wild birds. They were, and are today, many turkeys in the woods that are only part wild." Someone once said Woodmont was "his magnificent hobby." That, or obsession.

Harold Smith Kolmer, Assistant Director of State of Maryland Game and Inland Fish Commission, wrote Shelby that her late husband was, "without a doubt the most outstanding conservationist not only in Maryland but the United States and his loss is surely going to be keenly felt by all who had the privilege of knowing him." Henry Jr. saw the man from a more personal perspective, "Henry P. was a loving husband and father. He was a gracious host, marvelous storyteller and generous friend. He annually sent bushel baskets of peaches and boxes of game to friends all over the country. Shelbridge and Woodmont were charmed treasures. I have fond memories growing up in this supportive environment which was beneficial beyond compare."

James A. Roemer of the Niles Rolling Mill Company in Niles Ohio was an early member of Woodmont. He first joined the club in the late 1930s. At the age of 96, he recalled Henry as "a person unto himself. I had a lot of admiration and respect for Bridges because of what he did to resurrect Woodmont and without him it would not have been a Woodmont as it was in ways unique, unusual and different."

Henry P. Bridges was a giant of a businessman in the silica mining industry. He was masterful at entertaining his business relations and financial backers at The Woodmont Road and Gun Club. He utilized the Club by having hunting parties of friends, family and clients. The "*Old English Style*" hunting at the Club was first conceived by the European aristocracy. In Europe hunting was a privilege and only the wealthy nobles, landowners and kings hunted from medieval times forward. This tradition found its way to America and Bridges established *"Old English"* hunting at his beloved Woodmont.

Woodmont's hunting was for the experienced hunter and the non-experienced hunter. The hunters bonded on the sporting field and had warm fellowship in the Clubhouse around the two massive solid wood tables in the dinning hall. Business deals, politics and cultural events were all subjects of conversation for members and their guests. Bridges' love of the wild turkey inspired him to raise tens of thousands of turkey during his lifetime. The bird was both hunted and released to reestablish the once endangered game bird in the United States to healthy populations. Bridges interior conviction led him to inspire many other men to follow in his mission of game management and conservation.

Thoreau once said, "I learned this, at least, by my experiment; that if one advances confidently in the direction of his dreams, and endeavors to live the life which he has imagined, he will meet with a success unexpected in common hours." And this Henry Bridges did.

The *"Sage of Woodmont."*

EPILOGUE

WOODMONT ROD & GUN CLUB: 1958-2011:

When Henry returned to Woodmont in early 1951 following surgery, he employed a Pennsylvania lumber company to cut every tree on the property over twelve inches in diameter. He did this to encourage the growth of cover for game to make use of. The club used a portion of the proceeds to pay off loans that Bridges had accumulated personally in order to keep Woodmont financially viable.

Henry's executor, H. Graham Wood of the First National Bank of Maryland, wrote Henry Jr. in 1958:

> *Frank Wachter, Secretary of the Pennsylvania Glass Sand Corporation, stopped in to see me yesterday and told me that he had been authorized by Mr. Roemer to obtain an option on the Woodmont stock at a total purchase price of $50,000. ....No one can say what the stock is actually worth. While your family and the trusts own 50% of the outstanding stock. ....About six months ago Mr. Wachter and Mr. Andrews stopped in to see me and on behalf of Mr. Roemer indicated that Mr. Roemer's group might be interested in acquiring the stock for $40,000.00. At that time, I told them that the group should raise the offer to at least $50,000.00 but so much time expired that I was afraid the group had lost what interest it had in the proposition. We feel that the present figure of $50,000.00 is the best that we will be able to obtain, and our committee recommends that we grant an option of three weeks on the terms. Although your trust and Powell's trust each hold 1,414 shares, we will attempt to withhold from the number of shares to be covered by the option 30 shares to be delivered to you in accordance with your father's will. Powell has already received his by gift."*

Roemer ended up buying the specified shares of Woodmont Stock for the agreed upon price of $50,000. On September 2, 1958, Graham Wood again wrote Henry Jr., "We are enclosing 30 shares the Woodmont Rod and Gun Club, capital stock, Certificate No. 480, registered in your name representing distribution due you in accordance with the terms of your father's will." These transactions settled the sale of Woodmont Club stock from Bridges' estate. Although Henry had told his sons never to get involved with the daily operation of Woodmont, he wanted them to each have 30 shares of the stock.

After Henry's death the difficulties of running a club such as Woodmont became readily apparent. Two families, by word of mouth only, were designated to buy Bridges' controlling interest of club stock. The Roemers were initially entrusted with the future of Woodmont; later the Andrews family became involved in the operation of the Club. In 1957, E.T. Andrews was the president of the Pennsylvania Glass Sand. Henry Roemer Jr. had been a trusted friend and financial backer of Woodmont for many years. He was living in Sharon, Pennsylvania operating the Sharon Steel Corporation, one of the big eight steel firms in America. Historically, the club had relied upon the Pennsylvania Glass Sand Corporation electricians, plumbers and heavy equipment operators to maintain the grounds and clubhouse. In 1968, Pennsylvania Glass Sand was bought out by International Telephone and Telegraph Corporation. Even before the company had begun to distance itself from the club.

By the early 1980s clubs such as Woodmont were an increasing anachronism. Hunting no longer held such broad appeal among the wealthy, a change which made Woodmont's operating budget of $500,000 all the harder to meet. Membership declined to twenty by 1985, and the future looked uncertain at best. Then in 1986, branches of the Bridges' families from Chicago and Charlotte held a reunion at Woodmont. I was beginning my seminary education at Pittsburgh Theological Seminary. I could not imagine this wonderful placed slipping away.

Walter Exline continued to manage the club until his death, when his son King took over. Then, in 1985, Henry Roemer III was given the responsibility of manager. Henry and I formed an immediate bond because we were both third-generation family participants in the club. We became good friends over the next ten years even as Woodmont teetered on the brink of extinction.

By 1986, the Club was in obvious need of renovation and financial help. Timber was now being clear cut to reduce the $300,000 club debt. Somehow, Henry managed to inspire a rejuvenation of the club, and once again there seemed to be hope. The membership increased to nearly fifty. The clubhouse and grounds were improved and restored with the meager revenues produced from hunting parties. The club owes Henry A. Roemer, III a great deal of thanks for his effort to restore Woodmont to glory. If it had not been for Henry and the ten years he devoted to the restoration of the club, Woodmont surely would have been sold for commercial development.

I joined in spirit with Roemer and tried to help resurrect the club. I personally contacted members of families whose combined fortunes totaled more than $30 billion, including a DuPont, a Mellon, and a Cox, all descendents of former club members. No one showed any interest in helping.

Woodmont was able to forestall development until 1993, when, in the words of one account, "an historic meeting at the Club took place with members Robert Kunisch, Terry Randall, Maryland Department of Natural Resources (DNR) Torrey Brown and Mike Nelson, and Patrick F. Noonan, chairman of The Conservation Fund www.conservationfund.org, and David Sutherland that resulted in an agreement to work together to protect the Club." The Conservation Fund acts to protect the nation's legacy of land and water resources in partnership with other organizations, public agencies, foundations, corporations, and individuals. Founded in 1985 by Patrick F. Noonan, the Fund seeks innovative, market driven, conservation solutions that integrate economic and environmental goals. With 238 corporate partners who have contributed millions of dollars in support, the Fund has helped safeguard wildlife habitat, greenways, community "greenspace" and historic sites totaling three million acres throughout the nation.

In 1995, the Fund reported it "had been working jointly with the Maryland Department of Natural Resources and, had earlier presented the DNR's plans detailing interest in acquiring the Woodmont property to the State Board of Public Works for approval, said Jack Lynn, a spokesman of the Conservation Fund." The negotiations moved quickly and the Club was sold in a Bargain Sale for over $3,400,000 to The Conservation Fund and then resold to the State of Maryland. Richard Erdmann, general counsel for the Conservation Fund who helped to guide the negotiations, said, "All of us owe a debt of gratitude to the shareholders and members of the Woodmont Rod and Gun Club. Their commitment to retain the integrity of the land and to preserve the history of the club for future generations of Marylanders has been a key to success."

Henry and I spent countless hours around the kitchen table at Woodmont talking about ways to keep the club alive and preserve the heritage we had both come to love. The first attempt to transfer club membership to a new corporation failed for reasons that can best be described as political.

During this time I contributed funds to keep the wild turkey flock fed and alive; the idea of Woodmont without them was too much for me. The Conservation Fund and the state were determined to create a new hunting operation and preserve the heritage. It was the largest land acquisition for the Maryland in forty years.

The Conservation Fund wrote:

> *Richard Erdmann and David Sutherland of the Fund and key members of the Club led by Bob Kunisch and encouraged by club members Mike Batza, Larry Scriggins, Terry Randall and Calman "Buddy" Zamoiski continued extensive negotiations with the DNR to devise a private-public partnership that would meet all the goals of the interested parties....One of the issues facing the sale was double taxation because it was a social club for federal tax purposes, its sale would result in double taxation....the Fund sought a private letter ruling from the Internal Revenue Service (IRS) addressing whether it could merge Woodmont into a to-be-created Maryland nonprofit stock corporation, Sustainable Conservation, Inc (SCI), on a tax-free basis.*

The IRS ruled favorably, and in August of 1995 SCI acquired the stock of Woodmont with ninety-seven percent of the members tendering their shares below fair market value.

Thanks to the negotiating skills of the Fund's David Sutherland and club member Larry Scriggins, an agreement was reached in 1997 between the Izaak Walton League (IWL), the state of Maryland and a group of private corporate members; the IWL took charge of management. A renewable fifteen year lease was negotiated with the state to keep the hunting traditions and the club viable. For six months of the year the club would have exclusive use of the clubhouse and 1,400 acres of the preserve. The public would have hunting rights for ten days in the deer season and two weeks in the turkey season. During the six months off-season from hunting "the state DNR's State Forest and Park Service oversees conservation-related activities on about 1,000 of the 1,400 acres of the IWL Chapter's leased land. Activities, which are sponsored by various hunting and recreation groups, including hunting, trap shooting, hunter ethics programs, children's hunter education, guided nature walks, canoeing on the Potomac, bicycling, picnics, and lodge tours."

The club is operating at a profit and is booked six months of the year for turkey and pheasant hunting. Clint Mowen, former chief of police in Hagerstown, was the manager, with assistance from his son Jeff Mowen and daughter-in-law Diane. The family and the staff of fifteen men and women work to keep the tradition viable. In 2011, Mike Worden is the manager and the club resently signed a seccond 15 year lease with the State of Maryland. Woodmount Rod & Gun Club has a bright furture.

In 1997, at the October 1, dinner celebrating the opening hunt, I was asked to give the blessing and a short history of the Woodmont Club. In the middle of the speech, when I spoke the words, "if these walls could talk, they would tell us that the greatest years of The Woodmont Rod & Gun Club are ahead of us" the middle doors of the dinning room blew wide open! At that moment the dining hall fell silent, as if to listen for the spirit of Henry P. Bridges roaming the floor. I am certain the old man himself opened the doors to see his grandson proudly celebrating his Woodmont tradition. To this day, the radiator pipes still rattle with the spirit of Henry P. Bridges.

Maryland Governor Paris N. Glendening, author David P. Bridges and Woodmont Club member Calman "Buddy" Zamoiski, Jr. in Governor's Office, Annapolis.

MODERN WILD TURKEY CONSERVATION & NWTF:

Henry had made a substantial effort to repopulate the American wild turkey and his accomplishment has been held in high regard by the conservation community. His work was continued by the National Wild Turkey Federation, a national nonprofit conservation and education organization. In 1973, when the National Wild Turkey Federation was founded, there were an estimated 1.3 million wild turkeys and 1.5 million turkey hunters. Thanks to the work of state wildlife agencies and the NWTF's many volunteers and partners, today there are an estimated 5.6 million wild turkeys and approximately 2.6 million turkey hunters.

Since 1985, more than $164 million NWTF and cooperator dollars have been spent on over 21,000 projects benefiting wild turkeys throughout North America. The NWTF is a grassroots' organization with 450,000 members in the fifty states, Canada and eleven foreign countries. It supports scientific wildlife management on public, private and corporate lands as well as wild turkey hunting as a traditional North American sport. Every state but Alaska now has a spring season and many have a fall season as well. The federations' success has meant that Henry's efforts at Woodmont were not in vain.

Since 1973, the NWTF's conservation partners and members have trapped and released 173,000 turkeys into new habitat. Modern techniques have proved to be more effective than raising turkey in open pens as Henry did for sixty years. While restoration is nearly complete east of the Mississippi, the work continues in the western United States and Canada. The NWTF, in cooperation with state and federal agencies, is aggressively implementing regional habitat programs in virtually every state across the country. And with help from corporate partners, the NWTF has donated more than 120,000 wild turkey transport boxes in support of this effort. When birds are trapped in the wild, they are placed in transport boxes and moved to habitat where their populations are low or non-existent.

"*Making Tracks*" is the cooperative program between the NWTF and state, federal and provincial wildlife agencies to restore wild turkeys to all suitable habitats in North America. The NWTF works with the wildlife agencies, coordinating the trap and transfer of the birds. An increase of fifty-one percent in the wild turkey population since 1990 shows conservation at its best. Not only does wild turkey transfer help build local populations, it also creates hunting opportunities that provide a sizable boost to local economies. Henry's conservation effort, though pioneering and innovative for his time, has given way to ideas more modern. Rarely has an endangered creature found such able benefactors as Henry P. Bridges and The National Wild Turkey Federation, (www.nwtf.org.)

THE PENNSYLVANNIA GLASS SAND CORPORATION:

Throughout the 1950s and into the 1960s, The Pennsylvania Glass Sand Corporation expanded operations. As Robert and Henry Bridges understood, success in business depends on innovation. Then, on June 30, 1968, International Telephone and Telegraph Corporation bought Pennsylvania Glass Sand:

> *International Telephone and Telegraph and Pennsylvania Glass Sand Corporation in a joint statement Monday announced that agreement had been reached in principle on the terms under which Pennsylvania Glass Sand Corporation would become part of the ITT System. The transaction is subject to the approval of the Boards of Directors of both companies and the stockholders of Pennsyl-*

vania Glass Sand Corporation and the fulfillment of certain other conditions.

Terms of the transaction call for the exchange of .628 shares of ITT Common Stock and .27 shares of ITT Cumulative Preferred Stock, $4.50. Convertible Series I, for each share of Pennsylvania Glass Sand Corporation exchange ratio reflects the 2 for 1 split of the ITT Common Stock which became effective on January 26, 1968. The ITT Preferred Stock issuable in the transaction would be convertible into the new ITT transaction Stock at $61 per share.

Pennsylvania Glass Sand Corporation is a leading supplier of silica which is a basic ingredient of all glass products, including glass containers, and many items for the modern home such as ceramic fixtures, tile, mirrors, fiberglass textiles and porcelain enamel. Pennsylvania Glass Sand Corporation also produced attapulgite, i.e. "Fuller's Earth," which is used by the agricultural chemical industry and in oil well drilling and fire retardant chemicals.

In commenting on the transaction, Mr. Harold S. Geneen, Chairman and President of ITT, said, "Pennsylvania Glass Sand gives us a solid position in an industry whose products are basic to the growth of the American economy. We are please to welcome them into our organization." Mr. Earle Andrews, Chairman of the Board of Pennsylvania Glass Sand Corporation, said, "We are confident that the association with ITT will enable us to explore areas that hitherto have been out of reach of our company, both in terms of new domestic activities and increased sales abroad."

Geneen had now built a corporation with consolidated sales and revenues of $6.4 billion. He was one of the first corporate leaders to build a diversified conglomerate. Mining operations continued to expand under ITT. The first innovation brought about by ITT was the construction of a larger crusher to handle the amount of raw material and the use of massive, eighty-five ton trucks. Each one was capable of moving fifty loads per day, was the equivalent of 3,500 tons of sand. Long gone were the days of the mule-drawn cart.

In September 1985, ITT sold Pennsylvania Glass Sand to Pacific Coast Resources, a subsidiary of RTZ Corporation, based in London. RTZ was the premier mining house in the world. On June 1, 1987, Pacific Coast Resources changed its name to U.S. Borax and Chemical Corporation. U.S. Borax in 1996 changed the name of Pennsylvania Glass Sand to U.S. Silica

Company. That same year, the privately held D. George Harris & Associates sponsored the acquisition of U.S. Silica by an investor group. Today, twenty-four mining plants are operated by U.S. Silica Company, a subsidiary of Better Minerals and Aggregates Company. Under the careful leadership of Richard J. Shearer, president and chief operating officer of U.S. Silica, and Craig S. Cinalli, president, of Better Materials Corporation, the various facilities are operating at full capacity. Richard E. Goodell, past president and chief executive officer of the U.S. Silica Corporation, was yet another individual who grew the business started by Robert Bridges.

Better Materials Corporation in Berkeley Springs, West Virginia.

SHELBRIDGE:

In 1973, Shelbridge was sold in a bargain sale with 9.03 acres worth $100,000 to the state of Tennessee. After Henry's death, Shelby married Hal White, vice president of Standard Accident Insurance Company. Shelby died in October of 1972. She had lived to see six grandchildren born into the world and had the pleasure of spending many long days with them at Shelbridge. The decision to sell the home was made by sons Powell and Henry Jr. The home became the residence of the president of East Tennessee State University of Johnson City. Dr. D.P. Culp, then university president, was instrumental in the sale and became the first resident.

In June of 2000, East Tennessee State University President Dr. Paul Stanton invited the Bridges family to return to Shelbridge for a reunion. No doubt, Henry and Shelby approved.

The Bridges' family reunion at Shelbridge, June 2000.

ENDNOTES

CHAPTER 1

"hunters and trappers": M. Emily Leatherman, Hancock, 1776-1976 (Hancock, MD: privately published. 1985), 1.

"In 1820": Ibid, 4.

"declared his intention": Diary of Priscilla Williams Bridges (1826), Bridges Papers.

"Samuel L. Gregory": Washington County Land Records, Hagerstown, Maryland. Land Record NN 34, March 7, 1829.

"Jonathon Rowland": *Ibid*, Land Record SS 38, March 27, 1834.

"Nathaniel Summers": *Ibid*, Land Record WW 41, July 28, 1840.

"rose at last": J. William McIlvain,. "Early Presbyterianism in Maryland," in *Johns Hopkins University Studies in Historical and Political Science,* VIII (1890), 12. The author is a direct descendant of Beall.

"This Church was": Hancock Presbyterian Church Session Minutes, 1844-1890. Southern Presbyterian Church Archives Center. Montreat, NC. Volume I, 6.

"On August": *Ibid*, 8.

"This is the book": *The Bible*, Revised Standard Version, Book of Genesis.

"A large meeting": J. Thomas Schraf, *History of Western Maryland,* (Philadelphia PA: Regional Publishing Company,1882), Volume I, 194-95.

"Resolved, That we": *Ibid.*

"Colonel Ashby": Leatherman, *Hancock,* 23.

"At one o'clock": *Ibid.*

"It may be": C. John Backus, *A Discourse Delivered at the Opening of the Westminster Presbyterian Church, Baltimore, Maryland* (Baltimore MD: S. Guiteau, 1852), 17.

"In theory": Colleen McDannell, *Material Christianity, Religion and Popular Culture in America* (New Haven CT: Yale University Press, 1995), 74.

"My father was": Henry P. Bridges, *The Woodmont Story* (New York, A.S. Barnes and Company, 1953), 13-15.

"There were evenings": *Ibid.*

"Horse, cattle, sheep": Leatherman, *Hancock*, 25.

"It was known": Raymond C. Salter, *Tercentary History of Maryland* (Chicago IL: S.J. Clarke Publishing Company, 1925), 480.

CHAPTER 2

"Later the Bridges": F. Thomas Hahn and L. Emory Kemp, *Cement Mills Along the Potomac River* (Morgantown, WV: West Virginia University Institute for the History of Technology & Industrial Archaeology, 1994), Volume II, Number 1, 79.

"Thus the heavens": King James Version of the *Bible*, Genesis 2: 1-3.

"An ardent Sabbatarian": Priscilla Williams Bridges diary.

"Along with more investors": Siler Papers, University of West Virginia at Morgantown. June 21, 1892.

"In the making": Session Minutes, 1844-1890, Volume I, 538.

"Morgan County is": Morgan Messenger (Berkeley Springs, WV), November 11, 1893.

"The bridge over": Hahn and Kemp, *Cement Mills,* Volume II, Number, 78.

"What is a Trust?": J. A. Quarles, "The Ethics of Trade," in *Presbyterian Quarterly* Volume III (1889), 108.

"But when a": *Ibid*, 109.

"The Christian is": *Ibid*, 107.

"The company will": Charleston Gazette/Morgan County News, August 25, 1905.

"the repeat was": Morgan Messenger, (Berkeley Springs, WV), December 9, 1905.

"The party of said": Siler Papers, July 5, 1906.

"Hope you may": Robert to Henry Bridges, Henry Bridges diary, Bridges Collection.

"In time of": *Ibid,* 46.

"I hope this": *Ibid.*

"Dear Henry": Robert to Henry Bridges, December 13, 1907, Bridges Collection.

"My Dear Son": Robert to Henry Bridges, December 18, 1907, Bridges Collection.

"He will be": Hagerstown Morning Herald, January 11, 1908.

"When the pulpit": *Ibid.*

"every tub stands": Bridges, *Woodmont Story,* 15.

CHAPTER 3

"Suddenly the awful": Bridges, *Woodmont Story,* 9-10.

"Henry, you beat": *Ibid*, 18.

"Born in Ireland": Sherry H. Olson, *Baltimore: The Building of an American City.* (Baltimore: The John Hopkins University Press, 1997), 209.

"combination of people": Bridges, *Woodmont Story,* 33.

"The Woodmont Rod": C. J. Burnett, "The Woodmont R. and G. Club. Opening of the Bass Season on the Potomac," Washington Evening Star, April 25. 1882.

"The club was": *Ibid.*

"a large old estate": "Rod And Gun, The Woodmont Rod and Gun Club," Evening Star, Apr. 28, 1883.

"The group officially": Cynthia Ott, "A Sportsman's Paradise: The Woodmont Rod and Gun Club," *Maryland Historical Magazine,* Volume XCII (1997), 236.

"new club house": "The Woodmont Rod and Gun Club. Its Organization, Description of Club House, etc.," *American Angler,* Number 17 (Oct. 21, 1882).

"consisting of a large": Evening Star, April 28, 1883.

"In short, the year": *Ibid*, April 25, 1882.

"To the most": *Ibid*, April 28, 1883.

"The rules of": "Woodmont Rod and Gun Club," *Shooting and Fishing, A Weekly Journal of the Rifle, Gun and Rod,* Volume 10, Number 8, (June 18, 1891), 145.

"The rare sport" Evening Star, April 25, 1882.

"The locality affords": *Ibid*, April 28 1883.

"During the summer": *Ibid.*

"Senator Wade Hampton": *Ibid.*

"fire struck in": Bridges, *Woodmont Story,* 52.

"I wanted the": *Ibid*, 57.

"And it all": *Ibid,* 39.

CHAPTER 4

"But the wild": "Trails of a Turkey Hunter, Fur, Fin and Feather" *Field & Stream,* April 5, 1874, Volume IL, Number 8, 256-257.

"Prairie Chickens were": "Game, Fur, Hide and Poultry Market," *Ibid,* January 23, 1875, Volume II, Number 23, 616.

"To most of ": Paul Knight, "The School and The Conservation Movement" in *Maryland Conservationist,* Volume V (1928), 10.

"we have": *Ibid.*

"ravaging": *Ibid.*

"The rapidity of": *Ibid.*

"situation as it": *Ibid.*

"commission consisting": E. Lee LeCompte, "History of Conservation of the Natural Resources of Maryland 1785 to 1924, 139 Years," in *Maryland Conservationist,* Volume I (1924), 4.

"In 1919 the": *Ibid.*

"Leaving the big": *Ibid,* 3-5.

"the most successful": *Ibid.*

"The game of": *Ibid.*

"the club has": E. Digby Baltzell, *The Protestant Establishment, Aristocracy & Cast in America.* (New Haven, Connecticut: Yale University Press., 1964), 19-20.

"My dear Mr. Bridges": letters displayed on the walls of Woodmont Clubhouse.

"THE WHITE HOUSE": *Ibid.*

"Nov. 27, 1907": *Ibid.*

"A big dinner": Henry P. Bridges diary.

"Mr. Henry P. Bridges": *Ibid.*

"While driving down": *Ibid.*

"turned on the": *Ibid.*

"Early in November": "Wild Turkeys --Hunting We Go!," in *Maryland Conservationist*, Volume VI, (1929), 12.

"Article #6.": Robert Bridges, Last Will and Testament, Bridges Collection.

"We hear from": Hancock News, 1909.

"Boyd Casset met": Washington Post, April 14, 1910.

"W. Crosfield's team": *Ibid*, April 21, 1910.

"the matter of": Siler Papers, November 29,1910.

"there is enough": Hagerstown Mail, March 31,1911.

"The pipeline, 1,610": Washington Post, September 28,1911.

"present output of": Hancock News, July 28, 1911.

"proceeded to Hancock": *Ibid*, July 27, 1911.

"Mr. Marvin Everett": Morgan Messenger, March 4, 1915.

"A barge party": Priscilla Breathed Bridges diary, Bridges Collection.

"Henry P. Bridges, of": Henry P. Bridges diary, January 6, 1913.

"Our friend Henry": Hancock News, April 28, 1916.

"There are many": John Mash, *The Land of the Living: The Story of Maryland's Green Ridge Forest* (Cumberland, MD: Commercial Press, 1996), 65.

"the Berkeley Glass": Siler Papers, May 17, 1917.

"Company attorney": *Ibid*, December 10, 1919.

"Dear Mr. Siler": *Ibid*, Jan. 2, 1920.

"The general": *Ibid*, January 2, 1920.

"'Turc! Turc!' Calls": Bridges, *Woodmont Story,* 95.

"Now, a wild": *Ibid.*, 97.

"experts at killing": G. James Dickson (ed.), *The Wild Turkey: Biology & Management* (Harrisburg, PA: Stockpole Books., 1992), 8.

"[With] a little": Gene Smith, "The Evolution of the Diaphragm Turkey Call," in *Turkey Call,* Volume 19, Number 2 (1992), 37.

"These boxes enjoyed": Dwain Bland, "Turkeys of Yesteryear," in *Petersen's Hunting,* May 1990, 63.

"1) breath operated": Lovett E. Williams, *the Art & Science of Wild Turkey Hunting* (Gainesville, FL: Real Turkeys Publishers, 1989), 181.

"UNITED STATES PATENT": "Patent-Pending," *Field & Stream,* December 1923.

"by scattering": Bridges, *Woodmont Story*, 101.

"To scatter a": *Ibid,* 101.

"The time comes": *Ibid,* 101.

"The pupil is": The Peabody Conservatory of Music Records, Baltimore, Maryland, 1920-21.

"to my sweetheart": Henry P. Bridges diary, 98-99.

"a skilful tracker": Captain Paul A. Curtis, "turkey Ketchin'," in *Field & Stream,* September 1923, 587.

"one of the": *Ibid.*

"but it was": *Ibid.*

"Them birds'll hear": *Ibid,* 588.

"last falsetto squeak": *Ibid.*

"which turned out": *Ibid.*

"if they had": *Ibid.*

"All of these": *Ibid.*

"Dear commander-in chief": Henry P. Bridges Scrapbook, Bridges Collection,1924-1930.

"With the dynamite": "Six Lives Snuffed Out: Premature Explosion of 1,200 Pounds of Dynamite Takes Terrible Toll Late Monday Afternoon At Bridges Sand Mine," in Martinsburg Journal, June 8, 1926.

"All comrades, wives": S. John Newbraugh and John Douglas, "Sleeping Beneath the Sand, Songwriter John W. Unger of Morgan County," in *Goldenseal,* Winter 1993, 63.

"fit so naturally": Bridges, *Woodmont Story,* 155.

"an artificial lake,": LeCompte, "Inspection Of Game Refuges In Western Maryland" in *Maryland Conservationist,* Fall, Volume I (1927), 15.

"John B. Ferguson": "$80,000 Woodmont Club, Finest in Trophies, Scene of Dinner Party" in *Maryland Conservationist,* Volume VIII, Number 2 (1931), 24.

"While the matter": Morgan Messenger, March 24, 1927.

"Mrs. M. Mayuard": Henry P. Bridges personal record book 1928-1929, Bridges Collection.

"Mr. William Elkins": "The Woodmont Rod And Gun Club--A Famous Shooting Preserve," *Maryland Conservationist,* Volume VI, Number. 1 (1929).

"The average family": Henry P. Bridges diary.

"Love of nature": Bridges, *A Woodland Idyll* (Lancaster, PA: Press of the Lancaster Printing Co., 1922). 40.

"country atmosphere": *Ibid.,* p. 14.

"without molestation": H. J. Cookingham quoted in John F. Reiger, *American Sportsmen and the Origins of Conservation* (New York: Winchester Press, 1975), 58.

CHAPTER 5

"Fishermen, hunters, woodchoppers": Henry David Thoreau, *Walden* (Boston, MA: Beacon Press., 1997), 197.

"Oh, these forest": Fredrick Turner, *John Muir: Rediscovering America (*Cambridge, MA: Perseus Publishing, 1985), 139.

"For humans": Curt Meine and Richard L. Knight, *The Essential Aldo Leopold* (Madison: The University of Wisconsin Press, 1999), 223.

"Physical combat between": Aldo Leopold, *A Sand County Almanac* New York: Oxford University Press, 1949), 192.

"Our village life": Thoreau, *Walden,* 296-297.

"I know not": Jim Casada (ed.), *America's Greatest Game Bird* (Columbia: University of South Carolina Press, 1994), 102.

"Poets sing": Meine and Knight, *Leopold,* 225-26.

"To be a practitioner": *Ibid*, 1.

"Far back in": Peter C. Chambliss, "Stalking the Wild Turkey at Woodmont, A Famous Old Hunting Preserve Yields a Day of Sport" in *Maryland Conservationist,* Volume VIII, Number 1 (1931),10-13.

"Rounding the point": Meine and Knight, *Leopold,* 228.

"Successful hunting of": Casada, *Game Bird,* 19.

"The Woodmont Rod": "Woodmont Rod & Gun Club a Great Asset to Western Maryland Sportsmen" in *Maryland Conservationist,* Volume IX, Number 1 (1932), 20.

"The Propagation of": E. Lee LeCompte, "The Propagation of Game in Captivity," *Ibid,* Volume IX, Number 1 (1932), 18.

"There are still": Meine and Knight, *Leopold,* 59.

"Morning air!": Thoreau, *Walden,*131.

"The man-let": Bridges, *Woodmont Story,* 126-28.

"It is little": Morgan Messenger, August 30, 1934.

"I lay on": Bridges, *Woodmont Story,* 106.

"My dear": letter, Bridges Collection, December 20, 1934.

"So I lost": Bridges, *Woodmont Story,* 107.

"For in the": *Ibid,* 107.

"For the duration": Leopold, *Sand County,* 38-39.

"People from miles": Leatherman, *Hancock,* 82.

"He rubbed his": Bridges, *Woodmont Story,* 164.

"'Mr. President": *Ibid,* 167.

"Bridges, you may": *Ibid,* 170.

"Our jaunt around": *Ibid,* 170-71.

"Seeing these children": Baltimore Sun, May 13, 1935.

"Dear Mr. Bridges": letter, Bridges Collection, May 16, 1935.

"We'll call you": Bridges, *Woodmont Story*, 103.

"Frankly, I think": letter, Bridges Collection, November 25, 1935.

"Mr. Henry P. Bridges": "The Woodmont Rod & Gun Club" in *Maryland Conservationist,* Volume XIII, Number 2 (1936), 16.

"If you have": letter, Bridges Collection, April 22, 1936.

"With the exception": *Ibid*, May 18, 1936.

"After the big": letter, Bridges Collection, November 23, 1936.

"Your letter of 8th": *Ibid*, December 15, 1936.

"We will ship": *Ibid*, February 4, 1937.

"The other day": *Ibid*, July 7, 1937.

"Shelby and I": *Ibid*, July 13, 1937.

"Thanks for your": *Ibid*, July 14, 1937.

"In reading of": *Ibid*, August 30, 1937.

"Among the several": LeCompte, "Game Farms Are Essential," in *Maryland Conservationist,* Volume XIV, Number 4 (1938), 13.

"Dear Cousin Harry": letter, Bridges Collection, October 14, 1937.

"I received your": *Ibid*, October 19, 1937.

"It would give": *Ibid*, October 25, 1937.

"A lake is": Thoreau, *Walden,* 176.

"I forgot to": letter, Bridges Collection, January 16, 1937.

"You can tell": *Ibid*, February 23, 1938.

"The herd of": *Ibid*, April 8, 1938.

"I would like": *Ibid*, September 27, 1938.

"Your letter received": *Ibid,* September 30, 1938.

"When will you": *Ibid*, November 2, 1938.

"My companions were": *Outdoorsman Magazine*, June 1939, 17-18.

"Your letter of": letter, Bridges Collection, November 30, 1938.

"Suddenly, close to": Casada, *Game Bird*, 116.

"No, what I": Bridges, *Woodmont Story*, 178.

"Harvey was a": *Ibid*, 181.

"Why, Judge, I": *Ibid*, 187.

"One year when": *Ibid*, 187-88.

"'Harvey,' I said": *Ibid,* 190.

"I received your": letter, Bridges Collection, January 16, 1939.

"I received your letter": *Ibid*, January 19, 1939.

"The Government delivered": *Ibid*, Jan. 20, 1939.

"OUT FISHING": *Ibid.*

"It is clear": Meine and Knight, *Leopold*, 68.

"I notice in": letter, Bridges Collection, March 13, 1939.

"I am sure": *Ibid*, April 3, 1939.

"myself and": *Ibid*, April 5, 1939.

"As I understand": *Ibid*, June 10, 1939.

"There is a": *Ibid*, July 3, 1939.

"I have your": *Ibid*, July 7, 1939.

"When we built": *Ibid*, July 18, 1939.

"What a strange": *Ibid*, July 22, 1939.

"I received your": *Ibid*, July 28, 1939.

"Please advise me": *Ibid*, August 15, 1939.

"I have just": *Ibid*, September 18, 1939.

"For the past": *Ibid*, October 11, 1939.

"It was a great": *Ibid*, October 5, 1937.

"The Club has": *Ibid*.

"The wild turkey": *Survey,* United States Department of The Interior, Bureau of Biological Survey Division of Information, Nov. 6, 1939, in Bridges Collection .

"The Governor and": Peter C. Chambliss, Baltimore Sun, November 16, 1939.

"It might be": *Ibid*.

"I found Babe": Bridges, *Woodmont Story,* 128-29.

"I greatly appreciate": letter, Bridges Collection, November 21, 1939.

CHAPTER 6

"The hunt took": Bridges, *Woodmont Story,* 197-98.

"For the past": letter, Bridges Collection, January 22, 1940.

"First, was James": Bridges, *Woodmont Story,* 196.

"Mr. Matthews is": letter, Bridges Collection, August 28, 1940.

"I am enclosing": *Ibid*, Nov. 14, 1940.

"anything but ": Bridges, *Woodmont Story,*129.

"A thing is": Leopold, *Sand County,* xxvi.

"In wilderness": *Ibid*, 133.

"Shelby and I": letter, Bridges Collection, May 16, 1941.

"At the great": *Ibid*, July 28, 1941.

"Did you see": *Ibid*, October 31, 1941.

"I was interested": *Ibid*, December 3, 1942.

"Tomorrow the turkey": John G. Mock, "Wild Turkey Is Rapidly Diminishing in Numbers; Tame Variety Is Offspring" in Pittsburgh Press, December 3, 1942.

"Because of certain": letter, Bridges Collection, December 3, 1942.

"This is the first": *Ibid*, February 2, 1943.

"We will have": *Ibid*, July 2, 1943.

"Fillmore Bishop": *Ibid*, November 12, 1943.

"Don't think": *Ibid*, April 10, 1946.

"The wildlife conservation": Meine and Knight, *Leopold,* 67.

"First of all": *Ibid,* 53.

"Leopold also understood": *Ibid*, 47.

"In 40 years": letter, Bridges Collection, April 12, 1946.

"The wild-life": Meine and Knight, *Leopold*, 39.

"We have learned": *Ibid*, 46.

"understood that wildlife": *Ibid.*

"the art of making": *Ibid.*

 "In short": *Ibid*, 53.

"For 48 years": letter, Bridges Collection, May 21, 1946.

"I realize": *Ibid.*

"I appreciated most": *Ibid*, May 25, 1946.

"I received your letter": *Ibid*, June 7, 1946.

"I received your": *Ibid*, June 10, 1946.

"This was the": letter, Bridges Collection, July 6, 1946.

"I admire ": Jim Casada , *Game Bird*, 32.

"In reading your ": 1954 article "Raising Wild Turkeys" part of Bridges Collection.

"I am interested": letter, Bridges Collection, November 25, 1954.

"I received your": *Ibid*, November 27, 1954.

"Governor McKeldin has": *Ibid*, September 7, 1955.

"I was much": *Ibid*, November 25, 1955.

"That was a": *Ibid*, December 5, 1955.

"Those of us": *Ibid*, April 9, 1956.

"Let me put": Bridges, *Woodmont Story,* 138.

"Now, when": *Ibid*, 96.

"his magnificent": letter, Bridges Collection, May 15, 1946.

"without a doubt": *Ibid*, April 29, 1957.

"Henry P. was": interview with Henry P. Bridges Jr., Charlotte, N.C., Spring 1999.

"a person unto": Interview with James A. Roemer, February 21, 2001.

"I learned this": Thoreau, *Walden,* 303.

EPILOGUE

"Frank Wachter, Secretary": letter, Bridges Collection, July 25, 1958.

"We are enclosing": *Ibid.*

"An historic meeting": Case Study of The Woodmont Rod and Gun Club, The Conservation Fund, Arlington Virginia, 2002.

"had been working": *Ibid.*

"All of us": Sondra Bishop. Hancock News, "State to own historic local Woodmont Rod and Gun Club," July 6, 1995.

"Richard Erdmann and": Case Study.

"The state DNR's": *Ibid.*

"International Telephone and": Morgan Messenger, "ITT Announces Acquisition of Pennsylvania Glass Sand," February 1, 1968.

INDEX